The Art of C:
Elegant Programming Solutions

The Art of C: Elegant Programming Solutions

Herbert Schildt

Osborne **McGraw-Hill**

Berkeley New York St. Louis San Francisco
Auckland Bogotá Hamburg London Madrid
Mexico City Milan Montreal New Delhi Panama City
Paris São Paulo Singapore Sydney
Tokyo Toronto

Osborne **McGraw-Hill**
2600 Tenth Street
Berkeley, California 94710
U.S.A.

Osborne **McGraw-Hill** offers software for sale. For information on software, translations, or book distributors outside of the U.S.A., please write to Osborne **McGraw-Hill** at the above address.

The Art of C: Elegant Programming Solutions

1234567890 DOC 9987654321

ISBN 0-07-881691-2

Publisher

Kenna S. Wood

Acquisitions Editor

Frances Stack

Associate Editor

Jill Pisoni

Project Editor

Madhu Prasher

Copy Editor

Dusty Bernard

Proofreading Coordinator

Erica Spaberg

Proofreaders

Linda Medoff
Paul Medoff
Dianne Walber

Indexer

Valerie Robbins

Computer Designers

Fred Lass
Jani Beckwith

Typesetting

Helena Charm
Erick Christgau
Marcela Hancik
Peter Hancik
Susie Kim
Stefany Otis
Lance Ravella
Michelle Salinaro

Cover Design

Bay Graphics Design, Inc.

Cover Illustration

Jim Carpenter

CONTENTS AT A GLANCE

CONTENTS

If you want to create world-class programs written in C, this book is for you!

My name is Herb Schildt. I am a veteran programmer and have programmed in C for many years. Before I began writing this book, I looked at a number of successful software products, trying to determine what common feature or features they had that others did not. I wanted to know what it was that made one product so much more successful than another of similar functionality. After a while, a thread connecting them began to show itself. It became clear that the successful products had been designed by someone who had not only a firm grasp of the specific application, but also complete mastery over the entire computing environment. This environment includes the operating system and the hardware itself. Only by having total control of these things can you hope to produce programs with snappy user interfaces that execute efficiently and offer the user the greatest possible flexibility.

This book unlocks many of the secrets used by master programmers to achieve the professional results users have come to expect. It explores the techniques and methods that make programs sizzle. When you have finished this book, you will be able to write programs that deserve attention. Among the topics covered are

- Direct video RAM accessing for lightning-fast screen displays
- Pop-up and pull-down menus
- Pop-up window routines
- Terminate-and-stay-resident programs
- Mouse interfacing
- Graphics functions, including object rotations
- Language interpreters
- File transfers via the serial port

This book is for any and every C programmer, from novice to pro. Even if you are just a beginner, you will be able to use the functions and programs in this book without having to understand all the subtle details of their operation. More advanced readers can use the routines as a basis for their own applications.

This book also contains profiles of ten world-class C programmers. They describe their personal views of C, what makes a great C programmer, and their own design philosophies. These programmers were chosen either because they had been directly involved in the creation of very successful C programs or because they have contributed to the advancement of the C language. (Of course, it was not possible to profile every worthy C programmer.) Interviewing the programmers profiled was one of the most enjoyable writing tasks that I have performed, and I thank all who participated for their time, effort, and insight.

The code in this book conforms to the ANSI C standard except where some PC-specific functions are employed. Therefore, all the routines should compile without change by any compiler that supports the ANSI standard. For development, I used both Turbo C and Microsoft C. (I also compiled the examples using Turbo C++.)

The programs contained in this book are also on the companion disk that accompanies this book. For an explanation of the contents of the disk, examine the README file or just enter **README** to see the contents of the file displayed on the screen.

CHAPTER ONE

Pop-up and Pull-down Menus

One of the most obvious trademarks of a professionally written program is the use of pop-up and pull-down menus. When correctly implemented, these menus give programs the snappy feel that users have come to expect. Although conceptually simple, creating pop-up and pull-down menus presents some substantial programming challenges.

Creating pop-up and pull-down menus requires direct control of the screen. Although the actual menu routines are quite portable, the routines to access the screen are intrinsically hardware- and operating system-dependent and must bypass C's normal console I/O functions. The video access routines developed here work with any computer that uses DOS and has an IBM-compatible BIOS for its operating system. DOS was chosen because it is the operating system in widest use, but you can generalize the basic concept to other systems.

Even if you are not interested in pop-up or pull-down menus at this time, you should still read the parts of this chapter that discuss video adapters; many of the basic concepts presented will be used again in the chapters on windows and graphics.

1

JIM BRODIE

Accomplished author and C programmer, Jim Brodie is probably best known for starting the ANSI committee, X3J11, that created the first standard for C. Jim convened the first meeting in the summer of 1983 and has served as its chairman ever since. During the several years that the committee labored towards the now adopted C standard, Jim contributed leadership, stability and an even-handed treatment, which helped the committee successfully resolve many very difficult issues. There is little question that the standardization of C has helped broaden its acceptance.

Given Jim's work on the ANSI C standard, I wanted his thoughts on C's future. "I think the future of C is alive and well. There will always be a class of programs which are most easily and effectively written in C. For example, C is excellent for real-time programs in which performance remains a very high priority. However, some types of programs that are currently being coded in C will move to C++ or other newer languages. For example, I think that C++ will dominate the arena of very large programs—especially those developed by moderate to large scale teams."

Because of Jim's background, I was curious which feature of C he regarded as the most interesting. "I don't know that I have a real 'favorite'," Jim replied. "But, I find pointers and their effective use fascinating. They combine power with flexibility but also create the opportunity for error and confusion. I believe that a minority of C programmers understand or know how to safely use pointers to their fullest advantage."

Jim describes his personal design philosophy as "hard to easy." "I usually do the high-level architecture and then do detail design work on the difficult parts. Solving the difficult parts first may make the schedule look bad for a while, but in the end, the overall development effort is shorter. Generally, the difficult parts of a program have wide ranging impact on the whole program. If you don't tackle them first, you usually end up doing a lot of rework," Jim elaborated.

Jim Brodie holds a BS in Psychology and an MA in Mathematics/Computer Science. He currently lives with his wife and three children in Chandler, Arizona.

WHAT ARE POP-UP AND PULL-DOWN MENUS?

It is important to understand what pop-up and pull-down menus are and how they differ from standard menus. When a standard menu is used, the screen is either cleared or scrolled and the menu is presented. When a selection is made, the screen is again cleared or scrolled and the program continues. The selection is made by using either the number or the first letter of each option.

When a pop-up or pull-down menu is activated, it overwrites what is currently on the screen. After the selection is made from the menu, the screen is restored to its previous state. You select an option from a pop-up or pull-down menu in one of two ways: (1) by pressing a *hot key*, which is a letter or number associated with one of the various menu options or (2) by using the arrow keys to move a highlight to the option you want and then pressing ENTER. Generally, the highlighted option is shown in reverse video or in a different color.

The key difference between standard menus and pop-up or pull-down menus is that activating a standard menu stops the program. A pop-up or pull-down menu, however, appears to "suspend" the current activity of the program. From a user's point of view, a standard menu can cause a break in concentration, while pop-up or pull-down menus are simply slight interruptions; the user's concentration is not impaired.

The difference between pop-up and pull-down menus is simple. Only one pop-up menu may be on the screen at any one time. It is used when the menu is only one level deep, that is, when the selections in the menu have no subselections. On the other hand, several pull-down menus may be active simultaneously. They are used when a selection from one menu may require the use of another menu to determine certain options. For example, you might use pull-down menus if you are designing a program that orders fruit. If the user selects "apple," the next menu prompts for the color of the apple, and a third menu displays apples that meet the previously determined specifications.

You can think of a pop-up menu as simply a pull-down menu that doesn't have any submenus, but developing separate routines for these two types of menus has certain advantages because the pull-down menus require much more overhead in a program than the simple pop-up menus.

Although there are many ways to actually structure a menu on the screen, the functions developed in this chapter use the most common form. This method places each menu item on a new line. This is the approach illustrated in the following simple mailing list top-level menu.

```
Load file
Save file
Print
Enter addresses
Delete addresses
Find
Modify
Quit
```

UNDERSTANDING THE VIDEO ADAPTERS

Because the creation of pop-up and pull-down menus requires direct control of the screen, it is important to understand the video display adapters. The four most common types of adapters are the monochrome adapter, the color/graphics adapter (CGA), the enhanced graphics adapter (EGA), and the video graphics array (VGA). The CGA, EGA, and VGA have several modes of operation, including 40- or 80-column text or graphics operation. These modes are shown in Table 1-1. The menu routines developed in this chapter are designed to be used in 80-column text mode. This means that the video mode of the system must be 2, 3, or 7. No matter what mode is used, the upper-left corner is 0,0.

The characters displayed on the screen are held in some reserved RAM on the display adapters. The location of the monochrome memory is B000:0000 and the CGA/EGA/VGA video RAM starts at B800:0000. (They are different in order to allow separate graphics and text screens to be used—but this is seldom done in practice.) Although the CGA and EGA function differently in some modes, they are the same in modes 2 and 3.

Each character displayed on the screen requires 2 bytes of video memory. The first byte holds the actual character, and the second holds its screen attribute. For color adapters, the attribute byte is interpreted as shown in Table 1-2. If you have a CGA, EGA, or VGA, the default video mode is 3, and the characters are displayed with an attribute byte value of

---

Table 1-1

The Video Modes for the IBM Line of Microcomputers

Mode	Type	Dimensions	Adapters
0	Text, b/w	40x25	CGA, EGA, VGA
1	Text, 16 colors	40x25	CGA, EGA, VGA
2	Text, b/w	80x25	CGA, EGA, VGA
3	Text, 16 colors	80x25	CGA, EGA, VGA
4	Graphics, 4 colors	320x200	CGA, EGA, VGA
5	Graphics, 4 gray tones	320x200	CGA, EGA, VGA
6	Graphics, b/w	640x200	CGA, EGA, VGA
7	Text, b/w	80x25	Monochrome
8	Graphics, 16 colors	160x200	PC*jr*
9	Graphics, 16 colors	320x200	PC*jr*
10	Graphics, 4 colors	640x200	PC*jr*
11	Reserved		
12	Reserved		
13	Graphics, 16 colors	320x200	EGA, VGA
14	Graphics, 16 colors	640x200	EGA, VGA
15	Graphics, 4 colors	640x350	EGA, VGA
16	Graphics, 16 colors	640x350	VGA
17	Graphics, 2 colors	640x480	VGA
18	Graphics, 16 colors	640x480	VGA
19	Graphics, 256 colors	640x200	VGA

7. This turns the three foreground colors on, producing white. To produce reverse video, the foreground bits are turned off and the three background bits are turned on, producing a value of 0x70.

The monochrome adapter recognizes the blinking and intensity bits. Fortunately, it is designed to interpret an attribute of 7 as normal video and to interpret 0x70 as reverse video. Also, a value of 1 produces underlined characters.

Each adapter actually has four times as much memory as it needs to display text in 80-column mode. There are two reasons for this. First, the extra memory is needed for graphics (except in the monochrome adapter, of course). The second is to allow multiple screens to be held in RAM and then simply switched in when needed. Each region of memory is called a *video page*, and the effect of switching the active video page is quite dramatic. By default, page 0 is used when DOS initializes, and virtually all applications use page 0. For this reason it is used in the routines in this chapter. However, you can use other pages if you desire.

Table 1-2

The Video Attribute Byte

Bit	Binary Value	Meaning When Set
0	1	Blue foreground
1	2	Green foreground
2	4	Red foreground
3	8	Low intensity
4	16	Blue background
5	32	Green background
6	64	Red background
7	128	Blinking character

There are three ways to access the video adapter. The first is through DOS calls, which is far too slow for pop-up or pull-down menus. The second is through BIOS routines, which is quicker and may be fast enough on faster machines if the menus are small. The third way is by reading and writing the video RAM directly, which is very fast, but it requires more work on your part. This chapter develops two separate sets of video routines. One uses the BIOS and the other accesses the video RAM directly.

ACCESSING THE SCREEN THROUGH BIOS

Because pop-up and pull-down menu functions must save what is on their portion of the screen and restore it after the selection has been made, you must have routines that save and load a portion of the screen. The method of saving and restoring a portion of the screen developed in this section relies on calls to two built-in BIOS functions that read and write characters on the screen.

As you may know, calls into the BIOS can be quite slow. However, they are (more or less) guaranteed to work on any computer that has an IBM-compatible BIOS even if the actual screen hardware is different. Therefore, the BIOS menu routines should be used in applications that require the widest portability. (Frankly, virtually all DOS-based computers manufactured today are 100 percent IBM compatible, but many older systems are not.)

Using int86()

Calls are made to the BIOS by using software interrupts. The BIOS has several different interrupts for varying purposes. The one used here to access the screen is interrupt 0x10, which is used to access the video display. (If you are not familiar with accessing the BIOS, you will find a good discussion of the subject in my book, *C: The Complete Reference*, 2d. ed. [Berkeley: Osborne/McGraw-Hill, 1990.]) Like many BIOS interrupts, interrupt 0x10 has several options that are selected based on the value of the AH register. If the function returns a value, it is generally returned in AL. However, sometimes other registers are used if several values are returned. To access the BIOS interrupts, you need to use a C function called **int86()**. (Some compilers call this function by a different name, but both Microsoft C and Turbo C call it **int86()**. The following discussion applies specifically to these compilers, but you should be able to generalize.)

The **int86()** function takes this general form:

int int86(int *num*, /* the interrupt number */
        union REGS **inregs*, /* the input register values */
        union REGS **outregs*) /* the output register values */

The return value of **int86()** is the value of the AX register. The type **REGS** is supplied in the header **BIOS.H**. The type **REGS** shown here is defined by Turbo C*; however, it is similar to those defined by Microsoft C and other compilers.

```
/*
    Copyright (c) Borland International 1987,1988,1990,1991
    All Rights Reserved.
*/

struct WORDREGS {
    unsigned int    ax, bx, cx, dx, si, di, cflag, flags;
};

struct BYTEREGS {
    unsigned char   al, ah, bl, bh, cl, ch, dl, dh;
};
```

*Copyright © 1991, Borland International, Inc. Printed with permission from the header file of DOS.H in the Turbo C compiler. All rights reserved.

```
union   REGS   {
    struct  WORDREGS x;
    struct  BYTEREGS h;
};
```

As you can see, **REGS** is a union of two structures. Using the **WORDREGS** structure allows you to access the registers of the CPU as 16-bit quantities. **BYTEREGS** gives you access to the individual 8-bit registers. For example, to access interrupt 0x10, function 5, you would use this code sequence:

```
union REGS in, out;

in.h.ah = 5;
int86(0x10, &in, &out);
```

Saving a Portion of the Screen

To save what is on the screen, the current value at each screen location must be read and stored. To read a character from a specific screen location, you use interrupt 0x10, function 8, which returns the character and its associated attribute that are at the current position of the cursor. Therefore, to read characters from a specific portion of the screen, you must have a way of positioning the cursor. Although most C compilers supply such a function, some may not. Therefore, the one shown here, called **goto_xy()**, can be used. It uses the interrupt 0x10, function 2, with the column coordinate in DL and the row coordinate in DH. The video page is specified in BH (using the default page 0).

```
/* Send the cursor to specified X,Y coordinates. */
void goto_xy(int x, int y)
{
  union REGS r;

  r.h.ah = 2; /* cursor addressing function */
  r.h.dl = x; /* column coordinate */
  r.h.dh = y; /* row coordinate */
  r.h.bh = 0; /* video page */
  int86(0x10, &r, &r);
}
```

The read character interrupt 0x10, function 8, requires that the video page be in BH when called and returns the character at the current cursor position in AL and its attribute in AH. The function **save_video()**, shown here, reads a portion of the screen, saves the information into a buffer, and clears that portion of the screen:

```
/* Save a portion of the screen. */
void save_video(int startx, int endx, int starty, int endy,
                unsigned int *buf_ptr)
{
  union REGS r;
  register int i,j;

  for(i=startx; i<endx; i++)
    for(j=starty; j<endy; j++) {
      goto_xy(i, j);
      r.h.ah = 8; /* read character */
      r.h.bh = 0; /* assume active display page is 0 */
      *buf_ptr++ = int86(0x10, &r, &r); /* save in buffer */
      putchar(' '); /* clear the screen */
    }
}
```

The first four parameters of **save_video()** specify the X,Y coordinates of the upper-left and lower-right corners of the region to be saved. The parameter **buf_ptr** is an integer pointer to the region of memory that will hold the current contents of the screen. The region must be large enough to hold the amount of information being read from the screen.

The programs in this chapter allocate the buffer dynamically, but you could use some other scheme if it makes more sense for your own specific application. Remember, however, that the buffer must remain in existence until the screen is restored to its previous condition. The function also clears the specified region by writing spaces to each location.

Restoring the Screen

Restoring the screen once the menu selection has been made is simply a matter of writing the previously stored information back into the video RAM. To do this, use interrupt 0x10, function 9, which requires the character to be in AL, its attribute in BL, the video page in BH, and the number of times to write the character in CX (1, in this case). The function shown here, **restore _ video()**, puts the information in the buffer pointed to by **buf _ ptr** on the screen, given the beginning and ending X,Y coordinates:

```
/* Restore a portion of the screen. */
void restore_video(int startx, int endx, int starty, int endy,
                unsigned char *buf_ptr)
{
  union REGS r;
  register int i, j;

  for(i=startx; i<endx; i++)
    for(j=starty; j<endy; j++) {
      goto_xy(i, j);
      r.h.ah = 9; /* write character */
      r.h.bh = 0; /* assume active display page is 0 */
      r.x.cx = 1; /* number of times to write the character */
      r.h.al = *buf_ptr++; /* character */
      r.h.bl = *buf_ptr++; /* attribute */
      int86(0x10, &r, &r);
  }
}
```

CREATING POP-UP MENUS

Several pieces of information must be passed to a function that creates a pop-up menu. The first is a list of the menu options. The menu entries are strings to be displayed, and the easiest way to pass a list of strings to a function is to put the strings in a two-dimensional array and pass a pointer to that array. As stated earlier, a menu item may be selected either by moving the highlight to the desired entry and pressing ENTER or by pressing the key indicated for that entry. For the function to know which keys are "hot" and what they mean, the keys must be passed to it. The best way to do this is to pass a string that contains the hot-key characters in the same order as the menu strings.

The **pop-up()** function must also know how many items are in the menu, so this number must be passed to it. The **pop-up()** function also needs to know where to put the menu, so the X,Y coordinates of the upper-left corner are needed. Finally, it may be desirable to place a border around the menu in some situations but not in others. Therefore, a border on/off value has to be passed. From this description, the **popup()** function will have this prototype:

```
int popup(
  char *menu[],   /* menu text */
  char *keys,     /* hot keys */
  int count,      /* number of menu items */
  int x, int y,   /* X,Y coordinates of left-hand corner */
  int border      /* no border if 0 */
)
```

The **popup()** function must do the following:

- Save the part of the screen used by the menu
- Display the border if requested
- Display the menu
- Input the user's response
- Restore the screen to its original condition

Two of these goals are accomplished by the **save_video()** and **restore_video()** functions discussed in the previous section. Let's see how to accomplish the other three now.

Displaying the Menu

The key to displaying the menu is to keep in mind that **popup()** is passed a pointer to an array of string pointers. To display the individual strings, you simply index the pointer like an array. Each entry in the array is a pointer to the corresponding menu entry. The following function, called **display_menu()**, displays each menu item by using this method.

```
/* Display the menu in its proper location. */
void display_menu(char *menu[], int x, int y, int count)
{
  register int i;

  for(i=0; i<count; i++, y++) {
    goto_xy(x, y);
    printf(menu[i]);
  }
}
```

As you can see, the function is passed a pointer to the array of strings to be displayed, the X,Y coordinates at which to begin displaying them, and the number of entries in the menu.

By far the easiest way to create the two-dimensional array that holds the menu selection strings is to create global variables by using this general form:

```
char * <menu-name>[] = {
    "first selection",
    "second selection",
        .
        .
        .
    "Nth selection"
}
```

This declaration automatically causes the C compiler to place the strings in the run-time string table of the program. The variable then points to the first character of the first string in the table. For example, this declaration creates a variable called **fruit** that points to the A in "Apple":

```
char *fruit[]= {
    "Apple",
    "Orange",
    "Pear",
    "Grape",
    "Raspberry",
    "Strawberry"
};
```

Displaying the Border

If a border is desired, the following routine can put a border around a menu, given the coordinates of the upper-left and lower-right corners. It uses the vertical and horizontal line characters that are part of the standard character set on a PC or compatible. You may substitute others if you like.

```
/* Draw a border around the menu. */
void draw_border(int startx, int starty, int endx, int endy)
```

```
{
  register int i;

  /* draw vertical lines */
  for(i=starty+1; i<endy; i++) {
     goto_xy(startx, i);
     putchar(179);
     goto_xy(endx, i);
     putchar(179);
  }

  /* draw horizontal lines */
  for(i=startx+1; i<endx; i++) {
    goto_xy(i, starty);
    putchar(196);
    goto_xy(i, endy);
    putchar(196);
  }

  /* draw the corners */
  goto_xy(startx, starty); putchar(218);
  goto_xy(startx, endy); putchar(192);
  goto_xy(endx, starty); putchar(191);
  goto_xy(endx, endy); putchar(217);

}
```

Inputting the User's Response

As stated, the user may enter a response in one of two ways. First, the UP ARROW and DOWN ARROW keys can be used to move the highlight to the desired item, and then ENTER is pressed to actually select it. (For the menus developed here, the highlighted item will be displayed in reverse video.) The SPACEBAR may also be used to move the highlight. The second way an item can be selected is by pressing the hot key associated with it. The function **get_resp()**, shown here, accomplishes these goals:

```
/* Input user's selection. */
get_resp(int x, int y, int count, char *menu[], char *keys)
{
  union inkey {
```

```
  char ch[2];
  int i;
} c;
int arrow_choice=0;
char *key_choice;

x++;
y++;

/* highlight the first selection */
goto_xy(x, y);
write_video(x, y, menu[0], REV_VID); /* reverse video */

for(;;) {
  c.i = readkey();     /* read the key */

  /* reset the selection to normal video */
  goto_xy(x, y+arrow_choice);
  write_video(x, y+arrow_choice,
            menu[arrow_choice], NORM_VID); /* redisplay */

  if(c.ch[0]) { /* is normal key */
    /* see if it is a hot key */
    key_choice = strchr(keys, tolower(c.ch[0]));
    if(key_choice) return key_choice-keys;

    /* check for Enter or spacebar */
    switch(c.ch[0]) {
      case '\r': return arrow_choice;
      case ' ' : arrow_choice++;
        break;
      case ESC : return -1; /* cancel */
    }
  }
  else {  /* is special key */
    switch(c.ch[1]) {
      case 72: arrow_choice--; /* up arrow */
        break;
      case 80: arrow_choice++; /* down arrow */
        break;
    }
  }
  if(arrow_choice==count) arrow_choice = 0;
  if(arrow_choice<0) arrow_choice = count-1;
```

```
    /* highlight the next selection */
    goto_xy(x, y+arrow_choice);
    write_video(x, y+arrow_choice, menu[arrow_choice], REV_VID);
  }
}
```

When **get_resp()** begins execution, the first menu item is highlighted. The macro **REV_VID** is defined elsewhere as 0x70, and **NORM_VID** is defined as 7. After the first menu item is highlighted, the routine enters the loop that waits for the user's response. First, it uses **readkey()** to input a keystroke. The **readkey()** function is shown here:

```
/* Return the 16-bit scan code from the keyboard. */
readkey(void)
{
  union REGS r;

  r.h.ah = 0;
  return int86(0x16, &r, &r);
}
```

The **readkey()** function uses interrupt 0x16, function 0, to return the full 16-bit scan code generated by the keyboard when a key is pressed. (Interrupt 0x16 is the entry point for the BIOS keyboard services.) Each time a key is pressed, two 8-bit codes are produced, encoded into a 16-bit integer. If the key pressed is a character key, the character is returned in the low-order eight bits. However, if a special key is pressed, such as an arrow key, the low-order byte is 0 and the high-order byte contains that key's position code. The position codes for the UP ARROW and DOWN ARROW keys are 72 and 80. Functions like **getchar()** return only the character code, so it is necessary to bypass them and read the scan code directly. (Some compilers supply a function like **readkey()** in their libraries. For example, Turbo C's similar function is called **bioskey()**. If your compiler supplies a similar function, feel free to use it.)

Each time an arrow key is pressed, the item that is currently highlighted is redisplayed in normal video and the next one is highlighted. Pressing the DOWN ARROW key when the highlight is already at the bottom of the screen causes the highlight to wrap around to the first item. The same thing applies in reverse when the UP ARROW key is pressed with the first item already highlighted. Pressing the SPACEBAR causes the next lower item to be highlighted. The ESC key is used to abort from a menu. The value of ESC is 27.

The function **write_video()** is used by **get_resp()** to write a string to the video display at the specified X,Y position, using the specified attribute. The **write_video()** function, shown here, displays a menu entry in reverse video when highlighted or returns it to normal video when not highlighted:

```
/* Display a string with specified attribute. */
void write_video(int x, int y, char *p, int attrib)
{
  union REGS r;
  register int i;

  for(i=x; *p; i++) {
    goto_xy(i, y);
    r.h.ah = 9; /* write character */
    r.h.bh = 0; /* assume active display page is 0 */
    r.x.cx = 1; /* number of times to write the character */
    r.h.al = *p++; /* character */
    r.h.bl = attrib; /* attribute */
    int86(0x10, &r, &r);
  }
}
```

The popup() Function

Now that all the pieces have been created, the **popup()** function can be assembled as shown here:

```
/* Display a pop-up menu and return selection.
   This function returns -2 if menu cannot be constructed;
   it returns -1 if user hits escape key;
   otherwise the item number is returned starting
   with 0 as the first (topmost) entry.
*/
int popup(
  char *menu[], /* menu text */
  char *keys,  /* hot keys */
  int count,   /* number of menu items */
  int x, int y, /* X,Y coordinates of left-hand corner */
  int border   /* no border if 0 */
)
{
```

```
register int i, len;
int endx, endy, choice;
unsigned int *p;

if((y>24) ¦¦ (y<0) ¦¦ (x>79) ¦¦ (x<0)) {
  printf("range error");
  return -2;
}

/* make sure that the menu will fit */
len = 0;
for(i=0; i<count; i++)
 if(strlen(menu[i]) > len) len = strlen(menu[i]);
endx = len + 2 + x;
endy = count + 1 + y;
if((endy+1>24) ¦¦ (endx+1>79)) {
  printf("menu won't fit");
  return -2;
}

/* allocate enough memory to hold the current contents
   of the screen */
p = (unsigned int *) malloc((endx-x+1) * (endy-y+1));
if(!p) exit(1);  /* install your own error handler here */

/* save what is currently on the screen */
save_video(x, endx+1, y, endy+1, p);

if(border) draw_border(x, y, endx, endy);

/* display the menu */
display_menu(menu, x+1, y+1, count);

/* get the user's response */
choice = get_resp(x, y, count, menu, keys);

/* restore the original screen */
restore_video(x, endx+1, y, endy+1, (char *) p);
free(p);

return choice;
}
```

As you can see, **popup()** checks for an out-of-range location and for an oversized menu. It returns −2 if one of these situations exists. Because get_resp() returns a −1 when the user presses the ESC key, a return value of −1 by popup() should be considered as a "cancel menu" request. If the user makes a selection, the return value will be in the range 0 through count−1, with the first menu entry corresponding to 0. As written, popup() uses C's dynamic allocation routines to provide temporary storage for the screen information. This is usually the best approach, but feel free to change it if it makes sense for your specific application.

Putting It All Together

The sample program shown here uses the pop-up menu routines to display three pop-up menus. The only function you haven't seen is called cls(), which clears the screen. Some C compilers do not include a function to do this, so if your compiler doesn't, you can use the one shown in the program.

```
/* Pop-up menu routines for text mode operation that use DOS
   video services. */

#include "stdio.h"
#include "dos.h"
#include "stdlib.h"
#include "bios.h"
#include "string.h"
#include "ctype.h"

#define BORDER 1
#define ESC 27
#define REV_VID 0x70
#define NORM_VID 7

int popup(char *menu[], char *keys, int count,
          int x, int y, int border);
void save_video(int startx, int endx, int starty, int endy,
                unsigned int *buf_ptr);
void restore_video(int startx, int endx, int starty, int endy,
                   unsigned char *buf_ptr);
void goto_xy(int x, int y), cls(void);
void write_video(int x, int y, char *p, int attrib);
void display_menu(char *menu[], int x, int y, int count);
void draw_border(int startx, int starty, int endx, int endy);
int get_resp(int x, int y, int count, char *menu[], char *keys);
```

```
int readkey(void);

char *fruit[]= {
  "Apple",
  "Orange",
  "Pear",
  "Grape",
  "Raspberry",
  "Strawberry"
};

char *color[]= {
  "Red",
  "Yellow",
  "Orange",
  "Green",
};

char *apple_type[]= {
  "Red delicious",
  "Jonathan",
  "Winesap",
  "Rome"
};

main(void)
{
  int i;

  cls();
  goto_xy(0, 0);

  for(i=0; i<25; i++)
    printf("This is a test of the pop-up window routines.\n");

  popup(fruit, "aopgrs", 6, 3, 1, BORDER);
  popup(color, "ryog", 4, 10, 5, BORDER);
  popup(apple_type, "rjwr", 4, 18, 10, BORDER);

  return 0;
}

/* Display a pop-up menu and return selection.
   This function returns -2 if menu cannot be constructed;
   it returns -1 if user hits escape key;
```

```
    otherwise the item number is returned starting
    with 0 as the first (topmost) entry.
*/
int popup(
  char *menu[], /* menu text */
  char *keys,  /* hot keys */
  int count,   /* number of menu items */
  int x, int y, /* X,Y coordinates of left hand corner */
  int border   /* no border if 0 */
)
{
  register int i, len;
  int endx, endy, choice;
  unsigned int *p;

  if((y>24) || (y<0) || (x>79) || (x<0)) {
    printf("range error");
    return -2;
  }

  /* make sure that the menu will fit */
  len = 0;
  for(i=0; i<count; i++)
   if(strlen(menu[i]) > len) len = strlen(menu[i]);
  endx = len + 2 + x;
  endy = count + 1 + y;
  if((endy+1>24) || (endx+1>79)) {
    printf("menu won't fit");
    return -2;
  }

  /* allocate enough memory to hold the current contents
     of the screen */
  p = (unsigned int *) malloc((endx-x+1) * (endy-y+1));
  if(!p) exit(1);  /* install your own error handler here */

  /* save what is currently on the screen */
  save_video(x, endx+1, y, endy+1, p);

  if(border) draw_border(x, y, endx, endy);

  /* display the menu */
  display_menu(menu, x+1, y+1, count);

  /* get the user's response */
```

```
    choice = get_resp(x, y, count, menu, keys);

    /* restore the original screen */
    restore_video(x, endx+1, y, endy+1, (char *) p);
    free(p);

    return choice;
}

/* Display the menu in its proper location. */
void display_menu(char *menu[], int x, int y, int count)
{
  register int i;

  for(i=0; i<count; i++, y++) {
    goto_xy(x, y);
    printf(menu[i]);
  }
}

/* Draw a border around the menu. */
void draw_border(int startx, int starty, int endx, int endy)
{
  register int i;

  /* draw vertical lines */
  for(i=starty+1; i<endy; i++) {
    goto_xy(startx, i);
    putchar(179);
    goto_xy(endx, i);
    putchar(179);
  }

  /* draw horizontal lines */
  for(i=startx+1; i<endx; i++) {
    goto_xy(i, starty);
    putchar(196);
    goto_xy(i, endy);
    putchar(196);
  }

  /* draw the corners */
  goto_xy(startx, starty); putchar(218);
  goto_xy(startx, endy); putchar(192);
  goto_xy(endx, starty); putchar(191);
```

```
    goto_xy(endx, endy); putchar(217);

}

/* Input user's selection. */
get_resp(int x, int y, int count, char *menu[], char *keys)
{
  union inkey {
    char ch[2];
    int i;
  } c;
  int arrow_choice=0;
  char *key_choice;

  x++;
  y++;

  /* highlight the first selection */
  goto_xy(x, y);
  write_video(x, y, menu[0], REV_VID); /* reverse video */

  for(;;) {
    c.i = readkey();     /* read the key */

    /* reset the selection to normal video */
    goto_xy(x, y+arrow_choice);
    write_video(x, y+arrow_choice,
                menu[arrow_choice], NORM_VID); /* redisplay */

    if(c.ch[0]) { /* is normal key */
      /* see if it is a hot key */
      key_choice = strchr(keys, tolower(c.ch[0]));
      if(key_choice) return key_choice-keys;

      /* check for Enter or spacebar */
      switch(c.ch[0]) {
        case '\r': return arrow_choice;
        case ' ' : arrow_choice++;
          break;
        case ESC : return -1; /* cancel */
      }
    }
    else {  /* is special key */
      switch(c.ch[1]) {
        case 72: arrow_choice--; /* up arrow */
```

```
        break;
      case 80: arrow_choice++; /* down arrow */
        break;
    }
  }
  if(arrow_choice==count) arrow_choice = 0;
  if(arrow_choice<0) arrow_choice = count-1;

  /* highlight the next selection */
  goto_xy(x, y+arrow_choice);
  write_video(x, y+arrow_choice, menu[arrow_choice], REV_VID);
  }
}


/* Display a string with specified attribute. */
void write_video(int x, int y, char *p, int attrib)
{
  union REGS r;
  register int i;

  for(i=x; *p; i++) {
    goto_xy(i, y);
    r.h.ah = 9; /* write character */
    r.h.bh = 0; /* assume active display page is 0 */
    r.x.cx = 1; /* number of times to write the character */
    r.h.al = *p++; /* character */
    r.h.bl = attrib; /* attribute */
    int86(0x10, &r, &r);
  }
}


/* Save a portion of the screen. */
void save_video(int startx, int endx, int starty, int endy,
                unsigned int *buf_ptr)
{
  union REGS r;
  register int i,j;

  for(i=startx; i<endx; i++)
    for(j=starty; j<endy; j++) {
      goto_xy(i, j);
      r.h.ah = 8; /* read character */
      r.h.bh = 0; /* assume active display page is 0 */
      *buf_ptr++ = int86(0x10, &r, &r); /* save in buffer */
      putchar(' '); /* clear the screen */
```

```
    }
}

/* Restore a portion of the screen. */
void restore_video(int startx, int endx, int starty, int endy,
                unsigned char *buf_ptr)
{
  union REGS r;
  register int i, j;

  for(i=startx; i<endx; i++)
    for(j=starty; j<endy; j++) {
      goto_xy(i, j);
      r.h.ah = 9; /* write character */
      r.h.bh = 0; /* assume active display page is 0 */
      r.x.cx = 1; /* number of times to write the character */
      r.h.al = *buf_ptr++; /* character */
      r.h.bl = *buf_ptr++; /* attribute */
      int86(0x10, &r, &r);
  }
}

/* Clear the screen. */
void cls(void)
{
  union REGS r;

  r.h.ah = 6; /* screen scroll code */
  r.h.al = 0; /* clear screen code */
  r.h.ch = 0; /* start row */
  r.h.cl = 0; /* start column */
  r.h.dh = 24; /* end row */
  r.h.dl = 79; /* end column */
  r.h.bh = 7;  /* blank line is black */
  int86(0x10, &r, &r);
}

/* Send the cursor to specified X,Y coordinates. */
void goto_xy(int x, int y)
{
  union REGS r;

  r.h.ah = 2; /* cursor addressing function */
  r.h.dl = x; /* column coordinate */
```

```
  r.h.dh = y; /* row coordinate */
  r.h.bh = 0; /* video page */
  int86(0x10, &r, &r);
}

/* Return the 16-bit scan code from the keyboard. */
readkey(void)
{
  union REGS r;

  r.h.ah = 0;
  return int86(0x16, &r, &r);
}
```

You should enter this program into your computer and try it. As it runs, each menu is displayed in turn. (In this program the responses are discarded, but a real application would, of course, process them.) A series of the screens produced is shown in Figure 1-1. Unless you have a very fast computer, you will probably notice that the pop-up action is somewhat sluggish. The only way to solve this problem is to read and write characters directly to and from the video RAM, which is the subject of the next section. Again, the only advantage of using the BIOS approach is that the pop-up menu routines work on any computer that supports BIOS-level compatibility with the IBM BIOS, even if the computer is not 100 percent hardware compatible.

ACCESSING THE VIDEO RAM DIRECTLY

To create menus that really "pop" up, you must bypass the BIOS function calls and directly access the video RAM. Doing this allows characters to be displayed on the screen blindingly fast. By directly reading and writing from and to the video RAM, you can turn the rather sluggish pop-up menus into highly efficient routines.

Reading and writing the video RAM requires the use of **far** pointers. If your C compiler does not support **far** pointers, you cannot directly access the video RAM. **far** pointers can be supported in one of two ways by a C compiler. First, the common **far** keyword extension is used by a great many compilers. It allows a pointer to be declared as **far**. The other way is to use a large memory model compiler in which all pointers are **far** by default. The routines used in this chapter use the **far** type modifier. If you desire, you can remove it and simply compile the code by using a large memory model compiler.

Figure 1-1a

Sample output of the pop-up menu program

```
This is a test of the pop-up window routines.
Thi                    f the pop-up window routines.
Thi Apple             f the pop-up window routines.
Thi Orange            f the pop-up window routines.
Thi Pear              f the pop-up window routines.
Thi Grape             f the pop-up window routines.
Thi Raspberry         f the pop-up window routines.
Thi Strawberry        f the pop-up window routines.
Thi                    f the pop-up window routines.
This is a test of the pop-up window routines.
This is a test of the pop-up window routines.
This is a test of the pop-up window routines.
This is a test of the pop-up window routines.
This is a test of the pop-up window routines.
This is a test of the pop-up window routines.
This is a test of the pop-up window routines.
This is a test of the pop-up window routines.
This is a test of the pop-up window routines.
This is a test of the pop-up window routines.
This is a test of the pop-up window routines.
This is a test of the pop-up window routines.
```

Figure 1-1b

Sample output of the pop-up menu program

```
This is a test of the pop-up window routines.
This is a test of the pop-up window routines.
This is a test of the pop-up window routines.
This is a test of the pop-up window routines.
This is a test of the pop-up window routines.
This is a          he pop-up window routines.
This is a Red      he pop-up window routines.
This is a Yellow   he pop-up window routines.
This is a Orange   he pop-up window routines.
This is a Green    he pop-up window routines.
This is a          he pop-up window routines.
This is a test of the pop-up window routines.
This is a test of the pop-up window routines.
This is a test of the pop-up window routines.
This is a test of the pop-up window routines.
This is a test of the pop-up window routines.
This is a test of the pop-up window routines.
This is a test of the pop-up window routines.
This is a test of the pop-up window routines.
This is a test of the pop-up window routines.
This is a test of the pop-up window routines.
This is a test of the pop-up window routines.
This is a test of the pop-up window routines.
```

Figure 1-1c

Sample output of the pop-up menu program

```
This is a test of the pop-up window routines.
This is a test of the pop-up window routines.
This is a test of the pop-up window routines.
This is a test of the pop-up window routines.
This is a test of the pop-up window routines.
This is a test of the pop-up window routines.
This is a test of the pop-up window routines.
This is a test of the pop-up window routines.
This is a test of the pop-up window routines.
This is a test of the pop-up window routines.
This is a test of         w routines.
This is a test of  Red delicious  w routines.
This is a test of  Jonathan       w routines.
This is a test of  Winesap        w routines.
This is a test of  Rome           w routines.
This is a test of                 w routines.
This is a test of the pop-up window routines.
This is a test of the pop-up window routines.
This is a test of the pop-up window routines.
This is a test of the pop-up window routines.
This is a test of the pop-up window routines.
This is a test of the pop-up window routines.
```

Determining the Location of the Video RAM

The monochrome adapter has its video RAM at B000:0000, while the others are located at B800:0000. For the menu routines to operate correctly for each adapter, they need to know which adapter is in the system. Fortunately, there is an easy way to do this. The BIOS interrupt 0x10, function 15, returns the current video mode. As mentioned earlier, the routines developed in this chapter require that the mode be 2, 3, or 7. The CGA, EGA, and VGA adapters can use modes 2 and 3 but not mode 7; only the monochrome adapter can use this mode. Therefore, if the current video mode is 7, a monochrome adapter is in use; otherwise, it is a CGA, EGA, or VGA. For our purposes, the CGA, EGA, and VGA function the same in text mode, so it doesn't matter which is in the system. Therefore, the **popup()** function must see which adapter is in the system and set a global pointer variable to the proper address. This fragment of code accomplishes just that:

```
vmode = video_mode();
if((vmode!=2) && (vmode!=3) && (vmode!=7)) {
  printf("video must be in 80 column text mode");
  exit(1);
```

```
}
/* set proper address of video RAM */
if(vmode==7) vid_mem = (char far *) 0xB0000000;
else vid_mem = (char far *) 0xB8000000;
```

The function **video_mode()** returns the current video mode and the variable **vid_mem** is declared as a global **char far** elsewhere.

Converting save_video() and restore_video()

Once the variable **vid_mem** has been given the proper address, it is a simple matter to use it to read or write characters to or from the video RAM. Remember, the video memory requires 2 bytes for each character, one for the character itself and one for its attribute. The character byte is first and the attribute is second; therefore, it takes 160 bytes for each line on the screen. Hence, to find the address of a specific character position, you must use this formula:

address = address of adapter + Y*160 + X*2

The functions **save_video()** and **restore_video()** look like the ones shown here when direct video RAM accessing is used:

```
/* Save a portion of the screen using direct
   video RAM accessing.
*/
void save_video(int startx, int endx, int starty, int endy,
                unsigned char *buf_ptr)
{
  register int i,j;
  char far *v, far *t;

  v = vid_mem;
  for(i=startx; i<endx; i++)
    for(j=starty; j<endy; j++) {
      t = v + (j*160) + i*2; /* compute the address */
      *buf_ptr++ = *t++; /* read the character */
      *buf_ptr++ = *t;   /* read the attribute */
      *(t-1) = ' ';  /* clear the window */
    }
}
```

```
/* Restore a portion of the screen using direct
   video RAM accessing.
*/
void restore_video(int startx, int endx, int starty, int endy,
                   unsigned char *buf_ptr)
{
  register int i,j;
  char far *v, far *t;

  v = vid_mem;
  t = v;
  for(i=startx; i<endx; i++)
    for(j=starty; j<endy; j++) {
      v = t;
      v += (j*160) + i*2; /* compute the address */
      *v++ = *buf_ptr++;  /* write the character */
      *v = *buf_ptr++;    /* write the attribute */
  }
}
```

As you can see, the characters and attributes to be written or read are accessed through the use of pointers to the video memory. The other functions that read and write characters are converted in the same way.

One new function (shown next) is required if all accesses to the video display are to be done directly. Called **write _ char()**, this function writes one character to the specified screen location with the specified attribute.

```
/* Write character with specified attribute. */
void write_char(int x, int y, char ch, int attrib)
{
  char far *v;

  v = vid_mem;
  v += (y*160) + x*2; /* compute the address */
  *v++ = ch; /* write the character */
  *v = attrib;  /* write the attribute */
}
```

The complete direct memory access version of the pop-up menu functions are shown here along with the same sample test program. You should enter it into your computer and compare its performance to that

of the BIOS version. As you will see, the difference is quite dramatic. The
menus seem to appear and disappear instantaneously.

```c
/* Pop-up menu routines for text mode operation
   using direct video RAM reads and writes. */

#include "stdio.h"
#include "dos.h"
#include "stdlib.h"
#include "ctype.h"
#include "bios.h"
#include "string.h"

#define BORDER 1
#define ESC 27
#define REV_VID 0x70
#define NORM_VID 7

int popup(char *menu[], char *keys, int count,
          int x, int y, int border);
void save_video(int startx, int endx, int starty, int endy,
                unsigned char *buf_ptr);
void restore_video(int startx, int endx, int starty, int endy,
                   unsigned char *buf_ptr);
void goto_xy(int x, int y), cls(void);
void write_video(int x, int y, char *p, int attrib);
void display_menu(char *menu[], int x, int y, int count);
void draw_border(int startx, int starty, int endx, int endy);
void write_string(int x, int y, char *p, int attrib);
void write_char(int x, int y, char ch, int attrib);
int get_resp(int x, int y, int count, char *menu[], char *keys);
int video_mode(void);
int readkey(void);

char far *vid_mem;

char *fruit[]= {
  "Apple",
  "Orange",
  "Pear",
  "Grape",
  "Raspberry",
  "Strawberry"
};
```

```c
char *color[]= {
  "Red",
  "Yellow",
  "Orange",
  "Green",
};

char *apple_type[]= {
  "Red delicious",
  "Jonathan",
  "Winesap",
  "Rome"
};

main(void)
{
  int i;

  cls();
  goto_xy(0, 0);
  for(i=0; i<25; i++)
    printf("This is a test of the pop-up window routines.\n");

  popup(fruit, "aopgrs", 6, 3, 1, BORDER);
  popup(color, "ryog", 4, 10, 5, BORDER);
  popup(apple_type, "rjwr", 4, 18, 10, BORDER);

  return 0;
}

/* Display a pop-up menu and return selection.
   This function returns -2 if menu cannot be constructed;
   it returns -1 if user hits escape key;
   otherwise the item number is returned starting
   with 0 as the first (topmost) entry.
*/
int popup(
  char *menu[], /* menu text */
  char *keys,  /* hot keys */
  int count,   /* number of menu items */
  int x, int y, /* X,Y coordinates of left-hand corner */
  int border    /* no border if 0 */
)
{
  register int i, len;
```

```
int endx, endy, choice, vmode;
unsigned char *p;

if((y>24) || (y<0) || (x>79) || (x<0)) {
  printf("range error");
  return -2;
}

vmode = video_mode();
if((vmode!=2) && (vmode!=3) && (vmode!=7)) {
  printf("video must be in 80 column text mode");
  exit(1);
}
/* set proper address of video RAM */
if(vmode==7) vid_mem = (char far *) 0xB0000000;
else vid_mem = (char far *) 0xB8000000;

/* make sure that menu will fit */
len = 0;
for(i=0; i<count; i++)
 if(strlen(menu[i]) > len) len = strlen(menu[i]);
endx = len + 2 + x;
endy = count + 1 + y;
if((endy+1>24) || (endx+1>79)) {
  printf("menu won't fit");
  return -2;
}

/* allocate enough memory to hold current contents of
   the screen */
p = (unsigned char *) malloc(2 * (endx-x+1) * (endy-y+1));
if(!p) exit(1); /* install your own error handler here */

/* save the current screen data */
save_video(x, endx+1, y, endy+1, p);

if(border) draw_border(x, y, endx, endy);

/* display the menu */
display_menu(menu, x+1, y+1, count);

/* get the user's response */
choice = get_resp(x, y, count, menu, keys);

/* restore the original screen */
```

```
    restore_video(x, endx+1, y, endy+1, p);
    free(p);
    return choice;
}

/* Display the menu in its proper location. */
void display_menu(char *menu[], int x, int y, int count)
{
    register int i;

    for(i=0; i<count; i++, y++)
        write_string(x, y, menu[i], NORM_VID);
}

/* Draw a border around the window. */
void draw_border(int startx, int starty, int endx, int endy)
{
    register int i;
    char far *v, far *t;

    v = vid_mem;
    t = v;

    /* draw vertical lines */
    for(i=starty+1; i<endy; i++) {
        v += (i*160) + startx*2;
        *v++ = 179;
        *v = NORM_VID;
        v = t;
        v += (i*160) + endx*2;
        *v++ = 179;
        *v = NORM_VID;
        v = t;
    }
    /* draw horizontal lines */
    for(i=startx+1; i<endx; i++) {
        v += (starty*160) + i*2;
        *v++ = 196;
        *v = NORM_VID;
        v = t;
        v += (endy*160) + i*2;
        *v++ = 196;
        *v = NORM_VID;
        v = t;
```

```
  /* draw corners */
  write_char(startx, starty, (char) 218, NORM_VID);
  write_char(startx, endy, (char) 192, NORM_VID);
  write_char(endx, starty, (char) 191, NORM_VID);
  write_char(endx, endy, (char) 217, NORM_VID);
}

/* Input user's selection. */
get_resp(int x, int y, int count, char *menu[], char *keys)
{
  union inkey {
    char ch[2];
    int i;
  } c;
  int arrow_choice=0;
  char *key_choice;

  x++;
  y++;

  /* highlight the first selection */
  goto_xy(x, y);
  write_string(x, y, menu[0], REV_VID); /* reverse video */

  for(;;) {
    c.i = readkey();     /* read the key */

    /* reset the selection to normal video */
    goto_xy(x, y+arrow_choice);
    write_string(x, y+arrow_choice,
               menu[arrow_choice], NORM_VID); /* redisplay */

    if(c.ch[0]) { /* is normal key */
      /* see if it is a hot key */
      key_choice = strchr(keys, tolower(c.ch[0]));
      if(key_choice) return key_choice-keys;

    /* check for Enter or spacebar */
    switch(c.ch[0]) {
      case '\r': return arrow_choice;
      case ' ' : arrow_choice++;
        break;
      case ESC : return -1;  /* cancel */
    }
```

```
  }
  else {  /* is special key */
    switch(c.ch[1]) {
      case 72: arrow_choice--; /* up arrow */
        break;
      case 80: arrow_choice++; /* down arrow */
        break;
    }
  }
  if(arrow_choice==count) arrow_choice=0;
  if(arrow_choice<0) arrow_choice = count-1;

  /* highlight the next selection */
  goto_xy(x, y+arrow_choice);
  write_string(x, y+arrow_choice, menu[arrow_choice], REV_VID);
  }
}

/* Display a string with specified attribute. */
void write_string(int x, int y, char *p, int attrib)
{
  register int i;
  char far *v;

  v = vid_mem;
  v += (y*160) + x*2;  /* compute the address */
  for(i=y; *p; i++) {
    *v++ = *p++;  /* write the character */
    *v++ = attrib;    /* write the attribute */
  }
}

/* Write character with specified attribute. */
void write_char(int x, int y, char ch, int attrib)
{
  char far *v;

  v = vid_mem;
  v += (y*160) + x*2; /* compute the address */
  *v++ = ch; /* write the character */
  *v = attrib;  /* write the attribute */
}

/* Save a portion of the screen using direct
   video RAM accessing.
```

```
*/
void save_video(int startx, int endx, int starty, int endy,
               unsigned char *buf_ptr)
{
  register int i,j;
  char far *v, far *t;

  v = vid_mem;
  for(i=startx; i<endx; i++)
    for(j=starty; j<endy; j++) {
      t = v + (j*160) + i*2; /* compute the address */
      *buf_ptr++ = *t++; /* read the character */
      *buf_ptr++ = *t;   /* read the attribute */
      *(t-1) = ' ';  /* clear the window */
    }
}


/* Restore a portion of the screen using direct
   video RAM accessing.
*/
void restore_video(int startx, int endx, int starty, int endy,
                  unsigned char *buf_ptr)
{
  register int i,j;
  char far *v, far *t;

  v = vid_mem;
  t = v;
  for(i=startx; i<endx; i++)
    for(j=starty; j<endy; j++) {
      v = t;
      v += (j*160) + i*2; /* compute the address */
      *v++ = *buf_ptr++;  /* write the character */
      *v = *buf_ptr++;    /* write the attribute */
    }
}

/* Clear the screen. */
void cls(void)
{
  union REGS r;

  r.h.ah = 6; /* screen scroll code */
  r.h.al = 0; /* clear screen code */
```

```
    r.h.ch = 0; /* start row */
    r.h.cl = 0; /* start column */
    r.h.dh = 24; /* end row */
    r.h.dl = 79; /* end column */
    r.h.bh = 7;  /* blank line is black */
    int86(0x10, &r, &r);
}

/* Send the cursor to X,Y. */
void goto_xy(int x, int y)
{
  union REGS r;

  r.h.ah = 2; /* cursor addressing function */
  r.h.dl = x; /* column coordinate */
  r.h.dh = y; /* row coordinate */
  r.h.bh = 0; /* video page */
  int86(0x10, &r, &r);
}

/* Returns the current video mode. */
video_mode(void)
{
  union REGS r;

  r.h.ah = 15;  /* get video mode */
  return int86(0x10, &r, &r) & 255;
}

/* Return the 16-bit scan code from the keyboard. */
readkey(void)
{
  union REGS r;

  r.h.ah = 0;
  return int86(0x16, &r, &r);
}
```

CREATING PULL-DOWN MENUS

Pull-down menus are fundamentally different from simple pop-up menus
in that two or more pull-down menus may appear to be active at any

one time. Generally, pull-down menus allow the user to select options within options and are used to support a system of menus. Unlike the **popup()** function that saved the screen, displayed the menu, and then restored the screen, the **pulldown()** function developed in this section only saves the screen (if necessary), displays the menu, and returns the user's selection. The restoration of the screen is handled as a separate task elsewhere in the program. Before you can create pull-down menus, you must change the way you think about the menu.

Menu Frames

Central to the creation of pull-down, multilevel menus is the *menu frame.* Unlike the **popup()** function, which only needs access to the menu information while that menu is actually being used, the **pulldown()** function will have to have access to the information about the various menus as they are activated. In essence, the pull-down menu routines require that each menu have its frame of reference defined the entire time the program that is using the menus is running. Each menu is activated by its frame number, and the necessary information is loaded as needed by the various menu support functions.

The best way to support the menu frame approach is to create an array of structures that will hold all information relevant to a menu. The structure is defined as shown here:

```
struct menu_frame {
  int startx, endx, starty, endy;
  unsigned char *p; /* pointer to screen info */
  char **menu; /* pointer to menu strings */
  char *keys;  /* pointer to hot keys */
  int border;  /* border on/off */
  int count;   /* number of selections */
  int active;  /* is menu already active */
} frame[MAX_FRAME];
```

where **MAX_FRAME** is a macro that determines how many menus you can have. The only additional information required by the pull-down routines that is not needed by the pop-up functions is the **active** flag. It is used to signal when a menu is already on the screen and to prevent the original screen information from being overwritten.

Creating a Menu Frame

Before a menu can be used, a frame must be created for it. The function **make_menu()**, shown here, creates this frame:

```
/* Construct a pull-down menu frame.
   It returns 1 if the menu frame can be constructed;
   otherwise 0 is returned.
*/
make_menu(
  int num,      /* menu number */
  char *menu[], /* menu text */
  char *keys,   /* hot keys */
  int count,    /* number of menu items */
  int x, int y, /* X,Y coordinates of left-hand corner */
  int border    /* no border if 0 */
)
{
  register int i, len;
  int endx, endy;
  unsigned char *p;

  if(num>MAX_FRAME) {
    printf("Too many menus\n");
    return 0;
  }

  if((y>24) || (y<0) || (x>79) || (x<0)) {
    printf("range error");
    return 0;
  }

  /* compute the size */
  len = 0;
  for(i=0; i<count; i++)
   if(strlen(menu[i]) > len) len = strlen(menu[i]);
  endx = len + 2 + x;
  endy = count + 1 + y;
  if((endy+1>24) || (endx+1>79)) {
    printf("menu won't fit");
    return 0;
  }

  /* allocate enough memory to hold current contents
```

```
      of the screen */
   p = (unsigned char *) malloc(2 * (endx-x+1) * (endy-y+1));
   if(!p) exit(1); /* put your own error handler here */

   /* construct the frame */
   frame[num].startx = x; frame[num].endx = endx;
   frame[num].starty = y; frame[num].endy = endy;
   frame[num].p = p;
   frame[num].menu = (char **) menu;
   frame[num].border = border;
   frame[num].keys = keys;
   frame[num].count = count;
   frame[num].active = 0;
   return 1;
}
```

You call **make_menu()** with the same arguments that were used with **popup()** except that the number of the menu must be specified in the first argument. This number is used to identify the menu.

The pulldown() Function

The **pulldown()** function is shown here:

```
/* Display a pull-down menu and return selection. */
int pulldown(int num)
{
  int  vmode;

  vmode = video_mode();
  if((vmode!=2) && (vmode!=3) && (vmode!=7)) {
    printf("video must be in 80 column text mode");
    exit(1);
  }
  /* set proper address of video RAM */
  if(vmode==7) vid_mem = (char far *) 0xB0000000;
  else vid_mem = (char far *) 0xB8000000;

  /* get active window */
  if(!frame[num].active) { /* not currently in use */
    save_video(num);        /* save the current screen */
```

```
    frame[num].active = 1; /* set active flag */
  }

  if(frame[num].border) draw_border(num);

  display_menu(num);    /* display the menu */
  return get_resp(num); /* return response */
}
```

To use **pulldown()**, simply pass it the number of the menu you want displayed. However, be sure to restore the screen by using **restore_video()** elsewhere in your program. Remember, the point of pull-down menus is to allow two or more menus to remain on the screen, and potentially active, as the user selects various options. Therefore, you do not want to restore the screen until the entire selection process is complete.

Notice that the portion of the screen used by the menu is saved only if the **active** flag is 0. Since a pull-down menu must be able to be reentered, the screen must not be saved multiple times. (Otherwise, the menu itself would be saved, thus overwriting the original contents of the screen, which was already saved.)

Restoring the Screen

As noted earlier, **pulldown()** does not restore the screen. This is necessary to allow multiple menus on the screen at the same time. Your program must explicitly restore the screen by calling **restore_video()** with the menu number. The modified **restore_video()** function is shown here:

```
/* Restore a portion of the screen. */
void restore_video(int num)
{
  register int i,j;
  char far *v, far *t;
  char *buf_ptr;

  buf_ptr = frame[num].p;
  v = vid_mem;
  t = v;
  for(i=frame[num].startx; i<frame[num].endx+1; i++)
```

```
    for(j=frame[num].starty; j<frame[num].endy+1; j++) {
      v = t;
      v += (j*160) + i*2; /* compute the address */
      *v++ = *buf_ptr++;  /* write the character */
      *v = *buf_ptr++;    /* write the attribute */
  }
  frame[num].active = 0; /* deactivate */
}
```

Like the other menu support functions, the modified **restore_video()** function shown here has been converted to work with frames. As such, only the menu number is now passed to **restore_video()**, which makes for a clean interface.

A Sample Program Using the Pull-down Routines

All the pull-down menu functions along with a simple sample program are shown here and should be entered into your computer:

```
/* Pull-down menu routines for text mode operation and
   short sample program.
*/

#include "stdio.h"
#include "dos.h"
#include "stdlib.h"
#include "bios.h"
#include "ctype.h"
#include "string.h"

#define BORDER 1
#define ESC 27
#define MAX_FRAME 10
#define REV_VID 0x70
#define NORM_VID 7

void save_video(int num);
void restore_video(int num);
void goto_xy(int x, int y), cls(void);
void write_video(int x, int y, char *p, int attrib);
void display_menu(int num);
void write_string(int x, int y, char *p, int attrib);
```

```
void write_char(int x, int y, char ch, int attrib);
void pd_driver(void);
int make_menu(int num, char *menu[], char *keys,
              int count, int x, int y, int border);
int get_resp(int num), pulldown(int num);
int video_mode(void);
void display_menu(int num), draw_border(int num);
char far *vid_mem;
int readkey(void);

struct menu_frame {
  int startx, endx, starty, endy;
  unsigned char *p;
  char **menu;
  char *keys;
  int border, count;
  int active;
} frame[MAX_FRAME], i;

char *fruit[]= {
  "Apple",
  "Orange",
  "Pear",
  "Grape",
  "Raspberry",
  "Strawberry"
};

char *color[]= {
  "Red",
  "Yellow",
  "Orange",
  "Green",
};

char *apple_type[]= {
  "Red delicious",
  "Jonathan",
  "Winesap",
  "Rome"
};

char *grape_type[]= {
  "Concord",
  "cAnadice",
```

```
      "Thompson",
      "Red flame"
};

main(void)
{
  cls();
  goto_xy(0, 0);

  /* first, create the menu frames */
  make_menu(0, fruit, "aopgrs", 6, 20, 5, BORDER);
  make_menu(1, color, "ryog", 4, 28, 9, BORDER);
  make_menu(2, apple_type, "rjwr", 4, 32, 12, BORDER);
  make_menu(3, grape_type, "catr", 4, 10, 9, BORDER);

  printf("Select your fruit:");

  pd_driver(); /* activate the menu system */

  return 0;
}

/* Demonstrate the pull-down menu functions. */
void pd_driver(void)
{
  int choice1, choice2, selection;

  /* now, activate as needed */
  while((choice1=pulldown(0)) != -1) {
    switch(choice1) {
      case 0: /* wants an apple */
        while((choice2=pulldown(1)) != -1) {
          if(choice2==0) {
            selection = pulldown(2); /* red apple */
            restore_video(2);
          }
        }
        restore_video(1);
        break;
      case 1:
      case 2: goto_xy(0, 1);
        printf("out of that selection");
        break;
      case 3: /* wants a grape */
        selection = pulldown(3);
```

```
        restore_video(3);
        break;
      case 4:
      case 5: goto_xy(0, 1);
        printf("out of that selection");
        break;
    }
  }
  restore_video(0);
}

/* Display a pull-down menu and return selection. */
int pulldown(int num)
{
  int  vmode;

  vmode = video_mode();
  if((vmode!=2) && (vmode!=3) && (vmode!=7)) {
    printf("video must be in 80 column text mode");
    exit(1);
  }
  /* set proper address of video RAM */
  if(vmode==7) vid_mem = (char far *) 0xB0000000;
  else vid_mem = (char far *) 0xB8000000;

  /* get active window */
  if(!frame[num].active) { /* not currently in use */
    save_video(num);        /* save the current screen */
    frame[num].active = 1; /* set active flag */
  }

  if(frame[num].border) draw_border(num);

  display_menu(num);     /* display the menu */
  return get_resp(num); /* return response */
}

/* Construct a pull-down menu frame.
   It returns 1 if the menu frame can be constructed;
   otherwise 0 is returned.
*/
make_menu(
  int num,      /* menu number */
  char *menu[], /* menu text */
  char *keys,  /* hot keys */
```

```
  int count,    /* number of menu items */
  int x, int y, /* X,Y coordinates of left-hand corner */
  int border    /* no border if 0 */
)
{
  register int i, len;
  int endx, endy;
  unsigned char *p;

  if(num>MAX_FRAME) {
    printf("Too many menus\n");
    return 0;
  }

  if((y>24) || (y<0) || (x>79) || (x<0)) {
    printf("range error");
    return 0;
  }

  /* compute the size */
  len = 0;
  for(i=0; i<count; i++)
   if(strlen(menu[i]) > len) len = strlen(menu[i]);
  endx = len + 2 + x;
  endy = count + 1 + y;
  if((endy+1>24) || (endx+1>79)) {
    printf("menu won't fit");
    return 0;
  }

  /* allocate enough memory to hold current contents
     of the screen */
  p = (unsigned char *) malloc(2 * (endx-x+1) * (endy-y+1));
  if(!p) exit(1); /* put your own error handler here */

  /* construct the frame */
  frame[num].startx = x; frame[num].endx = endx;
  frame[num].starty = y; frame[num].endy = endy;
  frame[num].p = p;
  frame[num].menu = (char **) menu;
  frame[num].border = border;
  frame[num].keys = keys;
  frame[num].count = count;
  frame[num].active = 0;
  return 1;
```

```
}

/* Display the menu in its proper location. */
void display_menu(int num)
{
  register int i, y;
  char **m;

  y = frame[num].starty+1;
  m = frame[num].menu;

  for(i=0; i<frame[num].count; i++, y++)
    write_string(frame[num].startx+1, y, m[i], NORM_VID);
}

/* Draw a border around the menu. */
void draw_border(int num)
{
  register int i;
  char far *v, far *t;

  v = vid_mem;
  t = v;

  /* draw vertical lines */
  for(i=frame[num].starty+1; i<frame[num].endy; i++) {
    v += (i*160) + frame[num].startx*2;
    *v++ = 179;
    *v = NORM_VID;
    v = t;
    v += (i*160) + frame[num].endx*2;
    *v++ = 179;
    *v = NORM_VID;
    v = t;
  }

  /* draw horizontal lines */
  for(i=frame[num].startx+1; i<frame[num].endx; i++) {
    v += (frame[num].starty*160) + i*2;
    *v++ = 196;
    *v = NORM_VID;
    v = t;
    v += (frame[num].endy*160) + i*2;
    *v++ = 196;
    *v = NORM_VID;
```

```
      v = t;
  }

  /* draw corners */
  write_char(frame[num].startx, frame[num].starty,
            (char) 218, NORM_VID);
  write_char(frame[num].startx, frame[num].endy,
            (char) 192, NORM_VID);
  write_char(frame[num].endx, frame[num].starty,
            (char) 191, NORM_VID);
  write_char(frame[num].endx, frame[num].endy,
            (char) 217, NORM_VID);
}

/* Input user's selection */
get_resp(int num)
{
  union inkey {
    char ch[2];
    int i;
  } c;
  int arrow_choice=0;
  char *key_choice;
  int x, y;

  x = frame[num].startx+1;
  y = frame[num].starty+1;

  /* highlight the first selection */
  goto_xy(x, y);
  write_string(x, y, frame[num].menu[0], REV_VID);

  for(;;) {
    c.i = readkey();     /* read the key */

    /* reset the selection to normal video */
    goto_xy(x, y+arrow_choice);
    write_string(x, y+arrow_choice,
      frame[num].menu[arrow_choice], NORM_VID); /* redisplay */

    if(c.ch[0]) { /* is normal key */
      /* see if it is a hot key */
      key_choice = strchr(frame[num].keys, tolower(c.ch[0]));
      if(key_choice) return key_choice-frame[num].keys;
```

```
      /* check for Enter or spacebar */
      switch(c.ch[0]) {
        case '\r': return arrow_choice;
        case ' ' : arrow_choice++;
          break;
        case ESC : return -1; /* cancel */
      }
    }
    else {  /* is special key */
      switch(c.ch[1]) {
        case 72: arrow_choice--; /* up arrow */
          break;
        case 80: arrow_choice++; /* down arrow */
          break;
      }
    }
    if(arrow_choice==frame[num].count) arrow_choice=0;
    if(arrow_choice<0) arrow_choice = frame[num].count-1;

    /* highlight the next selection */
    goto_xy(x, y+arrow_choice);
    write_string(x, y+arrow_choice,
      frame[num].menu[arrow_choice], REV_VID);
  }
}

/* Display a string with specified attribute. */
void write_string(int x, int y, char *p, int attrib)
{
  char far *v;

  v = vid_mem;
  v += (y*160) + x*2; /* compute the address */
  while(*p) {
    *v++ = *p++;  /* write the character */
    *v++ = attrib;    /* write the attribute */
  }
}

/* Write a character with specified attribute. */
void write_char(int x, int y, char ch, int attrib)
{
  char far *v;

  v = vid_mem;
```

```
  v += (y*160) + x*2; /* compute the address */
  *v++ = ch;  /* write the character */
  *v = attrib;    /* write the attribute */
}


/* Save a portion of the screen. */
void save_video(int num)
{
  register int i,j;
  char *buf_ptr;
  char far *v, far *t;

  buf_ptr = frame[num].p;
  v = vid_mem;
  for(i=frame[num].startx; i<frame[num].endx+1; i++)
    for(j=frame[num].starty; j<frame[num].endy+1; j++) {
      t = (v + (j*160) + i*2);
      *buf_ptr++ = *t++;
      *buf_ptr++ = *t;
      *(t-1) = ' ';  /* clear the window */
    }
}

/* Restore a portion of the screen. */
void restore_video(int num)
{
  register int i,j;
  char far *v, far *t;
  char *buf_ptr;

  buf_ptr = frame[num].p;
  v = vid_mem;
  t = v;
  for(i=frame[num].startx; i<frame[num].endx+1; i++)
    for(j=frame[num].starty; j<frame[num].endy+1; j++) {
      v = t;
      v += (j*160) + i*2; /* compute the address */
      *v++ = *buf_ptr++;  /* write the character */
      *v = *buf_ptr++;    /* write the attribute */
    }
  frame[num].active = 0; /* deactivate */
}

/* Clear the screen. */
void cls(void)
```

```
{
  union REGS r;

  r.h.ah = 6; /* screen scroll code */
  r.h.al = 0; /* clear screen code */
  r.h.ch = 0; /* start row */
  r.h.cl = 0; /* start column */
  r.h.dh = 24; /* end row */
  r.h.dl = 79; /* end column */
  r.h.bh = 7;  /* blank line is black */
  int86(0x10, &r, &r);
}

/* Send the cursor to X,Y. */
void goto_xy(int x, int y)
{
  union REGS r;

  r.h.ah = 2; /* cursor addressing function */
  r.h.dl = x; /* column coordinate */
  r.h.dh = y; /* row coordinate */
  r.h.bh = 0; /* video page */
  int86(0x10, &r, &r);
}

/* returns the current video mode */
video_mode(void)
{
  union REGS r;

  r.h.ah = 15;  /* get video mode */
  return int86(0x10, &r, &r) & 255;
}

/* Return the 16-bit scan code from the keyboard. */
readkey(void)
{
  union REGS r;

  r.h.ah = 0;
  return int86(0x16, &r, &r);
}
```

In this example, if the user selects "Apple," he or she is prompted for the color of the apple; if "Red" is chosen, the list of red apples is displayed. However, if "Grape" is selected, the user is prompted for the type of grape desired. The Apple selection menus are shown in Figure 1-2.

Look closely at the **pd_driver()** function that follows **main()**. When using pull-down menus, you must create a custom function that drives the menu system. The basic strategy of the the driver function will be much like **pd_driver()** in this example. Remember, this sample program only illustrates how to activate the menus. Your real application program will have to process the selections in a meaningful way. Keep in mind that the following sequence must be performed in order for a pull-down menu to be used:

1. Create the menu using **make_menu()**.

2. Activate the menu using **pulldown()**.

3. Restore the screen using **restore_video()** as each menu is exited.

ADDING OPTIONS

The menu routines developed in this chapter fit the needs of many situations. However, you might want to try adding some of the following options:

Figure 1-2

The Apple menus from the pull-down menu sample program

Select your fruit:

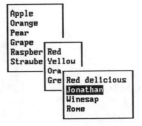

- Allow a menu title to be displayed
- Allow line menus (all options on one line)
- Use different colors for different menus
- Allow different types of borders to be specified

CHAPTER TWO

Pop-up Windows

Pop-up windows can give your programs a professional look and feel that cannot be achieved by other means. Pop-up windows leave the impression that you, the programmer, have mastery over the screen. Since the user generally judges a program by its user interface, this positive impression is generalized to the program as a whole.

This chapter develops a complete set of pop-up window functions that enable you to create and use multiple windows. The window routines make use of the direct video RAM accessing functions developed in Chapter 1. Because windows tend, in general, to be much larger than menus, the BIOS video functions simply cannot be used—even on the fastest computers. For pop-up windows to be effective they must come and go instantly.

Before developing window functions, it is important to understand exactly what a pop-up window is and how it is used.

MARTIN O'RIORDAN

Martin O'Riordan is Project Leader for Microsoft's C++ project. An honors graduate in Computer Science from Trinity College, Dublin, Ireland, he has been a prolific C programmer for a number of years. For example, in 1985, he created the first commercially available C++ translator.

To begin our discussion, I asked Martin what one single feature of C most impressed him. "Definitely the C expression. Expressions in C are truly wonderful. Combined with functions, no other construct can capture as much power and elegance," he said. "But remember," Martin quickly followed, "C also beats the heck out of assembler—both for structure and portability—and this is very important to the type of programming I do."

Since the creation of a C++ compiler is a very complex task, I asked Martin about his personal design philosophy. "First, understand the problem. Never start writing a program by coding. Instead, study the problem from many different angles. Then get the elements of the problem down on paper. Finally, begin coding." (The best C programmers have a lot of intuition and know how the machine thinks.)

When asked about the future of C, Martin responded, "The current future is C++. And, I don't know the future of C++," he mused. "It seems clear that over the next four or five years, C++ will replace C. After that, I think that language evolution is going to move away from the separate compilation model towards some sort of more integrated project development tool."

Martin O'Riordan is a person of many outside interests—a trait he shares with other world-class programmers. Some of his other interests include photography, robotics, medicine (particularly neurological and anatomical), psychology, and art. As Martin puts it, "I am interested in everything. I seldom consider anything I do wasted, because understanding problems means having a diverse approach to solving them."

Martin lives in Redmond, Washington, with his wife and three children.

POP-UP WINDOW THEORY

A *pop-up window* is a portion of the screen that is used for a specific purpose. When the window appears, what is currently on the screen is saved and the window is displayed. When the application using that window is finished, the window is removed and the original contents of the screen are restored. (This is similar to the pop-up menu process.) It is possible to have several windows on the screen at the same time.

Although not strictly necessary, all good window implementations allow the dimensions and screen position of a window to be changed interactively. Hence, the window functions cannot assume that a window will always be in the same place or of the same size.

Window routines are difficult to develop because the application using the window must not be allowed to write past the boundaries of the window. Because the size of the window may change without the application's knowledge, it is the job of the window routines—not the application—to prevent overwriting. Therefore, none of C's normal console I/O routines, such as **printf()** and **gets()**, can be used, and alternative window-specific I/O functions must be substituted. In fact, developing these window-specific I/O functions is the hardest part of creating window routines.

The theory behind using windows is quite simple. Each separate task of a program uses its own window. When the task is begun, its window is activated. When the task completes, its window is removed. If a task is interrupted, it is suspended but its own window is not removed, and the interrupting task simply activates its own window on top of the other window. (Without the use of windows, each task generally clears the screen. This causes the user to break concentration. However, when windows are used, the interrupting task is viewed as a temporary pause.)

To understand how windows might be used effectively, imagine that you have written a text editor that includes some extra features, including a notepad, a four-function calculator, and a decimal-to-hexadecimal converter. Because these functions are not directly related to the act of text editing, it makes sense to use a pop-up window whenever one of them is activated. Then, when one of the extra features is used, the main task of editing is simply suspended; it is not completely disrupted.

WINDOW FRAMES

Implementing pop-up windows correctly requires that all attributes needed for their frame of reference be available to all of the window functions at any time. To accomplish this, the frame concept, similar to that used by the pull-down menu routines, will be used. However, a window frame (no pun intended) contains some different information. To hold the frames, the array of structures shown here is used:

```
struct window_frame {
   int startx, endx, starty, endy; /* window position */
   int curx, cury; /* current cursor position in window */
   unsigned char *p; /* pointer to buffer */
   char *header; /* header message */
   int border; /* border on/off */
   int active; /* on screen yes/no */
} frame[MAX_FRAME];
```

The variables **startx**, **starty**, **endx**, and **endy** hold the coordinates of the upper-left corner and the lower-right corner of the window. The current position of the cursor inside the window is found in **curx** and **cury**. The cursor must be manually manipulated and maintained by the window routines. The pointer **p** points to the region of memory that holds what was previously on the portion of the screen overwritten by the window. Often, a window has a header that is a message identifying what the window is. This message is pointed to by **header**. The variable **border** is used to specify whether the window will have a border around it. The **active** variable is set to 1 if the window is currently on the screen and 0 otherwise.

From a programming point of view, using windows is quite easy. First, you create a window frame. Then, when you need the window, you activate it and use the special window-specific I/O functions to write to it. When the window is no longer needed, you deactivate it.

CREATING THE WINDOW FRAME

The function used to create a window frame is called **make_window()**, shown here:

```
/* Construct a pull-down window frame.
   1 is returned if window frame can be constructed;
   otherwise 0 is returned.
*/
make_window(
```

```
   int num, /* window number */
   char *header, /* header text */
   int startx, int starty, /* X,Y coordinates of upper-left corner */
   int endx, int endy, /* X,Y coordinates of lower-right corner */
   int border) /* no border if 0 */
{
  unsigned char *p;

  if(num>MAX_FRAME) {
    printf("Too many windows\n");
    return 0;
  }

  if((starty>24) || (starty<0) || (startx>78) || (startx<0)) {
    printf("range error");
    return 0;
  }

  if((endy>24) || (endx>79)) {
    printf("window won't fit");
    return 0;
  }

  /* allocate enough memory to hold it */
  p = (unsigned char *) malloc(2*(endy-starty+1)*(endx-startx+1));
  if(!p) exit(1); /* put your own error handler here */

  /* construct the frame */
  frame[num].startx = startx; frame[num].endx = endx;
  frame[num].starty = starty; frame[num].endy = endy;
  frame[num].p = p;
  frame[num].header = header;
  frame[num].border = border;
  frame[num].active = 0;
  frame[num].curx = 0; frame[num].cury = 0;
  return 1;
}
```

As you can see by looking at the function's declaration, it requires you to pass it the number of the window you wish to create a frame for and all other relevant information. For example, this call to **make_window()** creates a frame for window 0 that has the header "Editor [Esc to exit]", has the upper-left corner at 0,0 and the lower-right corner at 78,24, and uses a border:

```
make_window(0, " Editor [Esc to exit] ", 0, 0, 78, 24, BORDER);
```

Notice that the cursor position variables **curx** and **cury** are initialized to 0. This means that when the window is first activated, the cursor will be in the upper-left corner. The function also makes sure that the window fits on the screen.

ACTIVATING AND DEACTIVATING A WINDOW

To activate a window, use the **window()** function shown here, where **num** will contain the frame number of the window you want to use.

```
/* Display a pop-up window. */
void window(int num) /* window number */
{
  int  vmode;
  int x, y;

  vmode = video_mode();
  if((vmode!=2) && (vmode!=3) && (vmode!=7)) {
    printf("video must be in 80 column text mode");
    exit(1);
  }
  /* set proper address of video RAM */
  if(vmode==7) vid_mem = (char far *) 0xB0000000;
  else vid_mem = (char far *) 0xB8000000;

  /* get active window */
  if(!frame[num].active) { /* not currently in use */
    save_video(num);        /* save the current screen */
    frame[num].active = 1; /* set active flag */
  }

  if(frame[num].border) draw_border(num);
  display_header(num); /* display the window */

  x = frame[num].startx + frame[num].curx + 1;
  y = frame[num].starty + frame[num].cury + 1;
  goto_xy(x, y);
}
```

As you can see, it is very similar to the **menu()** function developed in the previous chapter. The **vid_mem** variable is a global **char far** pointer that is defined elsewhere.

The function **display_header()**, shown here, is used to display a header message at the top of the window. If the message does not fit, it will not be displayed.

```
/* Display the header message in its proper location. */
void display_header(int num)
{
  register int  x, len;

  x = frame[num].startx;

  /* Calculate the correct starting position to center
     the header message - if negative, message won't
     fit.
  */
  len = strlen(frame[num].header);
  len = (frame[num].endx - x - len) / 2;
  if(len<0) return; /* don't display it */
  x = x + len;

  write_string(x, frame[num].starty,
            frame[num].header, NORM_VID);
}
```

If you want the message displayed in reverse video, substitute **REV_VID** (defined as 0x70) for **NORM_VID** (defined as 7).

To deactivate a window, use the **deactivate()** function shown here, passing it the number of the window to remove:

```
/* Deactivate a window and remove it from the screen. */
void deactivate(int num)
{
  /* reset the cursor postion to upper-left corner */
  frame[num].curx = 0;
  frame[num].cury = 0;
  frame[num].active = 0;
  restore_video(num);
}
```

As shown, the function resets the cursor position to 0,0. However, since you may encounter some situations in which it is more desirable not to reset the cursor variables, feel free to change this feature if you like.

WINDOW I/O FUNCTIONS

Before a window can be used, it is necessary to develop a large number of window-specific console I/O functions. To understand why so many functions are needed, simply think about how many console I/O functions are in C's standard library. The functions developed in this chapter actually represent just a minimum set necessary to use windows. Although they do not include window-specific versions of all C's console I/O functions, these functions still entail a lot of code. As you will see, even the simplest operation, such as reading a character from the keyboard or putting a character on the screen, requires quite a bit of code because it must manually keep track of the current cursor position and not allow boundaries to be overwritten. Remember, none of the automatic features provided by DOS are available to manipulate the screen.

All of the window I/O functions begin with the word "window" for easy identification. Also, all the window I/O functions take as their first argument the number of the window being accessed.

The Window Cursor Positioning Function

It may seem like an unusual place to start, but the first function needed is a window equivalent of the **goto_xy()** function. The reason for this is simple. Since the window-specific I/O routines must manually maintain the cursor, there must be some way to put the cursor where it is supposed to be. The function **window_xy()**, shown here, does just that.

```
/* Position cursor in a window at specified location.
   Returns 0 if out of range;
   nonzero otherwise.
*/
window_xy(int num, int x, int y)
{
  if(x<0 || x+frame[num].startx>=frame[num].endx-1)
    return 0;
  if(y<0 || y+frame[num].starty>=frame[num].endy-1)
    return 0;
  frame[num].curx = x;
  frame[num].cury = y;
```

```
    goto_xy(frame[num].startx+x+1, frame[num].starty+y+1);
    return 1;
}
```

The key to understanding **window_xy()** is remembering that a specific X,Y coordinate is always in the same position inside the specified
window, no matter where the window is on the screen; that is, the X,Y
location is relative to the window, not to the screen. Stated a different
way, if you request the cursor to be at window location 2,2, it will be
placed two lines down and two characters over from the upper-left
corner, no matter where that window is actually positioned on the screen.
Physically placing the cursor at that relative position means translating it
into actual screen coordinates. That is what is done by **window_xy()**. In
addition, **window_xy()** does not allow the cursor to be positioned outside
the specified window.

The window_getche() Function

You cannot use **getche()**, which reads a keystroke and echoes it to the
screen, because it allows a window to be overrun, so an alternative
function called **window_getche()** must be developed. This function reads
a character from the current cursor position in the specified window.

```
/* Input keystrokes inside a window.
   Returns full 16-bit scan code.
*/
window_getche(int num)
{
  union inkey {
    char ch[2];
    int i;
  } c;

  if(!frame[num].active) return 0; /* window not active */

  window_xy(num, frame[num].curx, frame[num].cury);

  c.i = readkey(); /* read the key */

  if(c.ch[0]) {
```

```
    switch(c.ch[0]) {
      case '\r': /* the Enter key is pressed */
        break;
      case '\b': /* backspace */
        break;
      default:
        if(frame[num].cury+frame[num].starty < frame[num].endy-1) {
          write_char(frame[num].startx+ frame[num].curx+1,
            frame[num].starty+frame[num].cury+1, c.ch[0], NORM_VID);
          frame[num].curx++;
        }
    }
    if(frame[num].curx < 0) frame[num].curx = 0;
    if(frame[num].curx+frame[num].startx > frame[num].endx-2)
      frame[num].curx--;
    window_xy(num, frame[num].curx, frame[num].cury);
  }
  return c.i;
}
```

Unlike **getche()**, **window_getche()** returns the full 16-bit scan code. This means that you will have access to the standard character codes in the lower eight bits, as well as to the position code in the upper eight bits. If you want to ignore the position code, simply assign the return value of **window_getche()** to a character.

The function operates like this. First, if the frame is not active (that is, if it is not on the screen) the function returns 0. Since it is not possible to generate a 0 from the keyboard, your routines could check for this possible error. Next, the cursor is positioned to its current position in the window and the key is read. If it is a normal key and not a RETURN or BACKSPACE key, the current X cursor variable for that frame is incremented and the key is echoed. If the cursor is at a boundary, the X value is decremented to prevent the border of the window from being overrun. The final call to **window_xy()** advances the cursor on the screen to the next position.

The **window_getche()** function does not let you type past a window boundary. Keep in mind that all windows have borders, even if some are not explicitly displayed with lines. When the border is not displayed, blank space is used. This is because the window must be distinguished from the background. Even if the border is not drawn, characters may not be written outside the window.

The window_gets() Function

To read a string from within a window, use the **window_gets()** function shown here. It is not as sophisticated as most **gets()** functions, but it works for most applications. You can add functionality if you desire.

```
/* Read a string from a window. */
void window_gets(int num, char *s)
{
  char ch, *temp;

  temp = s;
  for(;;) {
    ch = window_getche(num);
    switch(ch) {
      case '\r': /* the Enter key is pressed */
        *s='\0';
        return;
      case '\b': /* backspace */
        if(s>temp) {
          s--;
          frame[num].curx--;
          if(frame[num].cury<0) frame[num].cury = 0;
            window_xy(num, frame[num].curx, frame[num].cury);
              write_char(frame[num].startx+ frame[num].curx+1,
            frame[num].starty+frame[num].cury+1, ' ', NORM_VID);
        }
        break;
      default: *s = ch;
        s++;
    }
  }
}
```

When the BACKSPACE key is pressed, it is necessary to back up the cursor, erase what is there, and write a space.

The window_putchar() Function

Writing a character to a window involves checking that the window is active and that the character will not cross the window boundary. After the character is written, the cursor position must be advanced. The function **window_putchar()**, shown here, accomplishes these tasks:

```c
/* Write a character at the current cursor position
   in the specified window.
   Returns 0 if window not active;
   1 otherwise.
*/
window_putchar(int num, char ch)
{
  register int x, y;
  char far *v;

  /* make sure window is active */
  if(!frame[num].active) return 0;

  x = frame[num].curx + frame[num].startx + 1;
  y = frame[num].cury + frame[num].starty + 1;

  v = vid_mem;
  v += (y*160) + x*2; /* compute the address */
  if(y>=frame[num].endy) {
    return 1;
  }
  if(x>=frame[num].endx) {
    return 1;
  }

  if(ch=='\n') { /* newline char */
    y++;
    x = frame[num].startx+1;
    v = vid_mem;
    v += (y*160) + x*2; /* compute the address */
    frame[num].curx = 0;  /* reset X */
    frame[num].cury++; /* increment Y */
  }
  else {
    frame[num].curx++;
    *v++ = ch;  /* write the character */
    *v++ = NORM_VID;    /* normal video attribute */
  }
  window_xy(num, frame[num].curx, frame[num].cury);
  return 1;
}
```

This function does not consider it an error condition if the character cannot be written because a window boundary would be crossed. This is because the size of a window can be dynamically changed, meaning that messages that previously fit may not fit at a later time. The function simply does not display a character that is outside the window.

Notice that a carriage return requires the cursor to be manually positioned down one line, if possible, and on the left side of the window.

The window _ puts() Function

The **window _ puts()** function writes the specified string to the indicated window by using **window _ putchar()**.

```
/* Write a string at the current cursor position
   in the specified window.
   Returns 0 if window not active;
   1 otherwise.
*/
window_puts(int num, char *str)
{
   /* make sure window is active */
   if(!frame[num].active) return 0;

   for( ; *str;  str++)
     window_putchar(num, *str);
   return 1;
}
```

Miscellaneous Screen-handling Functions

The window package also includes these screen functions:

Function	Purpose
window _ cls()	Clears a window
window _ cleol()	Clears from current cursor position to end of line
window _ upline()	Moves the cursor up one line
window _ downline()	Moves the cursor down one line
window _ bksp()	Moves the cursor back one space

These functions are shown next. You can create other, custom screen
functions by following the same general format used by these routines.

```c
/* Clear a window. */
void window_cls(int num)
{
  register int i,j;
  char far *v, far *t;

  v = vid_mem;
  t = v;
  for(i=frame[num].starty+1; i<frame[num].endy; i++)
    for(j=frame[num].startx+1; j<frame[num].endx; j++) {
      v = t;
      v += (i*160) + j*2;
      *v++ = ' '; /* write a space */
      *v = NORM_VID; /* normal */
    }
  frame[num].curx = 0;
  frame[num].cury = 0;
}

/* Clear to end of line. */
void window_cleol(int num)
{
  register int i, x, y;

  x = frame[num].curx;
  y = frame[num].cury;
  window_xy(num, frame[num].curx, frame[num].cury);

  for(i=frame[num].curx; i<frame[num].endx-1; i++)
    window_putchar(num,' ');
  window_xy(num, x, y);
}

/* Move cursor up one line.
   Returns nonzero if successful;
   0 otherwise.
*/
window_upline(int num)
{
  if(frame[num].cury > 0) {
    frame[num].cury--;
    window_xy(num, frame[num].curx, frame[num].cury);
```

```
      return 1;
  }
  return 0;
}


/* Move cursor down one line.
   Returns nonzero if successful;
   0 otherwise.
*/
window_downline(int num)
{
  if(frame[num].cury < frame[num].endy-frame[num].starty-1) {
    frame[num].cury++;
    window_xy(num, frame[num].curx, frame[num].cury);
    return 1;
  }
  return 0;
}


/* Back up one character. */
void window_bksp(int num)
{
  if(frame[num].curx>0) {
    frame[num].curx--;
    window_xy(num, frame[num].curx, frame[num].cury);
    window_putchar(num, ' ');
    frame[num].curx--;
    window_xy(num, frame[num].curx, frame[num].cury);
  }
}
```

CHANGING THE SIZE AND POSITION OF A WINDOW AT RUN TIME

Athough you use **make_window()** to define the initial size and position of the window, these parameters can be dynamically altered at run time. The basic theory behind altering a window is to change one or more of the frame parameters based on instructions from the user, erase the current window, and redraw it with the new parameters. The routines called **size()** and **move()**, shown here, are used to resize or reposition a specified window. The arrow keys as well as the HOME, END, PGDN, and PGUP keys are used to manipulate the shape or position of the window.

```
/* Interactively change the size of a window. */
void size(int num)
{
  char ch;
  int x, y, startx, starty;

  /* activate if necessary */
  if(!frame[num].active) window(num);

  startx = x = frame[num].startx;
  starty = y = frame[num].starty;
  window_xy(num, 0, 0);

  do {
    ch = get_special();
    switch(ch) {
      case 75: /* left */
        startx--;
        break;
      case 77: /* right */
        startx++;
        break;
      case 72: /* up */
        starty--;
        break;
      case 80: /* down */
        starty++;
        break;
      case 71: /* up left */
        starty--; startx--;
        break;
      case 73: /* up right */
        starty--; startx++;
        break;
      case 79: /* down left*/
        starty++; startx--;
        break;
      case 81: /* down right */
        starty++; startx++;
        break;
      case 60: /* F2: cancel and use original size */
        startx = x;
        starty = y;
        ch = 59;
    }
```

```
  /* see if out-of-range */
  if(startx<0) startx++;
  if(startx>=frame[num].endx) startx--;
  if(starty<0) starty++;
  if(starty>=frame[num].endy) starty--;
  deactivate(num);
  frame[num].startx = startx;
  frame[num].starty = starty;
  window(num);
} while(ch!=59); /* F1 to stop */
deactivate(num);
}

/* Interactively move a window. */
void move(int num)
{
  char ch;
  int x, y, ex, ey, startx, starty, endx, endy;

  /* activate if necessary */
  if(!frame[num].active) window(num);

  startx = x = frame[num].startx;
  starty = y = frame[num].starty;
  endx = ex = frame[num].endx;
  endy = ey = frame[num].endy;
  window_xy(num, 0, 0);

  do {
    ch = get_special();
    switch(ch) {
      case 75: /* left */
        startx--;
        endx--;
        break;
      case 77: /* right */
        startx++;
        endx++;
        break;
      case 72: /* up */
        starty--;
        endy--;
        break;
      case 80: /* down */
        starty++;
```

```
      endy++;
      break;
   case 71: /* up left */
     starty--; startx--;
     endy--; endx--;
     break;
   case 73: /* up right */
     starty--; startx++;
     endy--; endx++;
     break;
   case 79: /* down left*/
     starty++; startx--;
     endy++; endx--;
     break;
   case 81: /* down right */
     starty++; startx++;
     endy++; endx++;
     break;
   case 60: /* F2: cancel and use original size */
     startx = x;
     starty = y;
     endx = ex;
     endy = ey;
     ch = 59;
}

/* see if out-of-range */
if(startx<0) {
  startx++;
  endx++;
}
if(endx>=79) {
  startx--;
  endx--;
}
if(starty<0) {
  starty++;
  endy++;
}
if(endy>=25) {
  starty--;
  endy--;
}
deactivate(num);
```

```
    frame[num].startx = startx;
    frame[num].starty = starty;
    frame[num].endx = endx;
    frame[num].endy = endy;
    window(num);
  } while(ch!=59); /* F1 to stop */
  deactivate(num);
}
```

For both the **size()** and **move()** functions, when you have finished altering the window, press the F1 key. The new size or position of the window will be used whenever that window is activated unless you change it again. To abort either function, press the F2 key; the window returns to its former size or position.

CREATING APPLICATIONS THAT USE POP-UP WINDOWS

The most important thing to remember about using windows is to always use the window-specific I/O routines. Employing any of the standard C functions invites trouble by creating the possibility that the window boundary will be overwritten. Since no window equivalent of the **printf()** function was developed (you may want to develop one on your own, however), the easiest way to output data types other than characters and strings is as follows: use C's standard **sprintf()** function to transform whatever data type(s) you have into a formatted string and then use **window_puts()** to write the string to the window. The same method applies to inputting information other than characters and strings. Use **window_gets()** to read numbers and convert them into the desired data type by using C's standard **sscanf()** function, which takes a string as input instead of taking input from the keyboard.

Let's look at three simple window-based applications.

Decimal-to-Hexadecimal Converter

Examine the code for the decimal-to-hexadecimal converter shown here:

```
/* Decimal to hexadecimal converter. */
void dectohex(void)
{
  char in[80], out[80];
  int n;

  window(1);
  do {
    window_xy(1, 0, 0);  /* go to first line */
    window_cleol(1); /* clear the line */
    window_puts(1, "dec: "); /* prompt */
    window_gets(1, in); /* read the number */
    window_putchar(1, '\n'); /* go to next line */
    window_cleol(1); /* clear it */
    sscanf(in,"%d", &n); /* convert to internal format */
    sprintf(out, "%s%X", "hex: ",n); /* convert to hex */
    window_puts(1, out); /* output hex */
  } while(*in);
  deactivate(1);
}
```

This function activates its window and then loops, inputting decimal numbers and outputting their hexadecimal equivalents, until the user presses ENTER when prompted for the decimal number. The window is deactivated before the function returns.

Four-function Calculator

A very useful and popular pop-up window application is a calculator. The one developed here is *stack-based,* which means that you enter the operands first and then the operator (like postfix notation). The operands are placed on a stack. Each time an operator is encountered, the top two operands are removed and the operation is applied to them. The answer is printed and the result is pushed on the stack. For example, to find the answer to (10+5)/5 you would first enter **10**, then **5**, then the **+**. This results in the number 15 being displayed and also being put on the top of the stack. Next, enter **5** followed by the **/**. The answer 3 is displayed. The stack is 100 elements deep, which means that you can enter several operands before entering an operator.

The **calc()** function plus the **push()** and **pop()** stack routines are shown next. Although this version works only with integers, you can easily change it to work with real numbers.

```c
#define MAX 100

int *p;    /* pointer into the stack */
int *tos; /* points to top of stack */
int *bos; /* points to bottom of stack */

/* Stack based, postfix notation four-function calculator. */
void calc(void)
{
  char in[80], out[80];
  int answer, stack[MAX];
  int a,b;

  p = stack;
  tos = p;
  bos = p+MAX-1;

  window(2);
  do {
    window_xy(2, 0, 0);
    window_cleol(2);
    window_puts(2, ": "); /* calc prompt */
    window_gets(2, in);
    window_puts(2, "\n ");
    window_cleol(2);
    switch(*in) {
      case '+':
        a = pop();
        b = pop();
        answer = a+b;
        push(a+b);
        break;
      case '-':
        a = pop();
        b = pop();
        answer = b-a;
        push(b-a);
        break;
      case '*':
        a = pop();
```

```
      b = pop();
      answer = b*a;
      push(b*a);
      break;
    case '/':
      a = pop();
      b=pop();
      if(a==0) {
        window_puts(2, "divide by 0\n");
        break;
      }
      answer = b/a;
      push(b/a);
      break;
    default:
      push(atoi(in));
      continue;
  }
  sprintf(out, "%d", answer);
  window_puts(2, out);
} while(*in);
deactivate(2);
}


/* Place a number on the stack.
   Returns 1 if successful;
   0 if stack is full.
*/
push(int i)
{
  if(p>bos) return 0;

  *p=i;
  p++;
  return 1;
}

/* Retrieve top element from the stack.
   Returns 0 on stack underflows.
*/
pop(void)
{
  p--;
  if(p<tos) {
    p++;
```

```
    return 0;
  }
  return *p;
}
```

Pop-up Notepad

Another very useful pop-up application is the notepad. Often, when using a program, you may want to make a note. When a pop-up notepad is available, all you have to do is activate it, enter the note, and then return to whatever you were doing. A very simple notepad function is shown here:

```
/* Pop-up notepad. */
#define MAX_NOTE 10
char notes[MAX_NOTE][80];

void notepad(void)
{
  static first=1;
  register int i, j, k;
  union inkey {
    char ch[2];
    int i;
  } c;
  char ch;

  /* initialize notes array if necessary */
  if(first) {
    for(i=0; i<MAX_NOTE; i++)
      *notes[i] = '\0';
    first = !first;
  }

  window(3);
  /* display the existing notes */
  for(i=0; i<MAX_NOTE; i++) {
    if(*notes[i]) window_puts(3, notes[i]);
    window_putchar(3, '\n');
  }

  i=0;
```

```
window_xy(3, 0, 0);

for(;;) {
  c.i = readkey(); /* read the key */
  if(tolower(c.ch[1])==59) { /* F1 to quit */
    deactivate(3);
    break;
  }

  /* if normal key */
  if(isprint(c.ch[0]) || c.ch[0]=='\b') {
    window_cleol(3);
    notes[i][0] = c.ch[0];
    j = 1;
    window_putchar(3, notes[i][0]);
    do {
      ch = window_getche(3);
      if(ch=='\b') {
        if(j>0) {
          j--;
          window_bksp(3);
        }
      }
      else {
        notes[i][j] = ch;
        j++;
      }
    } while(notes[i][j-1]!='\r');
    notes[i][j-1] = '\0';
    if(i<MAX_NOTE-1) i++;
    window_putchar(3, '\n');
  }
  else {  /* is special key */
    switch(c.ch[1]) {
      case 72: /* up arrow */
        if(i>0) {
          i--;
          window_upline(3);
        }
        break;
      case 80: /* down arrow */
        if(i<MAX_NOTE-1) {
          i++;
          window_downline(3);
        }
```

```
      break;
    case 60: /* clear the notepad */
      window_cls(3);
      for(k=0; k<MAX_NOTE; k++) *notes[k] = '\0';
      window_xy(3, 0, 0);
    }
  }
 }
}
```

The **notepad()** function allows up to ten lines to be entered. You use the UP ARROW and DOWN ARROW keys to go to the line of your choice. If the line previously held a message, the line is erased. The F1 function key is used to exit the notepad. Pressing F2 clears the notepad.

PUTTING IT ALL TOGETHER

The sample program shown in this section includes all the window routines, the video support functions developed in Chapter 1, and the three window applications. It simulates an editor, and it allows you to use the function keys to activate the various window applications or to demonstrate different features of the window system. You should enter it into your computer at this time.

```
/* Window routines with simple demostration program.
   An editor is simulated. Three special pop-up window
   utilities illustrate both the power and magic of
   windowing software and also serve as examples of
   window programming. The pop-up window routines
   are a four-function calculator, a decimal to hex
   converter, and a pop-up notepad.
*/

#include "stdio.h"
#include "dos.h"
#include "bios.h"
#include "stdlib.h"
#include "string.h"

#define BORDER 1
#define ESC 27
#define MAX_FRAME 10
```

```
#define REV_VID 0x70
#define NORM_VID 7

void save_video(int num), restore_video(int num);
void goto_xy(int x, int y), cls(void);
void write_string(int x, int y, char *p, int attrib);
void write_char(int x, int y, char ch, int attrib);
void draw_border(int num);
void display_header(int num);
void window_gets(int num, char *s), size(int num);
void move(int num), window_cls(int num);
void window_cleol(int num), window(int num);
void dectohex(void), notepad(void), calc(void);
void deactivate(int num);
void window_bksp(int num);
int window_upline(int num), window_downline(int num);
int make_window(int num, char *header, int startx, int starty,
                int endx, int endy, int border);
int window_getche(int num);
int window_putchar(int num, char ch);
int window_xy(int num, int x, int y);
int video_mode(void), get_special(void);
int push(int i), pop(void);
int readkey(void);

char far *vid_mem;

struct window_frame {
  int startx, endx, starty, endy; /* window position */
  int curx, cury; /* current cursor position in window */
  unsigned char *p; /* pointer to buffer */
  char *header; /* header message */
  int border; /* border on/off */
  int active; /* on screen yes/no */
} frame[MAX_FRAME];

main(void)
{
  union inkey {
    char ch[2];
    int i;
  } c;
  int i;
  char ch;
```

```
cls();
goto_xy(0,0);

/* first, create the window frames */
make_window(0, " Editor [Esc to exit] ", 0, 0, 78, 24, BORDER);
make_window(1, " Decimal to Hex ", 40, 7, 70, 10, BORDER);
make_window(2, " Calculator ", 20, 8, 60, 12, BORDER);
make_window(3, " Notepad [F1 to exit] ", 20, 5, 60, 16, BORDER);

/* use window() to activate the specified window */
window(0);
do {
  c.i = window_getche(0);
  ch = c.i; /* use only low-order byte */
  if(ch=='\r') /* must do explicit crlf */
      window_putchar(0, '\n');

  switch(c.ch[1]) { /* see if arrow or function key */
    case 59: /* F1 demostrate the window_xy() function */
      window(1);
      for(i=0; i<10; i++)
        if(window_xy(1, i, i)) window_putchar(1,'X');
      window_getche(1);
      deactivate(1);
      break;
    case 60: /* F2 demonstrate sizing and moving a window */
      size(1);
      move(1);
      break;
    case 61: /* F3 invoke the calculator */
      calc();
      break;
    case 62: /* F4 invoke the dec to hex converter */
      dectohex();
      break;
    case 63: /* F5 invoke the notepad */
      notepad();
      break;
    case 72: /* up */
      window_upline(0);
      break;
    case 80: /* down */
      window_downline(0);
      break;
  }
```

```
  } while (ch!=ESC);
  deactivate(0); /* remove window */
  return 0;
}


/**********************************************************/
/* Window functions                                     */
/**********************************************************/

/* Display a pull-down window. */
void window(int num) /* window number */
{
  int  vmode;
  int x, y;

  vmode = video_mode();
  if((vmode!=2) && (vmode!=3) && (vmode!=7)) {
    printf("video must be in 80 column text mode");
    exit(1);
  }
  /* set proper address of video RAM */
  if(vmode==7) vid_mem = (char far *) 0xB0000000;
  else vid_mem = (char far *) 0xB8000000;

  /* get active window */
  if(!frame[num].active) { /* not currently in use */
    save_video(num);        /* save the current screen */
    frame[num].active = 1; /* set active flag */
  }

  if(frame[num].border) draw_border(num);
  display_header(num); /* display the window */

  x = frame[num].startx + frame[num].curx + 1;
  y = frame[num].starty + frame[num].cury + 1;
  goto_xy(x, y);
}

/* Construct a pull-down window frame.
   1 is returned if window frame can be constructed;
   otherwise 0 is returned.
*/
make_window(
  int num, /* window number */
  char *header, /* header text */
```

```
    int startx, int starty, /* X,Y coordinates of upper-left corner */
    int endx, int endy, /* X,Y coordinates of lower-right corner */
    int border) /* no border if 0 */
{
  unsigned char *p;

  if(num>MAX_FRAME) {
    printf("Too many windows\n");
    return 0;
  }

  if((starty>24) || (starty<0) || (startx>78) || (startx<0)) {
    printf("range error");
    return 0;
  }

  if((endy>24) || (endx>79)) {
    printf("window won't fit");
    return 0;
  }

  /* allocate enough memory to hold it */
  p = (unsigned char *) malloc(2*(endy-starty+1)*(endx-startx+1));
  if(!p) exit(1); /* put your own error handler here */

  /* construct the frame */
  frame[num].startx = startx; frame[num].endx = endx;
  frame[num].starty = starty; frame[num].endy = endy;
  frame[num].p = p;
  frame[num].header = header;
  frame[num].border = border;
  frame[num].active = 0;
  frame[num].curx = 0; frame[num].cury = 0;
  return 1;
}

/* Deactivate a window and remove it from the screen. */
void deactivate(int num)
{
  /* reset the cursor postion to upper-left corner */
  frame[num].curx = 0;
  frame[num].cury = 0;
  frame[num].active = 0;
  restore_video(num);
}
```

```
/* Interactively change the size of a window.
*/
void size(int num)
{
  char ch;
  int x, y, startx, starty;

  /* activate if necessary */
  if(!frame[num].active) window(num);

  startx = x = frame[num].startx;
  starty = y = frame[num].starty;
  window_xy(num, 0, 0);

  do {
    ch = get_special();
    switch(ch) {
      case 75: /* left */
        startx--;
        break;
      case 77: /* right */
        startx++;
        break;
      case 72: /* up */
        starty--;
        break;
      case 80: /* down */
        starty++;
        break;
      case 71: /* up left */
        starty--; startx--;
        break;
      case 73: /* up right */
        starty--; startx++;
        break;
      case 79: /* down left*/
        starty++; startx--;
        break;
      case 81: /* down right */
        starty++; startx++;
        break;
      case 60: /* F2: cancel and use original size */
        startx = x;
        starty = y;
```

```
        ch = 59;
    }
    /* see if out-of-range */
    if(startx<0) startx++;
    if(startx>=frame[num].endx) startx--;
    if(starty<0) starty++;
    if(starty>=frame[num].endy) starty--;
    deactivate(num);
    frame[num].startx = startx;
    frame[num].starty = starty;
    window(num);
  } while(ch!=59);  /* F1 to stop */
  deactivate(num);
}

/* Interactively move a window. */
void move(int num)
{
  char ch;
  int x, y, ex, ey, startx, starty, endx, endy;

  /* activate if necessary */
  if(!frame[num].active) window(num);

  startx = x = frame[num].startx;
  starty = y = frame[num].starty;
  endx = ex = frame[num].endx;
  endy = ey = frame[num].endy;
  window_xy(num, 0, 0);

  do {
    ch = get_special();
    switch(ch) {
      case 75: /* left */
        startx--;
        endx--;
        break;
      case 77: /* right */
        startx++;
        endx++;
        break;
      case 72: /* up */
        starty--;
        endy--;
        break;
```

```
    case 80: /* down */
      starty++;
      endy++;
      break;
    case 71: /* up left */
      starty--; startx--;
      endy--; endx--;
      break;
    case 73: /* up right */
      starty--; startx++;
      endy--; endx++;
      break;
    case 79: /* down left*/
      starty++; startx--;
      endy++; endx--;
      break;
    case 81: /* down right */
      starty++; startx++;
      endy++; endx++;
      break;
    case 60: /* F2: cancel and use original size */
      startx = x;
      starty = y;
      endx = ex;
      endy = ey;
      ch = 59;
  }

  /* see if out-of-range */
  if(startx<0) {
    startx++;
    endx++;
  }
  if(endx>=79) {
    startx--;
    endx--;
  }
  if(starty<0) {
    starty++;
    endy++;
  }
  if(endy>=25) {
    starty--;
    endy--;
  }
```

```
      deactivate(num);
      frame[num].startx = startx;
      frame[num].starty = starty;
      frame[num].endx = endx;
      frame[num].endy = endy;
      window(num);
   } while(ch!=59); /* F1 to stop */
   deactivate(num);
}

/* Display the header message in its proper location. */
void display_header(int num)
{
   register int  x, len;

   x = frame[num].startx;

   /* Calculate the correct starting position to center
      the header message - if negative, message won't
      fit.
   */
   len = strlen(frame[num].header);
   len = (frame[num].endx - x - len) / 2;
   if(len<0) return; /* don't display it */
   x = x + len;

   write_string(x, frame[num].starty,
                frame[num].header, NORM_VID);
}

/* Draw a window's border. */
void draw_border(int num)
{
   register int i;
   char far *v, far *t;

   v = vid_mem;
   t = v;
   for(i=frame[num].starty+1; i<frame[num].endy; i++) {
      v += (i*160) + frame[num].startx*2;
      *v++ = 179; /* vertical bar */
      *v = NORM_VID;
      v = t;
      v += (i*160) + frame[num].endx*2;
      *v++ = 179;
```

```
      *v = NORM_VID;
      v = t;
   }
   for(i=frame[num].startx+1; i<frame[num].endx; i++) {
      v += (frame[num].starty*160) + i*2;
      *v++ = 196; /* horizontal bar */
      *v = NORM_VID;
      v = t;
      v += (frame[num].endy*160) + i*2;
      *v++ = 196;
      *v = NORM_VID;
      v = t;
   }

   /* draw the corners of the border */
   write_char(frame[num].startx, frame[num].starty,
            (char) 218, NORM_VID);
   write_char(frame[num].startx, frame[num].endy,
            (char) 192, NORM_VID);
   write_char(frame[num].endx, frame[num].starty,
            (char) 191, NORM_VID);
   write_char(frame[num].endx, frame[num].endy,
            (char) 217, NORM_VID);
}


/*******************************************************/
/* Window I/O functions                             */
/*******************************************************/

/* Write a string at the current cursor position
   in the specified window.
   Returns 0 if window not active;
   1 otherwise.
*/
window_puts(int num, char *str)
{
   /* make sure window is active */
   if(!frame[num].active) return 0;

   for( ; *str;  str++)
     window_putchar(num, *str);
   return 1;
}

/* Write a character at the current cursor position
```

```
     in the specified window.
     Returns 0 if window not active;
     1 otherwise.
*/
window_putchar(int num, char ch)
{
  register int x, y;
  char far *v;

  /* make sure window is active */
  if(!frame[num].active) return 0;

  x = frame[num].curx + frame[num].startx + 1;
  y = frame[num].cury + frame[num].starty + 1;

  v = vid_mem;
  v += (y*160) + x*2; /* compute the address */
  if(y>=frame[num].endy) {
    return 1;
  }
  if(x>=frame[num].endx) {
    return 1;
  }

  if(ch=='\n') { /* newline char */
    y++;
    x = frame[num].startx+1;
    v = vid_mem;
    v += (y*160) + x*2; /* compute the address */
    frame[num].curx = 0;  /* reset X */
    frame[num].cury++; /* increment Y */
  }
  else {
    frame[num].curx++;
    *v++ = ch;  /* write the character */
    *v++ = NORM_VID;    /* normal video attribute */
  }
  window_xy(num, frame[num].curx, frame[num].cury);
  return 1;
}


/* Position cursor in a window at specified location.
   Returns 0 if out of range;
   nonzero otherwise.
*/
```

```
window_xy(int num, int x, int y)
{
  if(x<0 || x+frame[num].startx>=frame[num].endx-1)
    return 0;
  if(y<0 || y+frame[num].starty>=frame[num].endy-1)
    return 0;
  frame[num].curx = x;
  frame[num].cury = y;
  goto_xy(frame[num].startx+x+1, frame[num].starty+y+1);
  return 1;
}

/* Read a string from a window. */
void window_gets(int num, char *s)
{
  char ch, *temp;

  temp = s;
  for(;;) {
    ch = window_getche(num);
    switch(ch) {
      case '\r': /* the Enter key is pressed */
        *s='\0';
        return;
      case '\b': /* backspace */
        if(s>temp) {
          s--;
          frame[num].curx--;
          if(frame[num].cury<0) frame[num].cury = 0;
            window_xy(num, frame[num].curx, frame[num].cury);
              write_char(frame[num].startx+frame[num].curx+1,
            frame[num].starty+frame[num].cury+1, ' ', NORM_VID);
        }
        break;
      default: *s = ch;
        s++;
    }
  }
}

/* Input keystrokes inside a window.
   Returns full 16-bit scan code.
*/
window_getche(int num)
{
```

```
  union inkey {
    char ch[2];
    int i;
  } c;

  if(!frame[num].active) return 0; /* window not active */

  window_xy(num, frame[num].curx, frame[num].cury);

  c.i = readkey();        /* read the key */

  if(c.ch[0]) {
    switch(c.ch[0]) {
      case '\r': /* the Enter key is pressed */
        break;
      case '\b': /* backspace */
        break;
      default:
        if(frame[num].cury+frame[num].starty < frame[num].endy-1) {
          write_char(frame[num].startx+ frame[num].curx+1,
            frame[num].starty+frame[num].cury+1, c.ch[0], NORM_VID);
          frame[num].curx++;
        }
    }
    if(frame[num].curx < 0) frame[num].curx = 0;
    if(frame[num].curx+frame[num].startx > frame[num].endx-2)
      frame[num].curx--;
    window_xy(num, frame[num].curx, frame[num].cury);
  }
  return c.i;
}

/* Clear a window. */
void window_cls(int num)
{
  register int i,j;
  char far *v, far *t;

  v = vid_mem;
  t = v;
  for(i=frame[num].starty+1; i<frame[num].endy; i++)
    for(j=frame[num].startx+1; j<frame[num].endx; j++) {
      v = t;
      v += (i*160) + j*2;
      *v++ = ' ';  /* write a space */
```

```
      *v = NORM_VID;     /* normal */
  }
  frame[num].curx = 0;
  frame[num].cury = 0;
}

/* Clear to end of line. */
void window_cleol(int num)
{
  register int i, x, y;

  x = frame[num].curx;
  y = frame[num].cury;
  window_xy(num, frame[num].curx, frame[num].cury);

  for(i=frame[num].curx; i<frame[num].endx-1; i++)
    window_putchar(num,' ');
  window_xy(num, x, y);
}

/* Move cursor up one line.
   Returns nonzero if successful;
   0 otherwise.
*/
window_upline(int num)
{
  if(frame[num].cury > 0) {
    frame[num].cury--;
    window_xy(num, frame[num].curx, frame[num].cury);
    return 1;
  }
  return 0;
}

/* Move cursor down one line.
   Returns nonzero if successful;
   0 otherwise.
*/
window_downline(int num)
{
  if(frame[num].cury < frame[num].endy-frame[num].starty-1) {
    frame[num].cury++;
    window_xy(num, frame[num].curx, frame[num].cury);
    return 1;
  }
```

```
    return 0;
}

/* Back up one character. */
void window_bksp(int num)
{
  if(frame[num].curx>0) {
    frame[num].curx--;
    window_xy(num, frame[num].curx, frame[num].cury);
    window_putchar(num, ' ');
    frame[num].curx--;
    window_xy(num, frame[num].curx, frame[num].cury);
  }
}


/******************************************************/
/* Misc. functions                                   */
/******************************************************/

/* Display a string with specifed attribute. */
void write_string(int x, int y, char *p, int attrib)
{
  char far *v;

  v = vid_mem;
  v += (y*160) + x*2; /* compute the address */
  while(*p) {
    *v++ = *p++;  /* write the character */
    *v++ = attrib;    /* write the attribute */
  }
}

/* Write character with specified attribute. */
void write_char(int x, int y, char ch, int attrib)
{
  char far *v;

  v = vid_mem;
  v += (y*160) + x*2;
  *v++ = ch;  /* write the character */
  *v = attrib;    /* write the attribute */
}

/* Save a portion of the screen. */
void save_video(int num)
```

```
{
  register int i,j;
  char *buf_ptr;
  char far *v, far *t;

  buf_ptr = frame[num].p;
  v = vid_mem;
  for(i=frame[num].startx; i<frame[num].endx+1; i++)
    for(j=frame[num].starty; j<frame[num].endy+1; j++) {
      t = (v + (j*160) + i*2);
      *buf_ptr++ = *t++;
      *buf_ptr++ = *t;
      *(t-1) = ' ';  /* clear the window */
    }
}

/* Restore a portion of the screen. */
void restore_video(int num)
{
  register int i,j;
  char far *v, far *t;
  char *buf_ptr;

  buf_ptr = frame[num].p;
  v = vid_mem;
  t = v;
  for(i=frame[num].startx; i<frame[num].endx+1; i++)
    for(j=frame[num].starty; j<frame[num].endy+1; j++) {
      v = t;
      v += (j*160) + i*2;
      *v++ = *buf_ptr++;  /* write the character */
      *v = *buf_ptr++;    /* write the attribute */
    }
  frame[num].active = 0; /* restore_video */
}

/* Clear the screen. */
void cls(void)
{
  union REGS r;

  r.h.ah = 6; /* screen scroll code */
  r.h.al = 0; /* clear screen code */
  r.h.ch = 0; /* start row */
  r.h.cl = 0; /* start column */
```

```
  r.h.dh = 24; /* end row */
  r.h.dl = 79; /* end column */
  r.h.bh = 7;  /* blank line is black */
  int86(0x10, &r, &r);
}

/* Send the cursor to the specified X,Y position. */
void goto_xy(int x, int y)
{
  union REGS r;

  r.h.ah = 2; /* cursor addressing function */
  r.h.dl = x; /* column coordinate */
  r.h.dh = y; /* row coordinate */
  r.h.bh = 0; /* video page */
  int86(0x10, &r, &r);
}

/* Return the position code of arrow and function keys. */
get_special(void)
{
  union inkey {
    char ch[2];
    int i;
  } c;

  c.i = readkey(); /* read the key */

  return c.ch[1];
}

/* Returns the current video mode. */
video_mode(void)
{
  union REGS r;

  r.h.ah = 15;  /* get video mode */
  return int86(0x10, &r, &r) & 255;
}

/* Return the 16-bit scan code from the keyboard. */
readkey(void)
{
  union REGS r;
```

```
  r.h.ah = 0;
  return int86(0x16, &r, &r);
}

#include "ctype.h"
/*********************************************************/
/* pop-up window functions                             */
/*********************************************************/

#define MAX 100

int *p;   /* pointer into the stack */
int *tos; /* points to top of stack */
int *bos; /* points to bottom of stack */

/* Stack based, postfix notation four-function calculator. */
void calc(void)
{
  char in[80], out[80];
  int answer, stack[MAX];
  int a,b;

  p = stack;
  tos = p;
  bos = p+MAX-1;

  window(2);
  do {
    window_xy(2, 0, 0);
    window_cleol(2);
    window_puts(2, ": "); /* calc prompt */
    window_gets(2, in);
    window_puts(2, "\n ");
    window_cleol(2);
    switch(*in) {
      case '+':
        a = pop();
        b = pop();
        answer = a+b;
        push(a+b);
        break;
      case '-':
        a = pop();
        b = pop();
        answer = b-a;
```

```
        push(b-a);
        break;
      case '*':
        a = pop();
        b = pop();
        answer = b*a;
        push(b*a);
        break;
      case '/':
        a = pop();
        b = pop();
        if(a==0) {
          window_puts(2, "divide by 0\n");
          break;
        }
        answer = b/a;
        push(b/a);
        break;
      default:
        push(atoi(in));
        continue;
    }
    sprintf(out, "%d", answer);
    window_puts(2, out);
  } while(*in);
  deactivate(2);
}

/* Place a number on the stack.
   Returns 1 if successful;
   0 if stack is full.
*/
push(int i)
{
  if(p>bos) return 0;

  *p=i;
  p++;
  return 1;
}

/* Retrieve top element from the stack.
   Returns 0 on stack underflows.
*/
pop(void)
```

```
{
  p--;
  if(p<tos) {
    p++;
    return 0;
  }
  return *p;
}


/**********************************************************/

/* Decimal to hexadecimal converter. */
void dectohex(void)
{
  char in[80], out[80];
  int n;

  window(1);
  do {
    window_xy(1, 0, 0);  /* go to first line */
    window_cleol(1); /* clear the line */
    window_puts(1, "dec: "); /* prompt */
    window_gets(1, in); /* read the number */
    window_putchar(1, '\n'); /* go to next line */
    window_cleol(1); /* clear it */
    sscanf(in,"%d", &n); /* convert to internal format */
    sprintf(out, "%s%X", "hex: ",n); /* convert to hex */
    window_puts(1, out); /* output hex */
  } while(*in);
  deactivate(1);
}


/**********************************************************/

/* Pop-up notepad. */
#define MAX_NOTE 10
char notes[MAX_NOTE][80];

void notepad(void)
{
  static first=1;
  register int i, j, k;
  union inkey {
    char ch[2];
    int i;
```

```
  } c;
  char ch;

  /* initialize notes array if necessary */
  if(first) {
    for(i=0; i<MAX_NOTE; i++)
      *notes[i] = '\0';
    first = !first;
  }

  window(3);
  /* display the existing notes */
  for(i=0; i<MAX_NOTE; i++) {
    if(*notes[i]) window_puts(3, notes[i]);
    window_putchar(3, '\n');
  }

  i=0;
  window_xy(3, 0, 0);

  for(;;) {
    c.i = readkey();     /* read the key */
    if(tolower(c.ch[1])==59) { /* F1 to quit */
      deactivate(3);
      break;
    }

    /* if normal key */
    if(isprint(c.ch[0]) || c.ch[0]=='\b') {
      window_cleol(3);
      notes[i][0] = c.ch[0];
      j = 1;
      window_putchar(3, notes[i][0]);
      do {
        ch = window_getche(3);
        if(ch=='\b') {
          if(j>0) {
            j--;
            window_bksp(3);
          }
        }
        else {
          notes[i][j] = ch;
          j++;
        }
```

```
      } while(notes[i][j-1]!='\r');
      notes[i][j-1] = '\0';
      if(i<MAX_NOTE-1) i++;
      window_putchar(3, '\n');
    }
    else {   /* is special key */
      switch(c.ch[1]) {
        case 72: /* up arrow */
          if(i>0) {
            i--;
            window_upline(3);
          }
          break;
        case 80: /* down arrow */
          if(i<MAX_NOTE-1) {
            i++;
            window_downline(3);
          }
          break;
        case 60: /* clear the notepad */
          window_cls(3);
          for(k=0; k<MAX_NOTE; k++) *notes[k] = '\0';
          window_xy(3, 0, 0);
      }
    }
  }
}
```

The first five function keys do the following:

F1   Demonstrates the **window _ xy()** function
F2   Demonstrates sizing and moving a window
F3   Invokes the calculator
F4   Invokes the decimal to hexadecimal converter
F5   Invokes the notepad

Figures 2-1 through 2-3 illustrate the appearance of the pop-up menus on the screen. In Figure 2-4, the decimal-to-hexadecimal converter window has been enlarged and moved.

SOME THINGS TO TRY

With the window routines developed in this chapter, you must always specify the window to use. This approach gives you, the programmer, the

---

Figure 2-1

The calculator window

```
┌──────────────────── Editor [Esc to exit] ────────────────────┐
│To whom it may concern:                                        │
│                                                               │
│This is to inform you that D. W. Porkbellies will no longer    │
│be providing its customers with the following products:        │
│                                                               │
│                                                               │
│              ┌──────────── Calculator ────────────┐          │
│              │ :                                   │          │
│              │                                     │          │
│              │                                     │          │
│              └─────────────────────────────────────┘          │
│                                                               │
│                                                               │
│                                                               │
│                                                               │
│                                                               │
└───────────────────────────────────────────────────────────────┘
```

---

greatest flexibility. Another way of handling windows is the stack-based method. In this approach, the window-specified I/O routines do not take

---

Figure 2-2

The decimal-to-hexadecimal window

```
┌──────────────────── Editor [Esc to exit] ────────────────────┐
│To whom it may concern:                                        │
│                                                               │
│This is to inform you that D. W. Porkbellies will no longer    │
│be providing its customers with the following products:        │
│                                                               │
│         . meat and oats fake burgers                          │
│                                    ┌────── Decimal to Hex ──────┐
│         . lime cola drink pops     │ dec:                       │
│                                    └────────────────────────────┘
│         . syrup coated sizzle links                           │
│                                                               │
│                                                               │
│                                                               │
│                                                               │
│                                                               │
│                                                               │
└───────────────────────────────────────────────────────────────┘
```

Figure 2-3

The notepad window

```
┌──────────────────── Editor [Esc to exit] ────────────────────┐
│To whom it may concern:                                        │
│                                                               │
│This is to inform you that D. W. Porkbellies will no longer    │
│be providing its customers with the following products:        │
│                        ┌───────── Notepad [F1 to exit] ─────┐ │
│      . meat and oat    │call Sherry                         │ │
│                        │go to the store                     │ │
│      . lime cola dr    │                                    │ │
│                        │                                    │ │
│      . syrup coated    │                                    │ │
│                        │                                    │ │
│                        │                                    │ │
│                        │                                    │ │
│                        │                                    │ │
│                        └────────────────────────────────────┘ │
│                                                               │
│                                                               │
│                                                               │
│                                                               │
└───────────────────────────────────────────────────────────────┘
```

---

the window number as an argument. Instead, the window numbers are pushed on a stack in the order in which they are activated. The window

---
Figure 2-4

The decimal-to-hexadecimal window resized and moved

```
┌──────────────────── Editor [Esc to exit] ────────────────────┐
│To whom it may concern:                                        │
│                                                               │
│This is to inform you that D. W. Porkbellies will no longer    │
│be providing its customers with the following products:        │
│                                                               │
│      . meat and oats fake burgers                             │
│                                                               │
│      . lime    ┌────────── Decimal to Hex ──────────┐         │
│                │                                     │         │
│      . syrup   │                                     │         │
│                │                                     │         │
│                │                                     │         │
│                │                                     │         │
│                └─────────────────────────────────────┘         │
│                                                               │
│                                                               │
│                                                               │
└───────────────────────────────────────────────────────────────┘
```

routines always use the window that is on the top of the stack. When a window is deactivated, its number is popped off the stack. The advantage of this method is that you don't have to worry about which window number you are using. You might find it interesting to modify the window routines to work in this way.

Another variation is to allow a window to scroll when the cursor is at the bottom. As the routines are presently written, when the cursor is at the bottom of the window and RETURN is pressed, nothing happens. However, you can alter the routines so that the top line is scrolled off the screen and a blank one is brought up from the bottom.

Finally, for those readers who have color displays, using different color borders for different windows can, if applied correctly, add even more visual appeal to your application.

TSR Pop-up Programs

DOS is the most widely used operating system in the world. The success of DOS is due, in part, to the fact that it does what it is supposed to do: provide a single-user, single-tasking operating system for a personal computer. However, the one design flaw in DOS is the difficulty it has in supporting RAM-resident pop-up programs. RAM-resident programs are generally called *TSRs* because they use the DOS *terminate-and-stay-resident* function to stay resident in RAM. As you almost certainly know, a TSR program remains suspended in RAM awaiting execution. Generally, what activates a pop-up TSR is a special hot key. When the TSR is executed, it interrupts the currently executing process. When the TSR terminates, the interrupted program resumes execution.

It appears that the concept of TSR programs was essentially over-looked when DOS was created because there is virtually no *documented* support for them. However, over the years, several formally undocu-mented yet apparently stable features of DOS have been discovered that, when used correctly, can allow a TSR to coexist with DOS. Although the use of the undocumented DOS features is now more or less universally accepted when TSR programs are written, there are various ways these

NORMAN BARTEK

Norman Bartek is a senior member of the technical staff at Mark Williams Company. Mark Williams Company is well known to C programmers as the developer of C compilers and the COHERENT operating system, a low-priced UNIX clone designed especially for the PC environment. Norman was instrumental in bringing COHERENT to the PC marketplace. In addition to being the driving force behind the COHERENT system, Norman has also ported C compilers, linkers, and assemblers to a variety of diferent processors.

Norman told me he began programming in C in the late 1970s. "After having written device drivers and other systems level code at the assembler level for the nth time, I realized that C was a wonderful solution to the 'portable assembler' problem," he related. Echoing a comment often heard from C programmers, he said, "C allowed me to rewrite a low percentage of code when porting to a new environment."

I asked Norman what advice he had for other C programmers. "Avoid overly complex or 'cute' programming practices, such as nested ?s or expressions that depend on order of evaluation." He also had this advice, "Sanity check all input to your programs. Never use **scanf( )** or other routines that don't handle input errors." I completely agree with this philosophy.

Norman's approach to program design is a refreshing mix of practical wisdom and abstract philosophy. "Balance considerations such as portability and 'ideological purity' with the realities of life: deadlines, budgetary, and personnel constraints, product life cycles, and the like. But remember, your 'one shot' program may end up with more lives than you care to think about. A poor implementation may haunt you a long time."

Norman holds a BA and an MS in Computer Science from the Illinois Institute of Technology. He is the president of Bartek Associates Inc., a consulting firm specializing in the UNIX, C, and embedded control markets. He is married and has two children. Norman's other interests include high-end audio, teaching C, and enjoying his children.

features can be applied and various ways a TSR can be activated; there is still much debate as to what constitutes a "proper" TSR. This chapter* discusses the two most common undocumented features of DOS and explains the basic technology that makes TSRs possible. Its main focus is development of a TSR skeleton that you can use to create your own pop-up applications. However, three simple pop-up applications are included that illustrate how to use the TSR framework. The applications are a pop-up notepad, calculator, and file encryptor.

The code in this chapter is written for Turbo C. Although most of the examples in this book are intended to be reasonably compiler independent, this is not possible in this chapter for two reasons. First, creating a TSR program in C requires some special, non-ANSI-standard features. Because these features are not defined by ANSI, they differ widely among compilers. Second, not all compilers provide equal support for TSR programs. Turbo C and Microsoft C, as well as others, offer excellent support for TSRs, but there is not sufficient room in one chapter to show examples using all compilers. However, if you do not have Turbo C, you should be able to generalize easily to your compiler. (For example, converting to Microsoft C is basically a process of changing a few function names.) One reason that Turbo C is used here is that it is possible to fully implement a functional TSR without the use of any assembly code. Other compilers may require some assembly language modules.

Warning: For something that is so simple conceptually, creating TSR programs is one of the hardest programming tasks there is in the PC environment. For this chapter, you had better strap on your safety belt and put on your crash helmet! This chapter assumes that you have a basic knowledge of both DOS and its companion, the BIOS. (If you don't, you can still try the TSR program, but be careful how you change it.) Intrinsic to the development and use of a TSR program is the modification of the interrupt vector table. Any time you modify this table, you are flirting with a system crash. The program examples shown in this chapter were compiled by using Turbo C and run correctly with no known side effects. However, if you have a different compiler, they may not work correctly.

* Much of the material in this chapter is adapted from my book *Born to Code in C* (Berkeley, CA: Osborne/McGraw-Hill, 1989). If you are especially interested in TSRs, you might find the example applications in that book particularly interesting; they differ from the ones shown in this chapter.

Also, if you are typing the code by hand, you can easily create a small error. If either of these situations is the case, you must expect several system crashes. As you probably know, it is possible, in a worst-case scenario, to destroy data on your hard disk. You must be prepared for this. Make sure your backups are current.

WHY TSRs ARE SO TROUBLESOME

The main reason that TSR programs are as troublesome as they are desirable is that DOS is not *reentrant*. This means that if DOS is doing something for one program, it cannot suspend that operation, do something for another program, and return to finish the job for the first. If DOS were reentrant, then virtually all TSR problems would disappear.

Given that DOS is not reentrant, support for TSR programs could still have been included (cleanly) by having DOS set one (and only one) flag when it is okay to interrupt it and clear the flag when it can't be interrupted. As you will see, DOS does implement something similar, but in this case, similar is not close enough. In reality, for a TSR to know that DOS is able to be interrupted requires, minimally, the examination of a flag and the interception of an interrupt.

A third problem with DOS and TSRs involves disk activity. DOS transfers disk information in the DTA (disk transfer area) allocated to each program. The default DTA is part of the PSP (program segment prefix) that all programs have. When a TSR interrupts another program, it inherits the PSP of the other program. Therefore, if it performs any disk I/O, it runs the risk of overwriting information that is already in the other program's DTA. Hence, it is necessary for any TSR that accesses the disk to set the DTA to its own, perform the disk function, and then reset the DTA.

Another, different sort of problem with TSRs occurs when two or more attempt to exist together. Although a TSR may work correctly with DOS, it may not work well with another TSR. One potential trouble spot is that the hot keys used to activate one may also be needed by the other.

A final trouble with TSRs can occur when the program currently executing bypasses DOS (and even BIOS) for many functions. For example, it is possible for a program to perform its own disk I/O, bypassing both the DOS high-level functions and the BIOS low-level functions. If this happens and your TSR is activated and attempts to perform a disk access, a nasty crash could occur. The problem of programs circumventing

DOS and BIOS is the main reason why no TSR can be considered 100 percent safe in all situations. However, from a practical point of view, a TSR that follows the procedures described in this chapter will be reasonably safe to use.

TSRs AND INTERRUPTS

Virtually all TSR programs are activated by an interrupt. For interactive TSRs, the keystroke interrupt is commonly used. Before continuing the discussion of TSRs, it is important that you know how interrupts for the 8086 family of processors operate. (Henceforth, the term "8086" will be used to encompass the entire 8086 family, which includes the 8086, 8088, 80186, 80286, 80386, and 80486.)

The 8086 provides for 256 vectored interrupts. A *vectored interrupt* is an interrupt that is directed to its *interrupt service routine* (ISR) indirectly through an address held in a special location. The 8086 sets aside the first 1024 bytes of memory to hold the addresses of ISRs. This region is usually referred to as the *interrupt vector table.* Each address includes a segment and an offset portion and thus needs 4 bytes. Thus, the address of the ISR associated with interrupt 0 is location 0000:0000, the address of the ISR associated with interrupt 1 is 0000:0004, the ISR address of interrupt 2 is 0000:0008, and so on. For example, assume that the location of the ISR used by interrupt 2 is at 1000:0800. Then, this address would be stored in the interrupt vector table beginning at 0000:0008, and each time interrupt 2 was activated, the routine at 1000:0800 would be called.

Of the 256 available interrupts, a few are unused by DOS. For example, interrupt 0x64 is unused in all versions of DOS through version 5.00. This unallocated interrupt will be used as a flag to indicate whether or not the TSR is already loaded.

All interrupt service routines must be written as **far** procedures. In general, they must also terminate with an IRET (return from interrupt) instruction. All ISRs must preserve all registers. This means that at startup, the ISR must PUSH each register and, upon exit, POP each register.

All TSR programs must intercept one or more interrupts and provide their own interrupt service routines for these functions. You will see how this is done shortly.

THE INTERRUPT TYPE MODIFIER

Turbo C (and many other DOS-based compilers) provide one crucial element of support for TSRs: the **interrupt** function type modifier. Declaring a function to be of type **interrupt** tells the compiler to automatically preserve all registers and to terminate the function with an IRET instruction. For Turbo C, an **interrupt** function is passed all registers. However, you can simply declare **interrupt** functions as **void** if you don't need the values of the registers. (The ISRs developed in this chapter don't need them, for example.)

If your compiler does not include the **interrupt** type, then you must resort to an assembly language routine (or at least an assembly language interface) to handle the entry point to your TSR.

A QUICK LOOK AT THE PSP

The program segment prefix is used by TSRs for two main reasons. First, it provides the disk transfer area (DTA). This region is located 0x80 bytes from the start of the PSP. Second, it contains the segment address of the block of memory that holds a program's environmental information. This address is located 0x2C bytes from the start of the PSP. The PSP is also important to TSRs because it contains several other program-specific pieces of information. For these reasons, some TSR applications will need to reset the PSP when they pop up and restore it when they terminate.

Turbo C (and many other DOS-compatible C compilers) supply a built-in variable called **_psp** that is a **far** pointer to the start of a program's PSP. The TSR developed in this chapter makes use of this variable to access the contents of the PSP.

THE BASIC DESIGN OF AN INTERACTIVE TSR

All TSRs consist of three major parts: the initialization part, the ISRs used to support and activate the TSR, and the actual transient applications. Let's see what each piece consists of.

TSR Initialization

When a TSR program begins executing, it performs three basic functions. First, it initializes anything that the application portion requires. For example, in the TSR developed in this chapter, the initialization part of the TSR sets a pointer to the video RAM and creates three windows used by the pop-up applications. The second function that the initialization part of the TSR provides is the rerouting of various vectored interrupt addresses so that they point to the new routines provided by the TSR. Finally, the initialization part of the TSR terminates with a call to DOS function 0x31, which terminates the program but keeps it resident. Many C compilers provide their own functions for this. Turbo C calls this the **keep()** function. (Microsoft's parallel function is called **_dos_keep()**.) This function simply calls DOS function 0x31. The prototype for the **keep()** function is shown here:

void keep(unsigned char *status*, unsigned *mem_size*);

The value of *status* is returned to DOS. The amount of RAM to allocate to the TSR is specified in paragraphs by *mem_size*. (A paragraph is 16 bytes.) If your compiler does not provide a function like **keep()**, you can execute DOS function 0x31 with the return code in AL and the size of the program (in paragraphs) in DX. (Most DOS-based compilers provide some mechanism to access the various DOS functions.)

Determining the exact amount of RAM to set aside for your TSR program can be tricky. Generally, there will be some instructions given with your compiler. Keep in mind that the amount of memory needed by your application is greater than the size of its .EXE file. For the application developed in this chapter, 32K is set aside. This figure is used because it should work for a TSR created by virtually any compiler.

If you can find no instructions on how to compute the amount of RAM needed by your TSR, add the size of all the global data to the size of the .EXE file and then round up a few thousand bytes, and you should be safe. (If your TSR doesn't seem to run correctly, try increasing the amount of RAM you give it.)

The ISRs

All pop-up TSRs are activated by pressing a special hot key. You intercept this hot key by replacing the keyboard input interrupt with one of your own, which watches for this key. Since the TSR must intercept the hot key at the lowest level, it must replace the BIOS keyboard interrupt, which is interrupt 9, with its own, saving the address of the original interrupt 9 ISR.

Each time a key is pressed on the keyboard, interrupt 9 is generated. This causes your keyboard ISR to be called. The first thing your ISR must do is call the original keyboard input service. Next, your ISR must determine if the key that was pressed is the hot key. If it is, the pop-up TSR application must be activated if it is safe to do so. (How you determine whether it is safe to activate a TSR is discussed shortly.) Also, the hot key must be removed from the input queue so that it does not become input to the interrupted application.

In addition to the keyboard interrupt, your TSRs will need to provide at least one other ISR, which determines if DOS is safe to interrupt. Also, most interactive TSRs, including the one developed in this chapter, will need to intercept the timer interrupt (interrupt 8) to aid in the activation of the TSR. Finally, in some situations you may need to monitor the activity in a few other interrupts.

The Pop-up Application

Once you have determined that DOS is safe to interrupt, you can activate the pop-up application. However, the pop-up application is still not free to execute like a normal program for several reasons. First, since the TSR is popping up, possibly during the execution of another application, it must provide a mechanism for saving the current contents of the screen and restoring them when the pop-up is terminated. Second, in general, no pop-up application can use C's dynamic allocation functions, such as **malloc()**. This implies that functions like **printf()** and **fopen()** cannot be used since they call **malloc()** in the performance of their tasks. (Some compilers may differ in this regard, but it is generally accurate.) Hence, you will need to be careful about what standard C functions you use.

Although not strictly required, most pop-up TSRs operate through a window—that is, a portion of the screen. The advantage of this is that the user can still see part of the interrupted application. Since many TSRs are designed to provide support for other applications, this may be an important feature. Also, the amount of memory and time it takes to save and restore a screen is proportional to the amount of the screen saved. Hence, it is desirable to use a small window rather than the entire screen when appropriate. For this reason, most pop-up TSRs must include windowing software to support their screen I/O. However, even here, you may not be able to use "off the shelf" window routines because of the memory allocation problem. In addition, you will probably want the I/O routines to operate directly on the video RAM in order to obtain the fastest possible screen refreshes.

The TSR developed here includes many of the windowing routines developed in Chapter 2. (If you have not yet read Chapter 2, do so before proceeding with this chapter.) Some of the functions are slightly modified so as to be compatible with the TSR environment. For this reason, the windowing functions used in this chapter have been renamed by pre-fixing their names with "tsr."

Here is a brief description of the modifications to the windowing routines. First, it is necessary to statically allocate the memory necessary to store the current contents of the screen when an application pops up. A global array is used for this purpose. If you recall, this memory had been allocated dynamically, but this will not work here because the allocation functions use a DOS call, which is not allowed in a TSR application. The portion of the screen used by the window is saved into a global character array. This means that only one window can be active at a time. (If more than one were to be active, then multiple video buffers would be re-quired.) Second, the standard C functions **sscanf()** and **sprintf()** cannot be used because, at least in Turbo C, they appear to make calls to DOS, so **atoi()** and **itoa()** are substituted.

WHEN IS DOS SAFE TO INTERRUPT?

Put simply, DOS is safe to interrupt when it isn't doing anything very important. For example, you can interrupt DOS when it is simply display-ing the command prompt. However, you can't (well, you *shouldn't*) inter-rupt DOS when it is performing a disk access or writing to the screen, for example. The problem is that there are no documented DOS features that let you determine when DOS is idle. However, over the years, program-mers have discovered two very important undocumented DOS functions that allow TSRs to know (at least most of the time) when DOS is safe to interrupt. These two features were evidently implemented to support the PRINT command, which provides background printing. Why Microsoft chose not to document these features is unknown. Perhaps they simply didn't seem important at the time. Let's look at these two features now.

The DOS-idle Interrupt

Whenever DOS is waiting for user input, it essentially just loops, waiting for a keystroke. However, part of this loop executes an INT 0x28 instruc-tion. This interrupt has come to be known as the *DOS-idle interrupt*. INT

0x28 is called repeatedly by the first 12 DOS functions. (These functions provide for character I/O.) Therefore, each time interrupt 0x28 is executed, it means that DOS is safe to interrupt. Hence, your TSR should intercept interrupt 0x28 and use it to pop up the TSR if the hot key has been pressed. The trouble is that DOS executes interrupt 0x28 only when it is using one of the character I/O functions. This means that some mechanism other than 0x28 must be used to know when DOS is safe to interrupt in cases when these I/O functions are not being called. (Remember, many high-performance software packages bypass DOS and go directly to BIOS for console I/O, which means that interrupt 0x28 will never be called while these packages execute.) This trouble leads us to the second undocumented DOS feature: the *DOS-active flag*.

The DOS-active Flag

When DOS is active, it sets a byte inside itself to 1. When it becomes inactive, it resets this byte to 0. This byte is often called the *DOS-active flag* or sometimes the *inDOS flag*. The location of this flag can be determined only by using another undocumented DOS function: 0x34. This function returns the segment of the DOS-active flag in the ES register and the offset in the BX register. Before your TSR program pops up, it must interrogate the value of this flag. If it is 1, your TSR should not pop up. Instead, it must wait until this flag is 0.

The state of the DOS-active flag is insufficient in itself to indicate when a TSR can run because it is set to 1 when the DOS prompt is displayed. (After all, DOS *is* active when displaying its prompt.) This is why you must use the interrupt 0x28 as well.

THE TIMER INTERRUPT

As you will see, the timer interrupt is used to help activate the TSR developed in this chapter. On PCs and compatibles, the system clock causes interrupt 8 to be executed 18.2 times per second. This interrupt will be used to check the state of DOS. When DOS is safe and a hot key has been pressed, the TSR will be popped up.

TSRs AND GRAPHICS MODES

Although there is no fundamental reason why you cannot use pop-up TSR programs when the computer is in a graphics mode, it may be better (and is easier) to wait until the computer is in a text mode. There are several reasons for this. First, there are only a few text modes. The most common are video mode 2 (80-column black and white), mode 3 (80-column color text), and mode 7 (80-column monochrome). However, there are several different graphics modes. Further, in the 80-column text modes it takes 4000 bytes to hold the contents of the screen no matter what 80-column mode is being used. This means that as a worst case, your pop-up application needs to supply a buffer only 4000 bytes long in order to save the entire text screen when the TSR is activated. However, each graphics mode requires substantially more memory, and different graphics modes require differing amounts of RAM to hold an entire screen. Therefore, allowing a pop-up in a graphics mode means that your TSR will have to allocate enough memory to hold the worst-case storage requirements for the screen, which can be as large as 64K. Also, the time it takes to store and restore the old screen will be very noticeable to the user in the higher resolution graphics modes. For these reasons, the TSR examples developed in this chapter will pop up only when the computer is in a text mode. However, keep in mind that this is not a fundamental limitation of TSRs.

SOME SPECIAL TURBO C FUNCTIONS

The TSR program uses some special Turbo C-specific functions (although many compilers have their own equivalents). These functions are **int86()**, **int86x()**, **getvect()**, **setvect()**, and **freemem()**. Before continuing, a short discussion of these will help avoid confusion.

The **int86()** function was discussed in Chapter 1. Its relative, **int86x()** function, also generates a software interrupt. However, it also loads the values of the segment registers into a structure of type **SREGS**, which is its third argument. It has this prototype:

```
int int86x(int num, /* the interrupt number */
      union REGS *inregs, /* the input register values */
      union REGS *outregs, /* the output register values */
      struct SREGS *sregs /* segment registers */
)
```

The interrupt to generate is specified by *num*. You can specify the values of the registers at the time of the interrupt by using *inregs*. Upon return, *outregs* will hold the values of the registers as set by the ISR that handles the interrupt, and *sregs* will contain the value of the segment registers. The return value of **int86()** is the value of the AX register.

The types **REGS** and **SREGS** are supplied in the header **DOS.H**. Those shown here are defined by Turbo C; however, they are similar to those defined by Microsoft C and other compilers.

```
/*
    Copyright (c) Borland International 1987,1988,1990,1991
    All Rights Reserved.
*/
struct WORDREGS {
    unsigned int   ax, bx, cx, dx, si, di, cflag, flags;
};

struct BYTEREGS {
    unsigned char   al, ah, bl, bh, cl, ch, dl, dh;
};

union  REGS  {
    struct WORDREGS x;
    struct BYTEREGS h;
};

struct SREGS  {
    unsigned int   es;
    unsigned int   cs;
    unsigned int   ss;
    unsigned int   ds;
};
```

Copyright 1991, Borland International, Inc. Printed with permission from the header file of DOS.H in the Turbo C compiler. All rights reserved.

The **getvect()** and **setvect()** functions read and set, respectively, an address in the interrupt vector table, given the number of the interrupt. Their prototypes are

void interrupt *getvect(int *int_num*);
void setvect(int *int_num*, void interrupt (**ISR*)());

Here, *ISR* is a pointer to the new interrupt service routine. Its address will be installed in *int_num*'s vector table location.

For example, to return the address of the ISR that is used by interrupt 5, use this statement:

```
addr = getvect(5);
```

To set interrupt 5's ISR to the address of a function called **newint5()**, use this statement:

```
setvect(5, newint5);
```

The **freemem()** function is used to free memory previously allocated by DOS. This function translates to a call to DOS, function 0x49. Its only argument is the segment of the memory to free.

CREATING A TSR APPLICATION

Now that the theoretical groundwork has been laid, it is time to develop an actual, working example.

Initializing the TSR

Most of the initalization portion of the TSR is contained in **main()**, shown here. Take a close look at it now.

```
main(void)
{
  union REGS r;
  struct SREGS s;

  /* see if already loaded */
  old_int64 = getvect(0x64); /* unused interrupt */
  if(!old_int64) setvect(0x64, new_int8); /* set a flag */
  else {
    printf("TSR already loaded.");
    return 1;
  }

  /* obtain the dos_active flag address */
```

```
r.h.ah = 0x34;
int86x(0x21, &r, &r, &s);
dos_active = MK_FP(s.es, r.x.bx);

/* get old ISR addresses */
old_key = getvect(9); /* keystroke int */
old_int28 = getvect(0x28); /* int 28 */
old_int8 = getvect(8); /* timer interrupt */

 /* re-route interrupt vectors to new handlers */
setvect(9, tsr_keystroke);
setvect(0x28, dos_idle);
setvect(8, new_int8);

printf("F1: Notepad  F2: Calculator  F3: File Coder");
printf("  F4: Deactivate\n");

key = 0;
set_vid_mem(); /* get address of video memory */

/* initialize all windows */
make_tsrwindow(0, " Notepad [Esc to exit] ",
               20, 5, 60, 16, BORDER);
make_tsrwindow(1, " Calculator ", 20, 8, 60, 12, BORDER);
make_tsrwindow(2, " File Coder ", 20, 8, 60, 10, BORDER);

keep(0, 2000); /* terminate and stay resident */

return 0;
}
```

The first few lines of code are there to prevent the TSR from being loaded more than one time. Although it is not technically wrong to load a TSR more than once, it is not a good idea because it uses up the system's memory. As mentioned, interrupt 0x64 is not used for any other purpose, so you can use the memory reserved for it in the interrupt vector table as a flag. Before the TSR redirects any interrupts, it checks the value of interrupt 0x64's address vector. If this vector is 0, the TSR assumes that this is the first time it is being loaded, and it sets this value to non-zero. However, if it finds this vector to be set, it assumes that the TSR is already loaded, and it exits before redirecting any interrupts. (Remember, if the program exits after redirecting the interrupt vectors but before calling DOS function 49 to stay resident, then each time a redirected interrupt is executing, it will be jumping into nowhere.)

Next, the **main()** function determines the location of the DOS-active flag generating an interrupt to DOS function 0x34 by using **int86x()**. Once the values of ES and BX have been obtained, a **far** pointer is constructed by using Turbo C's **MK_FP()** function. If your compiler does not support these built-in register variables, you will need to write a short piece of assembly code that converts ES:BX into a **far** pointer. This pointer is then stored in the **dos_active** flag.

Next, the locations of the original ISRs for interrupts 8, 9, and 0x28 are saved by using Turbo C's **getvect()** function. The substitute ISRs will use these addresses to call the original ones. When you write a TSR, you must make sure that you link your replacement ISRs with the original ones because, as is the case with the keyboard interrupt and timer interrupts, the original ISRs may provide a crucial service. Also, if there is more than one TSR present in the system, you must make sure that you provide an unbroken chain between them. Finally, if you deactivate the TSR, you must replace the addresses of your ISRs with the original ones.

Once the addresses of the original ISRs for interrupts 8, 9, and 0x28 have been saved, the addresses of the new routines can be installed by using Turbo C's **setvect()** function. The name of the new keyboard function is **tsr_keystroke()**, the new timer function is called **new_int8()**, and the new interrupt 0x28 handler is called **dos_idle()**. Once this step has been accomplished, the new interrupt handlers are, in fact, active, so you must make sure that any initialization necessary to their functioning has been performed prior to this point.

In Turbo C, the pointers to the original ISRs are declared like this:

```
void interrupt (*old_int28)();
void interrupt (*old_key)();
void interrupt (*old_int8());
```

If you are using a different compiler, a somewhat different syntax may be required.

The next line of code initializes the value of the global variable **key**, which passes key codes to the **dos_idle()** and **new_int8()** functions. (You will see it in action shortly.) After that, the function **set_vid_mem()** is called to set the global **far** pointer **vid_mem** to point to the start of the video memory. This function is shown here along with the **video_mode()** function:

```
/* Set the vid_mem pointer to the start of video
   memory.
```

```
*/
void set_vid_mem(void)
{
  int vmode;

  vmode = video_mode();
  if((vmode!=2) && (vmode!=3) && (vmode!=7)) {
    printf("video must be in 80 column text mode");
    exit(1);
  }
  /* set proper address of video RAM */
  if(vmode==7) vid_mem = (char far *) MK_FP(0xB000, 0000);
  else vid_mem = (char far *) MK_FP(0xB800, 0000);
}

/* Returns the current video mode. */
video_mode(void)
{
  union REGS r;

  r.h.ah = 15; /* get video mode */
  return int86(0x10, &r, &r) & 255;
}
```

The TSR has three sample pop-up functions. Hence, the next section of code in **main()** initializes windows for these functions. Although the windowing system allows you to create windows "on the fly," in the interest of maintaining a snappy response to a pop-up request, all windows are created during intitialization.

Finally, the TSR terminates with a call to **keep()**, the Turbo C function that executes the DOS terminate-and-stay-resident function. After this, control returns to the command prompt.

The tsr_keystroke() ISR

The **tsr_keystroke()** function is shown next. This function is executed each time the keyboard interrupt (INT 9) is executed.

```
/* This is the function that intercepts the keystroke
   interrupt (int 9). */
void interrupt tsr_keystroke(void)
```

```
{
  int far *t2 = (int far *) 1050; /* address of head pointer */
  char far *t = (char far *) 1050; /* address of head pointer */

  (*old_key)(); /* first, call old keystroke ISR */

  if(*t != *(t+2)) {/* if not empty */
    t += *t-30+5; /* advance to the character position */
    if(*t>=59 && *t<=62) {
      switch(*t) { /* see what is in scan code */
        case 59: /* F1 - notepad */
          key = 1;
          break;
        case 60: /* F2 - calculator */
          key = 2;
          break;
        case 61: /* F3: file encrypter */
          key = 3;
          break;
        case 62: /* F4: deactivate TSR */
          key = 4;
          break;
      }
      *(t2+1) = *t2; /* zero buffer */
    }
  }
}
```

The function first calls the original keyboard ISR. The reason for this is easy to understand: the original keyboard ISR actually reads the key from the keyboard and puts it into the keyboard buffer. There is no reason for the replacement ISR to perform these functions. Once the keystroke is in the buffer, the **tsr_keystroke()** function takes over and determines if a hot key has been pressed. This function does not use any BIOS or DOS functions to read the key from the buffer. Instead, it directly interrogates the keyboard buffer. How and why it does this is the subject of the next section.

The Keystroke Character Buffer

As you know, standard versions of DOS buffer up to 15 characters entered at the keyboard, which allows typeahead. Each time a key is pressed, an interrupt 9 is generated. The keystroke input ISR reads the character from the port and places it in the buffer. When you call a DOS or BIOS keyboard character input function, only the contents of the buffer are examined—not the actual port. Therefore, it is possible for your routines to directly examine the contents of the keystroke buffer in a fashion similar to the way the BIOS and DOS routines do, thus allowing your TSR entry function to determine whether a hot key has been pressed or not.

The keystroke input buffer is located at 0000:041E (1054 in decimal). Because all keystrokes generate a 16-bit scan code, the buffer requires 30 bytes for the 15 characters. However, 32 bytes are actually used because the scan code for the carriage return key is automatically appended to the end of the buffer.

The buffer is organized as a circular queue that is accessed through a head pointer and a tail pointer. The head pointer points to the character last typed. The tail pointer points to the next character to be returned by an input request by DOS or BIOS. The head pointer is stored at location 0000:041A (1050 in decimal) and the tail pointer at 0000:041C (1052 in decimal). The values of the head and tail pointers are actually indexes into the queue, which means that their values are the index of the current position plus 30. (This is because of the way the 8086 processes indirect addressing.) The value of the head and tail pointer are the same when the queue is empty.

There are two reasons that **tsr_keystroke()** examines the keyboard buffer and does not call one of the standard input functions. First, it is faster to examine the keyboard buffer directly than it is to use an operating system call. If a computer has several TSRs running in it, sluggish response could result in slower systems. Second, this approach gives you the ability to modify the contents of the keyboard buffer. Although changing the contents of the buffer is not required by this TSR, it may be valuable to other applications.

The TSR uses the function keys F1 through F4 for its hot keys. You will probably want to change these to something like ALT-F1 through ALT-F4 for actual use so that you don't lose the DOS command-line editing functions associated with these keys. However, for testing and experimentation, it is simply easier to press one key than two. The scan code for F1 is 59, for F2 is 60, and so on. These values are encoded into the global variable **key**, beginning with 1. The reason for encoding the key rather than using its scan code is that you can change the hot key by changing only one line of code.

If a hot key has been encountered, you will want to remove it from the keystroke buffer. The fastest way to do this is to set the head pointer equal to the tail pointer, as is done in **tsr_keystroke()**.

Notice one important point about **tsr_keystroke()**: it does not, itself, actually activate the TSR. The reason for this is simple: some application software cannot be interrupted during the keystroke interrupt. For example, attempting to activate a TSR from the keystroke interrupt while the Turbo C integrated environment is active can lead to a system crash. This is why the timer interrupt is used to activate the TSR during those times when the DOS-idle interrupt is not being called.

The new_int8() interrupt

The function that intercepts the timer interrupt is quite simple. First, it calls the old timer routine. This is important. Failing to call the original timer ISR will cause your system to crash. Next, **new_int8()** checks to see if DOS is idle, if **busy** is cleared, and if a hot key is waiting in **key**. If these conditions have been met, the TSR is popped up by calling **activate_tsr()** (discussed shortly).

The global variable **busy** ensures that the TSR is not activated while it is already active. As stated, DOS is not reentrant. Further, the stack-switching scheme is not reentrant, so a second activation while the first activation of the TSR is still executing will crash the system and must be prevented. The value of **busy** is set by **activate_tsr()** when the TSR is activated and cleared upon exit. In this way, secondary activations are prevented.

The **new_int8()** interrupt is shown here along with the global variable **busy**:

```
/* busy is set to 1 when the program is active, 0 otherwise */
char busy = 0;

/* New interrupt 8. */
void interrupt new_int8(void)
{
  (*old_int8)(); /* call original int 8 */

  /* If DOS is idle, TSR is not already active,
     and if a hot key has been pressed, activate the TSR. */
  if(!*dos_active && !busy && key)
      activate_tsr();
}
```

Because the timer interrupt is executed 18 times a second, the TSR will still appear to be activated immediately when you press a hot key.

The dos_idle() ISR

The **dos_idle()** ISR is virtually the same as **new_int8()**. It first calls the original interrupt 0x28 ISR and then, if **busy** is cleared and there is a hot key waiting, the TSR is popped up. The **dos_idle()** function is shown here:

```
/* This function intercepts int 0x28 (the DOS-idle
   interrupt).
*/
void interrupt dos_idle(void)
{
  (*old_int28)(); /* call old int 0x28 ISR */
  if(!busy && key) activate_tsr();
}
```

The activate_tsr() Function

The entry point to the TSR utilities is through **activate_tsr()**. This function calls the function associated with the hot key pressed. However, before this is done, **activate_tsr()** has one very important job: it must reset the stack to one defined by the TSR. The reason for this is very simple. When an interrupt is executed, DOS automatically switches to one of its very small internal stacks. This internal stack is just barely large enough to hold the two **far** pointers declared in **tsr_keystroke()** plus the overhead created by the interrupt. It is far too small to support the stack requirements of the TSR applications. For this reason, **activate_tsr()** must reassign the stack upon entry and then reset it upon exit. This process requires the use of Turbo C's built-in register variables. If your compiler does not include this feature, you must use some assembly code to accomplish the stack switching. The TSR stack is held in an unsigned character array called **stack** that is 0x2000 bytes long. The **activate_tsr()** function is shown here:

```
/* Pop up the TSR. */
void activate_tsr(void)
{
  /* set up TSR stack */
```

```
  disable(); /* disable interrupts */
    ss = _SS;
    sp = _SP;
    _SS = _DS;
    _SP = (unsigned) &stck[STK_SIZE-2];
  enable();  /* enable interrupts */

  cursor_pos(); /* get current cursor position */

  /* check video mode - don't pop up if not in
     an 80-column text mode
  */
  video = video_mode();
  if(!busy && (video==7 || video==3 || video==2)) {
    busy = !busy; /* don't allow a second activation */
    switch(key) {
      case 1: notepad();
        break;
      case 2: calc();
        break;
      case 3: code();
        break;
  }
  busy = !busy;
  }
  if(key==4) /* deactivating TSR */
    write_string(old_col, old_row, "TSR deactivated", NORM_VID);

  goto_xy(old_col, old_row); /* reset cursor */

  /* restore old stack */
  disable();
    _SP = sp;
    _SS = ss;
  enable();

  if(key==4) { /* reset old ISR routines and free memory */
    setvect(8, old_int8);
    setvect(9, old_key);
    setvect(0x28, old_int28);
    setvect(0x64, old_int64);
    freemem(_psp); /* free program block */
  } else key = 0;
}
```

Notice that the stack-switching is preceded by a call to **disable()**. This Turbo C function disables interrupts. Until the entire stack switch is accomplished, no interrupts may occur. (If they do, the stack may not be set correctly.) Once the stack has been changed, interrupts are enabled by using a call to **enable()**. If your compiler does not have **disable()** and **enable()**, you will need to use their assembly code equivalent instructions, CLI and STI.

Next, **activate _ tsr()** finds out what video mode is currently in use. This value will be used to make sure that the TSR is not activated in a graphics mode.

Assuming the video mode is correct and the TSR is not currently active, **activate _ tsr()** next calls the function associated with the hot key. The value of **key** will be 0 unless a hot key has been pressed. If the F4 key has been pressed, the TSR is deactivated. The deactivation sequence is a little tricky because the stack must be restored to its original value before the original interrupt routines are restored. However, the deactivation message must be displayed prior to the stack change. This is why there are two comparisons for **key= =4**.

The function **cursor _ pos()** assigns to the global variables **old _ col** and **old _ row** the current value of the cursor. These values are then used by **write _ string()** to output a string to the console. The **write _ string()** function is a low-level routine included in the windowing system.

At the end of **activate _ tsr()**, the value of **key** is reset to 0.

THE TSR POP-UP APPLICATIONS

To illustrate the TSR skeleton, three short pop-up applications are developed here. Two are the notepad and calculator used to illustrate the window routines presented in Chapter 2. Aside from some very minor changes, these functions are identical to those described in Chapter 2, and no further discussion is needed. The third application is a simple file encryption function, and it is discussed here.

The file encryption function encodes a file by simply complementing each byte in the file. To decode the file, "encode" it a second time. As you probably know, two complements produce the original value. Keep in mind that this approach to file encryption is not very secure. (It is extremely easy for another programmer to break. However, this approach is quite effective when nonprogrammers are the concern.) For real security, you will obviously want to use a different encryption method. This simple approach is used here because it is quite short and doesn't "get in the way" of the parts of the function that relate to accessing disk files from a TSR application. The **code()** function is shown here:

```c
/*****************************************************/
/* A simple file encryption function.        */
/*****************************************************/
void code(void)
{
  int fd, num;
  char ch, fname[80];
  char far *old_dta;
  long sk;

  old_dta = getdta(); /* save old dta */
  setdta(MK_FP(_psp, 0x80)); /* construct new dta */

  /* prompt for file name */
  tsrwindow(2);
  tsrwindow_xy(2, 0, 0);
  tsrwindow_puts(2, "Enter name for file: ");
  tsrwindow_gets(2, fname);

  if((fd = _open(fname, O_RDWR)) < 0) {
    tsrwindow_xy(2, 0, 0);
    tsrwindow_cleol(2);
    tsrwindow_puts(2, "Cannot open file. Press a key.\n");
    tsrwindow_getche(2);
    tsrdeactive(2);
    setdta(old_dta); /* restore old dta */
    return;
  }

  num = 1;
  for(sk = 0; num==1 ; sk++) {
    lseek(fd, sk, SEEK_SET);
    num = _read(fd, &ch, 1);
    ch = ~ch; /* complement each byte */
    lseek(fd, sk, SEEK_SET);
    if(num==1) _write(fd, &ch , 1);
  }

  _close(fd);
  tsrdeactive(2);
  setdta(old_dta); /* restore old dta */
}
```

As you can see, the part of the function that actually encodes the file is quite small. What complicates the function is the fact that it is being executed inside a TSR. There are two reasons why accessing disk files from a TSR is so troublesome. First, as mentioned earlier, when an application pops up, the DTA is not automatically reset. Instead, the disk transfer address of the previously executing program is still in effect. This means that if the pop-up application accesses a disk file, the contents of the other application's data might (and probably will) be affected. Therefore, it is necessary to give the pop-up application a DTA separate from that used by the preempted program. To do this, you can use Turbo C's **getdta()** and **setdta()** functions. (If your compiler does not have equivalent functions, then you can call DOS functions 0x2F and 0x1A, respectively.) As stated, the default DTA is located at offset 0x80 in the program's PSP. Hence, this sequence of code resets the DTA to the TSR's default DTA:

```
char far *old_dta;

old_dta = getdta(); /* get the dta */
setdta(MK_FP(_psp, 0x80)); /* make TSR's dta current */
```

The value of **old_dta** resets the DTA to the value used by the interrupted program.

The second complication found in performing disk accesses is that for most compilers, you cannot use C's ANSI-standard I/O system. That is, functions like **fopen()**, **fread()**, and **fwrite()** will not work in a TSR because they all use C's dynamic memory allocation system. And, most implementations of C's dynamic memory system will not function in a TSR. Hence, you must use the UNIX-like functions **open()**, **close()**, **read()**, and **write()**. These functions are generally translated directly into equivalent DOS calls. Some compilers, like Turbo C, provide special versions of these functions, beginning with an underscore, that are guaranteed to be direct calls to DOS. If your compiler makes such a distinction, be sure to use these functions.

THE ENTIRE TSR PROGRAM LISTING

The entire listing to the TSR is shown here, along with its application functions and the modified windowing routines:

```
/* Terminate-and-stay-resident skeleton and sample
   applications.
*/

#include "stdio.h"
#include "stdlib.h"
#include "string.h"
#include "dos.h"
#include "ctype.h"
#include "fcntl.h"
#include "conio.h"
#include "bios.h"
#include "io.h"

#define BORDER 1
#define MAX_FRAME 3
#define REV_VID 0x70
#define NORM_VID 7
#define VID_SIZE 4000
#define STK_SIZE 0x2000

/* window function prototypes */
void save_video(int num), restore_video(int num);
void write_string(int x, int y, char *p, int attrib);
void write_char(int x, int y, char ch, int attrib);
void tsrdisplay_header(int num), tsrdraw_border(int num);
void tsrwindow_gets(int num , char *s);
void tsrwindow_cleol(int num), tsrwindow(int num);
void tsrwindow_cls(int num), set_vid_mem(void);
void tsrdeactive(int num);
void tsrwindow_bksp(int num);
void goto_xy(int x, int y);
int make_tsrwindow(int num, char *header, int startx,
                int starty, int endx, int endy, int border);
int tsrwindow_xy(int num, int x, int y);
int tsrwindow_puts(int num, char *str);
int video_mode(void), tsrwindow_putchar(int num, char ch);
int tsrwindow_getche(int num);
int tsrwindow_upline(int num), tsrwindow_downline(int num);
int readkey(void);

/* TSR function prototypes */
void cursor_pos(void);
void activate_tsr(void);
void interrupt tsr_keystroke(void);
```

```
void interrupt dos_idle(void);
void interrupt new_int8(void);
void interrupt (*old_int28)();
void interrupt (*old_int8)();
void interrupt (*old_key)();
void interrupt (*old_int64)();
void notepad(void), calc(void);
void code(void);
int push(int i), pop(void);

char far *vid_mem;
char video;

struct window_frame {
  int startx, endx, starty, endy; /* corners of window */
  int curx, cury; /* current cursor position in window */
  unsigned char *p; /* pointer to buffer */
  char *header; /* header message */
  int border; /* border on/off */
  int active; /* 1 if active, 0 if not */
} frame[MAX_FRAME];

char wp[VID_SIZE]; /* buffer to hold contents of the screen
                      when saved by save_video() */

/* busy is set to 1 when the program is active, 0 otherwise */
char busy = 0;

unsigned char stck[STK_SIZE];
unsigned int sp, ss;

int old_row, old_col;
int key;
char far *dos_active;

main(void)
{
  union REGS r;
  struct SREGS s;

  /* see if already loaded */
  old_int64 = getvect(0x64); /* unused interrupt */
  if(!old_int64) setvect(0x64, new_int8); /* set a flag */
  else {
    printf("TSR already loaded.");
```

```
    return 1;
  }

  /* obtain the dos_active flag address */
  r.h.ah = 0x34;
  int86x(0x21, &r, &r, &s);
  dos_active = MK_FP(s.es, r.x.bx);

  /* get old ISR addresses */
  old_key = getvect(9); /* keystroke int */
  old_int28 = getvect(0x28); /* int 28 */
  old_int8 = getvect(8); /* timer interrupt */

  /* reroute interrupt vectors to new handlers */
  setvect(9, tsr_keystroke);
  setvect(0x28, dos_idle);
  setvect(8, new_int8);

  printf("F1: Notepad    F2: Calculator    F3: File Coder");
  printf("    F4: Deactivate\n");

  key = 0;
  set_vid_mem(); /* get address of video memory */

  /* initialize all windows */
  make_tsrwindow(0, " Notepad [Esc to exit] ",
                 20, 5, 60, 16, BORDER);
  make_tsrwindow(1, " Calculator ", 20, 8, 60, 12, BORDER);
  make_tsrwindow(2, " File Coder ", 20, 8, 60, 10, BORDER);

  keep(0, 2000); /* terminate and stay resident */

  return 0;
}

/* This is the function that intercepts the keystroke
   interrupt (int 9). */
void interrupt tsr_keystroke(void)
{
  int far *t2 = (int far *) 1050; /* address of head pointer */
  char far *t = (char far *) 1050; /* address of head pointer */

  (*old_key)(); /* first, call old keystroke ISR */

  if(*t != *(t+2)) {/* if not empty */
```

```
    t += *t-30+5; /* advance to the character position */
    if(*t>=59 && *t<=62) {
      switch(*t) { /* see what is in scan code */
        case 59: /* F1: notepad */
          key = 1;
          break;
        case 60: /* F2: calculator */
          key = 2;
          break;
        case 61: /* F3: file encrypter */
          key = 3;
          break;
        case 62: /* F4: deactivate TSR */
          key = 4;
          break;
      }
      *(t2+1) = *t2; /* zero buffer */
    }
  }
}

/* New interrupt 8. */
void interrupt new_int8(void)
{
  (*old_int8)(); /* call original int 8 */

  /* If DOS is idle, TSR is not already active,
     and if a hot key has been pressed, activate the TSR. */
  if(!*dos_active && !busy && key)
        activate_tsr();
}

/* This function intercepts int 0x28 (the DOS-idle
   interrupt).
*/
void interrupt dos_idle(void)
{
  (*old_int28)(); /* call old int 0x28 ISR */
  if(!busy && key) activate_tsr();
}

/* Pop up the TSR. */
void activate_tsr(void)
{
  /* set up TSR stack */
```

```
disable(); /* disable interrupts */
  ss = _SS;
  sp = _SP;
  _SS = _DS;
  _SP = (unsigned) &stck[STK_SIZE-2];
enable();  /* enable interrupts */

cursor_pos(); /* get current cursor position */

/* check video mode - don't pop up if not in
   an 80-column text mode
*/
video = video_mode();
if(!busy && (video==7 ¦¦ video==3 ¦¦ video==2)) {
  busy = !busy; /* don't allow a second activation */
  switch(key) {
    case 1: notepad();
      break;
    case 2: calc();
      break;
    case 3: code();
      break;
  }
  busy = !busy;
}
if(key==4) /* deactivating TSR */
  write_string(old_col, old_row, "TSR deactivated", NORM_VID);

goto_xy(old_col, old_row); /* reset cursor */

/* restore old stack */
disable();
  _SP = sp;
  _SS = ss;
enable();

if(key==4) { /* reset old ISR routines and free memory */
  setvect(8, old_int8);
  setvect(9, old_key);
  setvect(0x28, old_int28);
  setvect(0x64, old_int64);
  freemem(_psp); /* free program block */
} else key = 0;
}
```

```
/*********************************************************/
/* Pop-up window application functions.                  */
/*********************************************************/

/*********************************************************/
/* Stack based, postfix notation four-function calculator */
/*********************************************************/
#define MAX 100

int *p;  /* pointer into the stack */
int *tos; /* points to top of stack */
int *bos; /* points to bottom of stack */
int stack[MAX];

void calc(void)
{
  int answer;
  int a, b;
  char in[80], out[80];

  p = stack;
  tos = p;
  bos = p+MAX-1;

  tsrwindow(1);
  do {
    tsrwindow_xy(1, 0, 0);
    tsrwindow_cleol(1);
    tsrwindow_puts(1, ": "); /* calc prompt */
    tsrwindow_gets(1, in);
    tsrwindow_puts(1, "\n ");
    tsrwindow_cleol(1);
    switch(*in) {
      case '+':
        a = pop();
        b = pop();
        answer = a+b;
        push(a+b);
        break;
      case '-':
        a = pop();
        b = pop();
        answer = b-a;
```

```
        push(b-a);
        break;
      case '*':
        a = pop();
        b = pop();
        answer = b*a;
        push(b*a);
        break;
      case '/':
        a = pop();
        b=pop();
        if(a==0) {
          tsrwindow_puts(0, "divide by 0\n");
          break;
        }
        answer = b/a;
        push(b/a);
        break;
      default:
        push(atoi(in));
    continue;
    }
    itoa(answer, out, 10);
    tsrwindow_puts(1, out);
  } while(*in);
  tsrdeactive(1);
}

/* Push a number on the stack.
   Returns 1 if successful, 0 if stack is full.
*/
push(int i)
{
  if(p>bos) return 0;

  *p=i;
  p++;
  return 1;
}

/* Retrieve top element from the stack.
   Returns 0 on stack underflows.
*/
```

```
pop(void)
{
  p--;
  if(p<tos) {
    p++;
    return 0;
  }
  return *p;
}


/*****************************************************/
/* Pop-up notepad.                                */
/*****************************************************/
#define MAX_NOTE 10
char notes[MAX_NOTE][80];

void notepad(void)
{
  static first=1;
  register int i, j, k;
  union inkey {
    char ch[2];
    int i;
  } c;
  char ch;

  /* initialize notes array if necessary */
  if(first) {
    for(i=0; i<MAX_NOTE; i++)
      *notes[i] = '\0';
    first = !first;
  }

  tsrwindow(0);
  /* display the existing notes */
  for(i=0; i<MAX_NOTE; i++) {
    if(*notes[i]) tsrwindow_puts(0, notes[i]);
    tsrwindow_putchar(0, '\n');
  }

  tsrwindow_xy(0, 0, 0);

  for(i=0;;) {
    c.i = readkey();  /* read the key */
```

```
if(tolower(c.ch[0])==27) { /* Esc to quit */
  tsrdeactive(0);
  break;
}

/* if normal key */
if(isprint(c.ch[0]) || c.ch[0]=='\b') {
  tsrwindow_cleol(0);
  notes[i][0] = c.ch[0];
  j = 1;
  tsrwindow_putchar(0, notes[i][0]);
  do {
ch = tsrwindow_getche(0);
if(ch=='\b') {
     if(j>0) {
        j--;
     tsrwindow_bksp(0);
  }
}
else {
  notes[i][j] = ch;
     j++;
   }
 } while(notes[i][j-1]!='\r');
  notes[i][j-1] = '\0';
  if(i<MAX_NOTE-1) i++;
  tsrwindow_putchar(0, '\n');
}
else { /* is special key */
  switch(c.ch[1]) {
    case 72: /* up arrow */
  if(i>0) {
    i--;
    tsrwindow_upline(0);
  }
  break;
    case 80: /* down arrow */
  if(i<MAX_NOTE-1) {
       i++;
    tsrwindow_downline(0);
  }
  break;
    case 63: /* F5: clear the notepad */
      tsrwindow_cls(0);
      for(k=0; k<MAX_NOTE; k++) *notes[k] = '\0';
```

```
        tsrwindow_xy(0, 0, 0);
    }
  }
 }
}

/*****************************************************/
/* A simple file encryption function.                */
/*****************************************************/
void code(void)
{
  int fd, num;
  char ch, fname[80];
  char far *old_dta;
  long sk;

  old_dta = getdta(); /* save old dta */
  setdta(MK_FP(_psp, 0x80)); /* construct new dta */

  tsrwindow(2);
  tsrwindow_xy(2, 0, 0);
  tsrwindow_puts(2, "Enter name for file: ");
  tsrwindow_gets(2, fname);

  if((fd = _open(fname, O_RDWR)) < 0) {
    tsrwindow_xy(2, 0, 0);
    tsrwindow_cleol(2);
    tsrwindow_puts(2, "Cannot open file. Press a key.\n");
    tsrwindow_getche(2);
    tsrdeactive(2);
    setdta(old_dta); /* restore old dta */
    return;
  }

  num = 1;
  for(sk = 0; num==1 ; sk++) {
    lseek(fd, sk, SEEK_SET);
    num = _read(fd, &ch, 1);
    ch = ~ch; /* complement each byte */
    lseek(fd, sk, SEEK_SET);
    if(num==1) _write(fd, &ch , 1);
  }

  _close(fd);
  tsrdeactive(2);
```

```
    setdta(old_dta); /* restore old dta */
}


/*********************************************************/
/* Window functions. These functions are adapted from   */
/* those developed in Chapter 2.                         */
/*********************************************************/

/* Display a pull-down window. */
void tsrwindow(int num) /* window number */
{
  /* get active window */
  if(!frame[num].active) { /* not currently in use */
    save_video(num);      /* save the current screen */
    frame[num].active = 1; /* set active flag */
  }

  if(frame[num].border) tsrdraw_border(num);
  tsrdisplay_header(num); /* display the window */
}


/* Construct a pull-down window frame.
   1 is returned if window frame can be constructed;
   otherwise 0 is returned.
*/
make_tsrwindow(
    int num, /* window number */
    char *header, /* header text */
    int startx, int starty, /* coordinates of upper-left corner */
    int endx, int endy, /* coordinates of lower-right corner */
    int border /* no border if 0 */
)
{
  if(num>MAX_FRAME) {
    tsrwindow_puts(0, "Too many windows\n");
    return 0;
  }

  if((startx>78) || (startx<0) || (starty>24) || (starty<0)) {
    tsrwindow_puts(0, "range error");
    return 0;
  }

  if((endx>79) || (endy>25)) {
    tsrwindow_puts(0, "window won't fit");
```

```
      return 0;
   }

   /* construct the frame */
   frame[num].startx = startx; frame[num].endx = endx;
   frame[num].starty = starty; frame[num].endy = endy;
   frame[num].p = wp;
   frame[num].header = header;
   frame[num].border = border;
   frame[num].active = 0;
   frame[num].curx = 0; frame[num].cury = 0;
   return 1;
}

/* Deactivate a window and remove it from the screen. */
void tsrdeactive(int num)
{
   /* reset the cursor postion to upper-left corner */
   frame[num].curx = 0;
   frame[num].cury = 0;
   frame[num].active = 0;
   restore_video(num);
}

/* Display the header message in its proper location. */
void tsrdisplay_header(int num)
{
   register int x, len;

   x = frame[num].startx;

   /* Calculate the correct starting position to center
      the header message - if negative, message won't
      fit.
   */
   len = strlen(frame[num].header);
   len = (frame[num].endx - x - len) / 2;
   if(len<0) return; /* don't display it */
   x = x +len;

   write_string(x, frame[num].starty,
        frame[num].header, NORM_VID);
}

/* Draw a window's border. */
```

```
void tsrdraw_border(int num)
{
  register int i;
  char far *v, far *t;

  v = vid_mem;
  t = v;
  for(i=frame[num].starty+1; i<frame[num].endy; i++) {
    v += (i*160) + frame[num].startx*2;
    *v++ = 179;
    *v = NORM_VID;
    v = t;
    v += (i*160) + frame[num].endx*2;
    *v++ = 179;
    *v = NORM_VID;
    v = t;
  }
  for(i=frame[num].startx+1; i<frame[num].endx; i++) {
    v += (frame[num].starty*160) + i*2;
    *v++ = 196;
    *v = NORM_VID;
    v = t;
    v += (frame[num].endy*160) + i*2;
    *v++ = 196;
    *v = NORM_VID;
    v = t;
  }

  /* draw the corners of the border */
  write_char(frame[num].startx, frame[num].starty, 218, NORM_VID);
  write_char(frame[num].startx, frame[num].endy, 192, NORM_VID);
  write_char(frame[num].endx, frame[num].starty, 191, NORM_VID);
  write_char(frame[num].endx, frame[num].endy, 217, NORM_VID);
}

/* Write a string at the current cursor position
   in the specified window.
   Returns 0 if window not active, 1 otherwise.
*/
tsrwindow_puts(int num, char *str)
{
  /* make sure window is active */
  if(!frame[num].active) return 0;

  for( ; *str; str++)
```

```
      tsrwindow_putchar(num, *str);
   return 1;
}


/* Write a character at the current cursor position
   in the specified window.
   Returns 0 if window not active, 1 otherwise.
*/
tsrwindow_putchar(int num, char ch)
{
   int x, y;
   char far *v;

   /* make sure window is active */
   if(!frame[num].active) return 0;

   x = frame[num].curx + frame[num].startx + 1;
   y = frame[num].cury + frame[num].starty + 1;

   v = vid_mem;
   v += (y*160) + x*2; /* compute the address */
   if(y>=frame[num].endy) return 1;
   if(x>=frame[num].endx) return 1;

   if(ch=='\n') { /* newline char */
      y++;
      x = frame[num].startx+1;
      v = vid_mem;
      v += (y*160) + x*2; /* compute the address */
      frame[num].cury++; /* increment Y */
      frame[num].curx = 0; /* reset X */
   }
   else {
      frame[num].curx++;
      *v++ = ch; /* write the character */
      *v++ = NORM_VID; /* normal video attribute */
   }
   tsrwindow_xy(num, frame[num].curx, frame[num].cury);
   return 1;
}


/* Position cursor in a window at specified location.
   Returns 0 if out of range; nonzero otherwise.
*/
tsrwindow_xy(int num, int x, int y)
```

```
{
  if(x<0 ¦¦ x+frame[num].startx>=frame[num].endx-1)
    return 0;
  if(y<0 ¦¦ y+frame[num].starty>=frame[num].endy-1)
    return 0;
  frame[num].curx = x;
  frame[num].cury = y;
  goto_xy(frame[num].startx+x+1, frame[num].starty+y+1);
  return 1;
}

/* Read a string from a window. */
void tsrwindow_gets(int num, char *s)
{
  char ch, *temp;

  temp = s;
  for(;;) {
    ch = tsrwindow_getche(num);
    switch(ch) {
      case '\r': /* the Enter key is pressed */
        *s = '\0';
        return;
      case '\b': /* backspace */
        if(s>temp) {
          s--;
          frame[num].curx--;
          if(frame[num].curx<0) frame[num].curx = 0;
          tsrwindow_xy(num, frame[num].curx, frame[num].cury);
          write_char(frame[num].startx+ frame[num].curx+1,
            frame[num].starty+frame[num].cury+1, ' ', NORM_VID);
        }
        break;
      default: *s = ch;
    s++;
    }
  }
}

/* Input keystrokes inside a window.
   Returns full 16-bit scan code.
*/
tsrwindow_getche(int num)
{
  union inkey {
```

```
    char ch[2];
    int i;
  } c;

  if(!frame[num].active) return 0; /* window not active */

  tsrwindow_xy(num, frame[num].curx, frame[num].cury);

  c.i = readkey();  /* read the key */

  if(c.ch[0]) {
    switch(c.ch[0]) {
      case '\r': /* the Enter key is pressed */
        break;
      case '\b': /* backspace */
        break;
      default:
        if(frame[num].cury+frame[num].starty < frame[num].endy-1) {
          write_char(frame[num].startx+frame[num].curx+1,
            frame[num].starty+frame[num].cury+1, c.ch[0], NORM_VID);
          frame[num].curx++;
        }
    }
    if(frame[num].curx < 0) frame[num].curx = 0;
    if(frame[num].curx+frame[num].startx > frame[num].endx-2)
      frame[num].curx--;
    tsrwindow_xy(num, frame[num].curx, frame[num].cury);
  }
  return c.i;
}

/* Clear to end of line. */
void tsrwindow_cleol(int num)
{
  register int i, x, y;

  x = frame[num].curx;
  y = frame[num].cury;
  tsrwindow_xy(num, frame[num].curx, frame[num].cury);

  for(i=frame[num].curx; i<frame[num].endx-1; i++)
    tsrwindow_putchar(num,' ');
  tsrwindow_xy(num, x, y);
}
```

```c
/* Clear a window. */
void tsrwindow_cls(int num)
{
  register int i, j;
  char far *v;

  for(i=frame[num].starty+1; i<frame[num].endy; i++)
    for(j=frame[num].startx+1; j<frame[num].endx; j++) {
      v = vid_mem;
      v += (i*160) + j*2;
      *v++ = ' '; /* write a space */
      *v++ = NORM_VID;
    }
  frame[num].curx = 0;
  frame[num].cury = 0;
}


/* Move cursor up one line.
   Returns nonzero if successful, 0 otherwise.
*/
tsrwindow_upline(int num)
{
  if(frame[num].cury > 0) {
    frame[num].cury--;
    tsrwindow_xy(num, frame[num].curx, frame[num].cury);
    return 1;
  }
  return 0;
}


/* Move cursor down one line.
   Returns nonzero if successful, 0 otherwise.
*/
tsrwindow_downline(int num)
{
  if(frame[num].cury < frame[num].endy-frame[num].starty-1) {
    frame[num].cury++;
    tsrwindow_xy(num, frame[num].curx, frame[num].cury);
    return 1;
  }
  return 1;
}


/* Back up one character. */
```

```
void tsrwindow_bksp(int num)
{
  if(frame[num].curx>0) {
    frame[num].curx--;
    tsrwindow_xy(num, frame[num].curx, frame[num].cury);
    tsrwindow_putchar(num, ' ');
    frame[num].curx--;
    tsrwindow_xy(num, frame[num].curx, frame[num].cury);
  }
}

/***********************************************/
/* Low-level video functions.                 */
/***********************************************/

/* Display a string with specifed attribute. */
void write_string(int x, int y, char *p, int attrib)
{
  char far *v;

  v = vid_mem;
  v += (y*160) + x*2; /* compute the address */
  for(; *p; ) {
    *v++ = *p++; /* write the character */
    *v++ = attrib; /* write the attribute */
    }
}

/* Write character with specified attribute. */
void write_char(int x, int y, char ch, int attrib)
{
  char far *v;

  v = vid_mem;
  v += (y*160) + x*2;
  *v++ = ch; /* write the character */
  *v = attrib;  /* write the attribute */
}

/* Save a portion of the screen. */
void save_video(int num)
{
  register int i,j;
  char *buf_ptr;
  char far *v, far *t;
```

```
  buf_ptr = frame[num].p;
  v = vid_mem;
  for(i=frame[num].startx; i<frame[num].endx+1; i++)
    for(j=frame[num].starty; j<frame[num].endy+1; j++) {
      t = (v + (j*160) + i*2);
      *buf_ptr++ = *t++;
      *buf_ptr++ = *t;
      *(t-1) = ' '; /* clear the window */
    }
}

/* Restore a portion of the screen. */
void restore_video(int num)
{
  register int i,j;
  char far *v, far *t;
  char *buf_ptr;

  buf_ptr = frame[num].p;
  v = vid_mem;
  t = v;
  for(i=frame[num].startx; i<frame[num].endx+1; i++)
    for(j=frame[num].starty; j<frame[num].endy+1; j++) {
      v = t;
      v += (j*160) + i*2;
      *v++ = *buf_ptr++; /* write the character */
      *v = *buf_ptr++;  /* write the attribute */
    }
  frame[num].active = 0; /* restore_video */
}

/* Returns the current video mode. */
video_mode(void)
{
  union REGS r;

  r.h.ah = 15; /* get video mode */
  return int86(0x10, &r, &r) & 255;
}

/* Return the 16-bit scan code from the keyboard. */
readkey(void)
{
  union REGS r;
```

```
  r.h.ah = 0;
  return int86(0x16, &r, &r);
}

/* Send the cursor to the specified X,Y position. */
void goto_xy(int x, int y)
{
  union REGS r;

  r.h.ah = 2; /* cursor addressing function */
  r.h.dl = x; /* column coordinate */
  r.h.dh = y; /* row coordinate */
  r.h.bh = 0; /* video page */
  int86(0x10, &r, &r);
}

/* Set the vid_mem pointer to the start of video
   memory.
*/
void set_vid_mem(void)
{
  int vmode;

  vmode = video_mode();
  if((vmode!=2) && (vmode!=3) && (vmode!=7)) {
    printf("video must be in 80 column text mode");
    exit(1);
  }
  /* set proper address of video RAM */
  if(vmode==7) vid_mem = (char far *) MK_FP(0xB000, 0000);
  else vid_mem = (char far *) MK_FP(0xB800, 0000);
}

/* Read and save cursor coordinates. */
void cursor_pos(void)
{
  union REGS i, o;

  i.h.bh = 0;
  i.h.ah = 3;
  int86(16, &i, &o);

  old_row = o.h.dh;
  old_col = o.h.dl;
}
```

SOME OTHER TSR CONSIDERATIONS

The TSR works fine on this author's systems, which include an early XT, an AT-clone, a model 60, and a model 80, with software that is mostly compilers and editors. It will probably work fine for you, too. However, just in case you experience some problems, here are a couple of things you might try.

Because some programs bypass DOS for much of their disk and screen I/O, some TSR programs watch for calls to interrupts 0x10 (BIOS screen routines) and 0x13 (BIOS disk I/O). These TSRs will not pop up while one of these interrupts is active. The TSR does not monitor these interrupts; however, in demanding situations, you may need to.

The TSR program relies upon the clock interrupt (INT 8) to trigger the pop-up application when interrupt 0x28 is not being called. Frankly, this approach degrades the overall system performance. However, popping up during a keyboard interrupt can cause problems when used with some application programs (such as the Turbo C integrated environment, for example), and the clock appears to be the only safe way to activate the TSR for these situations. However, you might want to experiment by using the keyboard interrupt to activate the TSR for your specific environment. If you experience no troubles, using this approach avoids slowing down your system.

CREATING YOUR OWN TSR APPLICATIONS

The best way to do TSR programming is to proceed deliberately. Get the core of your application running and then move ahead slowly. Then, if the program stops working, you will have a good idea of what has caused the error. Remember, you can find out only by trial and error which standard library functions are usable and which crash the system.

If you will be selling your TSR, be sure that it is compatible with other, popular TSRs. With a little effort, you can achieve this.

CHAPTER FOUR

Graphics

This chapter introduces a core set of graphics functions that allow the drawing of points, lines, boxes, and circles using a CGA, EGA, or VGA graphics adapter. These routines are then used as a foundation on which several higher level graphics functions are built.

Aside from briefly presenting the core graphics functions, this chapter develops the following routines:

- Saving a graphics image to a disk file

- Loading a graphics image from a disk file

- Rotating an object in two-dimensional space

- Copying or moving a graphics image to a new location

The chapter concludes with a "paint" program that allows the user to draw on the screen by using the cursor keys.

ANDREW KOENIG

Self-described as having "an eclectic, artistic temperament," Andrew Koenig has been programming in C at Bell Labs, New Jersey, since 1977. He wrote the first portable printf() library function for UNIX C and he has contributed to the first generic C++ libraries. He is also the author of the book *C Traps and Pitfalls*.

I asked Andrew if he would name one of his favorite programs written in C. He responded, "Dennis Ritchie's original PDP-11 C compiler and associated standard I/O libraries are works of art." In fact, many programmers still refer to Ritchie's initial compiler as one of the finest C programs ever written.

I mentioned to Andrew that many programmers have a proverb or saying that exemplifies their approach to programming, and I asked him about his. "Always remember: Most programs last far longer than their authors ever dreamed. If you get it right the first time, you don't have to worry about it later. This means avoiding arbitrary limits, magic numbers, and other sorts of sloppy programming. Also, you should be able to prove that your program works. It is generally impractical to generate an actual proof for every program you write, but you should be able to provide such a proof if called upon."

I asked Andrew if there was one piece of advice that he could offer to other programmers. He responded, "Don't guess! If you're not sure whether what you're doing will have the effect you want, study the problem until you are sure."

Like many programmers, Andrew has interests outside of programming. He is an instrument-rated private pilot, an accomplished musician, and an enthusiastic photographer. He holds a BA in mathematics from Columbia College and an MS in Computer Science from Columbia School of Engineering & Applied Science.

Once you have mastered the use of the graphics functions developed in this chapter, you will be able to create some very impressive programs. For example, using the image save and load functions, you will be able to create graphs or diagrams in advance and simply "pop" them up when needed. With the rotation function you can create "Star Wars"-type animated graphics that can be very exciting.

While most C compilers supply a graphics library, there are still several reasons why you might want to develop your own set of graphics routines. First, you have complete control over their operation because you have source code to them. (If you're like most programmers, you know there is nothing like being in full control of your program.) Second, you can modify your routines to work with new or different types of graphics adapters. Third, you can optimize your routines relative to your own specific application, thus avoiding the excess baggage that is often produced by generic graphics packages. In this chapter, you will find a core set of graphics routines that you can use and enhance as you see fit.

For the routines developed in this chapter to run correctly you need an IBM PC, XT, AT, PS/2, or compatible and a CGA, EGA, or VGA graphics adapter. However, beyond the writing of a point, the routines in the chapter are hardware independent, and you should have little trouble making them work on other types of graphics hardware.

This chapter begins with a brief discussion of the operation of the graphics adapters and the core graphics functions.

MODES AND PALETTES

Before any graphics functions can be used, the computer must be placed into the proper video mode. For the IBM PC, this means selecting the proper mode and palette.

Several different video modes are available on the IBM PC, as Table 4-1 shows. The functions developed in this chapter require screen mode 4, which is 320x200 four-color graphics. Although the EGA and VGA adapters allow greater resolution in other modes, mode 4 is used because it works with all color graphics adapters. This allows the graphics examples presented in this chapter to run on the widest variety of computers. To use a different EGA or VGA mode, you need only change the function that writes a point. Keep in mind that in all modes, the upper-left corner is location 0,0.

Table 4-1

The Screen Modes Available for the Various Video Adapters

Mode	Type	Dimensions	Adapters
0	Text, b/w	40x25	CGA, EGA, VGA
1	Text, 16 colors	40x25	CGA, EGA, VGA
2	Text, b/w	80x25	CGA, EGA, VGA
3	Text, 16 colors	80x25	CGA, EGA, VGA
4	Graphics, 4 colors	320x200	CGA, EGA, VGA
5	Graphics, 4 gray tones	320x200	CGA, EGA, VGA
6	Graphics, b/w	640x200	CGA, EGA, VGA
7	Text, b/w	80x25	monochrome
8	Graphics, 16 colors	160x200	PC*jr*
9	Graphics, 16 colors	320x200	PC*jr*
10	Graphics, 4 colors	640x200	PC*jr*
11	Reserved		
12	Reserved		
13	Graphics, 16 colors	320x200	EGA, VGA
14	Graphics, 16 colors	640x200	EGA, VGA
15	Graphics, 4 colors	640x350	EGA, VGA
16	Graphics, 16 colors	640x350	VGA
17	Graphics, 2 colors	640x480	VGA
18	Graphics, 16 colors	640x480	VGA
19	Graphics, 256 colors	640x200	VGA

BIOS interrupt 16, function 0, sets the video mode and is used by the the **mode()** function shown here:

```
/* Set the video mode. */
void mode(int mode_code)
{
  union REGS r;

  r.h.al = mode_code;
  r.h.ah = 0;
  int86(0x10, &r, &r);
}
```

Two palettes are available in mode 4 graphics. The *palette* determines which four colors are displayed. On the IBM PC, palette 0 provides the colors red, green, and yellow; palette 1 gives white, magenta, and cyan.

For each, the fourth color is the color of the background, usually black. The BIOS interrupt 16, function 11, sets the palette. The function **palette()**, shown here, selects the palette specified in its argument:

```
/* Set the palette. */
void palette(int pnum)
{
  union REGS r;

  r.h.bh = 1; /* code for palette select */
  r.h.bl = pnum;
  r.h.ah = 11; /* set palette function */
  int86(0x10, &r, &r);
}
```

WRITING PIXELS

The most fundamental graphics routine is the one that writes a *pixel,* the smallest addressable point on the video monitor screen. For the purposes of this discussion, however, the term "pixel" will be used to describe the smallest addressable point in a specific graphics mode. (In some literature, the term "pel" is also used.) Because the function that writes to a pixel is used by other, higher level routines, its efficiency is very important to the overall speed with which the graphics functions operate. On the IBM PC and compatibles, there are two ways to write information to a pixel. The first method, through the use of a BIOS interrupt, is the easiest but also the slowest—in fact, too slow for our purposes. The second and faster method is to write information directly into the video display RAM; this method is examined here.

Understanding Mode 4 Graphics

In graphics mode 4, the video RAM starts at location B800:0000. In mode 4, each byte holds the color information for 4 pixels. Therefore, 16K are needed for a resolution of 320x200. Because 2 bits can hold only four different values, there can be only four colors in mode 4. The value of each two-bit packet determines the color that is displayed according to this table:

Value	Color in Palette 0	Color in Palette 1
0	Background	Background
1	Yellow	Blue
2	Red	Purple
3	Green	White

A strange quirk in the CGA causes pixels in the even-numbered lines to be stored in memory beginning at B800:0000, but the pixels in the odd-numbered lines are stored 0x2000 (8152 in decimal) bytes higher, at B800:2000. Therefore, each row of pixels requires 80 bytes, 40 for the even pixels and 40 for the odd. Within each byte, the pixels are stored left to right as they appear on the screen. This means that pixel number 0 occupies bits 6 and 7, while pixel number 3 uses bits 0 and 1.

Creating the mempoint() Function

Given how the pixels are stored in the video RAM when mode 4 graphics is used, a function can now be developed that writes pixels directly to that memory. This function is called **mempoint()**.

To begin with, there is one very interesting feature of the BIOS write-pixel function that it is desirable for the **mempoint()** function to also support. If the BIOS write-pixel interrupt is called with the seventh bit (leftmost) of the color code set to 1, the color specified is XORed with the existing color at the specified location instead of simply overwriting the previous color. The advantage is that it guarantees that the pixel will be visible. It also allows the original contents of the screen to be easily restored. You will see the value of this feature a little later in this chapter.

Because 4 pixels are encoded into each byte, you must preserve the value of the other three when changing the value of one. The best way to do this is to create a bit mask with all bits set except those in the location of the pixel to be changed. This value is ANDed with the original byte, and then this value is ORed with the new information. However, the situation is slightly different if you want to XOR the new value with the old. In this case, you simply OR the original byte with 0 and then XOR that result with the new color.

The address of the proper byte is located by first multiplying the Y coordinate by 40 and then adding the value of the X coordinate divided by four. To determine whether the pixel is in the even or odd bank of memory, the remainder of the Y coordinate divided by 2 is used. If the outcome is 0, the number is even, so the first bank is used; otherwise, it is odd, and the second bank must be used. The proper bits within the byte are computed by performing a modulus division by 4. The remainder will be the number of the 2-bit packet that contains the information for the desired pixel. Bit shift operations are used to arrange the color code byte and the bit mask into their proper positions. Although the bit manipulations that take place in the function **mempoint()**, shown here, are fairly intimidating, if you study the code carefully, you should have no trouble understanding its operation. Notice that the pointer to the video memory is declared as **far**. This is necessary if you are compiling with a small data model.

```
/* Write a point directly to mode 4 graphics RAM. */
void mempoint(int x, int y, /* coordinate of point */
              int color) /* color */
{
  union mask {
    char c[2];
    int i;
  } bit_mask;
  int index, bit_position;
  unsigned char t;
  char xor; /* xor color in or overwrite */

  /* pointer to mode 4 graphics RAM */
  char far *ptr = (char far *) 0xB8000000;

  bit_mask.i = 0xFF3F; /* 11111111 00111111 in binary */

  /* check range */
  if(x<0 || x>XMAX || y<0 || y>YMAX) return;

  xor = color & 128; /* see if xor mode is set */
  color = color & 127; /* mask off high bit */

  /* set bit_mask and color bits to the right location */
  bit_position = x%4;
  color <<= 2*(3-bit_position);
  bit_mask.i >>= 2*bit_position;

  /* find the correct byte in screen memory */
  index = y*40 + (x >> 2);
  if(y % 2) index += 8152; /* if odd use 2nd bank */
```

```
/* write the color */
if(!xor) { /* overwrite mode */
  t = *(ptr+index) & bit_mask.c[0];
  *(ptr+index) = t | color;
}
else { /* xor mode */
  t = *(ptr+index) | (char) 0;
  *(ptr+index) = t ^ color;
}
}
```

Notice that the special XOR write mode available in the BIOS function has been preserved in **mempoint()**.

DRAWING LINES

The line-drawing function, a fundamental graphics routine, draws a line in the specified color, given the beginning and ending coordinates of the line. Although it is quite easy to draw lines that are either vertical or horizontal, it is more difficult to create a function that draws lines along any diagonal. For example, to draw a line from 0,0 to 80,120, what are the points in between?

One approach to creating a line-drawing function uses the ratio between the change in the X and Y dimensions. To see how this works, consider a line from 0,0 to 5,10. The change in X is 5 and the change in Y is 10. The ratio is 1/2, and it is used to determine the rate at which the X and Y coordinates change as the line is drawn. In this case, it means that the X coordinate is incremented only half as frequently as the Y coordinate. Novice programmers often choose this method when creating a line-drawing function. Although this method is mathematically sound and easy to understand, in order for it to work properly in all situations, floating-point variables and arithmetic must be used to avoid serious round-off errors. This means that the line-drawing function will run quite slowly unless there is a math coprocessor, such as the 8087, installed in the system. For this reason, it is seldom used.

By far the most common method used to draw a line employs Bresenham's algorithm. Although based conceptually on the ratios between the X and Y distances, no divisions or floating-point calculations are required. Instead, the ratio between the change in the X and Y directions is handled implicitly through a series of additions and subtractions. The basic idea behind Bresenham's approach is to record the amount of error between the ideal location of each point and where it is actually displayed. The error between the actual and ideal positions is due to the limitations of the hardware—the fact that no display has infinite resolution and that therefore the actual location of each dot on the line is the best approximation. In each iteration through the line-drawing loop, two variables, called **xerr** and **yerr**, are incremented by the changes in magnitude of the X and Y coordinates, respectively. When an error value reaches a predetermined limit, it is reset, and the appropriate coordinate counter is incremented. This process continues until the entire line is drawn. The **line()** function, shown here, implements this method; you should study it until you understand its operation. Notice that it uses the **mempoint()** function developed earlier to actually write a dot to the screen.

```
/* Draw a line in specified color
   using Bresenham's integer-based algorithm.
*/
void line(int startx, int starty, /* upper-left corner */
          int endx, int endy, /* lower-right corner */
          int color) /* color */
{
  register int t, distance;
  int x=0, y=0, delta_x, delta_y;
  int incx, incy;

  /* Compute the distances in both directions. */
  delta_x = endx-startx;
  delta_y = endy-starty;

  /* Compute the direction of the increment.
     An increment of 0 means either a vertical
     or horizontal line.
  */
  if(delta_x>0) incx = 1;
  else if(delta_x==0) incx = 0;
  else incx = -1;

  if(delta_y>0) incy = 1;
  else if(delta_y==0) incy = 0;
  else incy = -1;

  /* determine which distance is greater */
```

```
delta_x = abs(delta_x);
delta_y = abs(delta_y);
if(delta_x>delta_y) distance = delta_x;
else distance = delta_y;

/* draw the line */
for(t=0; t<=distance+1; t++) {
  mempoint(startx, starty, color);
  x += delta_x;
  y += delta_y;
  if(x>distance) {
    x -= distance;
    startx += incx;
  }
  if(y>distance) {
    y -= distance;
    starty += incy;
  }
 }
}
```

DRAWING AND FILLING BOXES

Once you have a line-drawing function, it is easy to create a box-drawing function. The one shown here draws the outline of a box in the specified color, given the coordinates of two opposing corners:

```
/* Draw a box. */
void box(int startx, int starty, /* upper-left corner */
        int endx, int endy, /* lower-right corner */
        int color) /* color */
{
  line(startx, starty, endx, starty, color);
  line(startx, starty, startx, endy, color);
  line(startx, endy, endx, endy, color);
  line(endx, starty, endx, endy, color);
}
```

Filling a box requires that you write to each pixel in the box. The **fill_box()** routine shown here fills a box with the specified color given the coordinates of two opposing corners. It uses the **line()** function to actually color in the box.

```
/* Fill box with specified color. */
void fill_box(int startx, int starty, /* upper-left corner */
          int endx, int endy, /* lower-right corner */
          int color) /* color */
{
  register int i, begin, end;

  begin = startx<endx ? startx : endx;
  end = startx>endx ? startx : endx;

  for(i=begin; i<=end;i++)
    line(i, starty, i, endy, color);
}
```

DRAWING CIRCLES

The easiest and fastest way to draw a circle is to use Bresenham's circle-drawing algorithm, similar to Bresenham's line-drawing algorithm. No floating-point calculations are required except for the aspect ratio, so it is quite fast. Essentially, the algorithm works by incrementing the X and Y coordinates as needed based upon the magnitude of the error between them. This value is held in the variable **delta**. The support function **plot_circle()** actually plots the points. You could place this code in line for extra speed, but it does make the **circle()** function harder to read and understand. The variable **asp_ratio** is global because it is used by both **circle()** and **plot_circle()**. Also, you may find it useful to set its value outside of the **circle()** function for some applications. By varying the **asp_ratio**, you can draw ellipses. The **circle()** function is called with the coordinates of the center of the circle, the radius (in pixels) of the circle, and its color. The **circle()** and **plot_circle()** functions are shown here:

```
double asp_ratio;

/* Draw a circle using Bresenham's integer-based algorithm. */
void circle(int x_center, int y_center, /* center */
          int radius, /* radius */
          int color) /* color */
{
  register int x, y, delta;

  asp_ratio = 1.0; /* for different aspect ratios, alter
```

```
                        this number */

  y = radius;
  delta = 3 - 2 * radius;

  for(x=0; x<y; ) {
    plot_circle(x, y, x_center, y_center, color);

    if (delta < 0)
      delta += 4*x+6;
    else {
      delta += 4*(x-y)+10;
      y--;
    }
    x++;
  }
  x = y;
  if(y) plot_circle(x, y, x_center, y_center, color);
}

/* Plot_circle() actually prints the points that
   define the circle.
*/
void plot_circle(int x, int y, /* point to plot */
                 int x_center, int y_center, /* center */
                 int color) /* color */
{
  int startx, endx, x1, starty, endy, y1;

  starty = y*asp_ratio;
  endy = (y+1)*asp_ratio;
  startx = x*asp_ratio;
  endx = (x+1)*asp_ratio;

  for (x1=startx; x1<endx; ++x1) {
    mempoint(x1+x_center, y+y_center, color);
    mempoint(x1+x_center, y_center-y, color);
    mempoint(x_center-x1, y_center-y, color);
    mempoint(x_center-x1, y+y_center, color);
  }

  for (y1=starty; y1<endy; ++y1) {
    mempoint(y1+x_center, x+y_center, color);
    mempoint(y1+x_center, y_center-x, color);
```

```
      mempoint(x_center-y1, y_center-x, color);
      mempoint(x_center-y1, x+y_center, color);
  }
}
```

It is possible to fill a circle by repeatedly calling **circle()** with increasingly smaller radiuses. This is the method used by **fill_circle()**, shown here:

```
/* Fill a circle by repeatedly calling circle()
   with smaller radius.
*/
void fill_circle(int x_center, int y_center,
                 int radius, int color)
{
  while(radius) {
    circle(x_center, y_center, radius, color);
    radius--;
  }
}
```

A SIMPLE TEST PROGRAM

The following program illustrates the previously described graphics functions. Its output is shown in Figure 4-1.

```
/* A short program to illustrate the core graphics
   functions.
 */
#include "dos.h"
#include "stdio.h"
#include "stdlib.h"
#include "conio.h"

#define XMAX 319
#define YMAX 199

void line(int startx, int starty, int endx, int endy,
        int color);
void box(int startx, int starty, int endx, int endy,
        int color);
```

```
void fill_box(int startx, int starty, int endx, int endy,
        int color);
void circle(int x_center, int y_center, int radius, int color);
void fill_circle(int x_center, int y_center, int radius, int color);
void plot_circle(int x, int y, int x_center, int y_center,
                int color);
void mempoint(int x, int y, int color);
void palette(int pnum);
void mode(int mode_code);

double asp_ratio; /* holds aspect ratio for circles */

main(void)
{
  mode(4);
  palette(0);

  line(0, 0, 100, 100, 1);
  box(50, 50, 80, 90, 2);
  fill_box(100, 0, 120, 40, 3);
  circle(100, 160, 30, 2);
  fill_circle(250, 150, 20, 1);

  getch();
  mode(3);

  return 0;
}

/* Set the palette. */
void palette(int pnum)
{
  union REGS r;

  r.h.bh = 1; /* code for palette select */
  r.h.bl = pnum;
  r.h.ah = 11; /* set palette function */
  int86(0x10, &r, &r);
}

/* Set the video mode. */
void mode(int mode_code)
{
  union REGS r;
```

```
  r.h.al = mode_code;
  r.h.ah = 0;
  int86(0x10, &r, &r);
}


/* Draw a box. */
void box(int startx, int starty, /* upper-left corner */
         int endx, int endy, /* lower-right corner */
         int color) /* color */
{
  line(startx, starty, endx, starty, color);
  line(startx, starty, startx, endy, color);
  line(startx, endy, endx, endy, color);
  line(endx, starty, endx, endy, color);
}


/* Draw a line in specified color
   using Bresenham's integer based algorithm.
*/
void line(int startx, int starty, /* upper-left corner */
          int endx, int endy, /* lower-right corner */
          int color) /* color */
{
  register int t, distance;
  int x=0, y=0, delta_x, delta_y;
  int incx, incy;

  /* Compute the distances in both directions. */
  delta_x = endx-startx;
  delta_y = endy-starty;

  /* Compute the direction of the increment.
     An increment of 0 means either a vertical
     or horizontal line.
  */
  if(delta_x>0) incx = 1;
  else if(delta_x==0) incx = 0;
  else incx = -1;

  if(delta_y>0) incy = 1;
  else if(delta_y==0) incy = 0;
  else incy = -1;

  /* determine which distance is greater */
```

```
delta_x = abs(delta_x);
delta_y = abs(delta_y);
if(delta_x>delta_y) distance = delta_x;
else distance = delta_y;

/* draw the line */
for(t=0; t<=distance+1; t++) {
  mempoint(startx, starty, color);
  x += delta_x;
  y += delta_y;
  if(x>distance) {
    x -= distance;
    startx += incx;
  }
  if(y>distance) {
    y -= distance;
    starty += incy;
  }
}
}

/* Fill box with specified color. */
void fill_box(int startx, int starty, /* upper-left corner */
        int endx, int endy, /* lower-right corner */
        int color) /* color */
{
  register int i, begin, end;

  begin = startx<endx ? startx : endx;
  end = startx>endx ? startx : endx;

  for(i=begin; i<=end;i++)
    line(i, starty, i, endy, color);
}

/* Draw a circle using Bresenham's integer-based algorithm. */
void circle(int x_center, int y_center, /* center */
        int radius, /* radius */
        int color) /* color */
{
  register int x, y, delta;

  asp_ratio = 1.0; /* for different aspect ratios, alter
                    this number */
```

```
  y = radius;
  delta = 3 - 2 * radius;

  for(x=0; x<y; ) {
    plot_circle(x, y, x_center, y_center, color);

    if (delta < 0)
      delta += 4*x+6;
    else {
      delta += 4*(x-y)+10;
      y--;
    }
    x++;
  }
  x = y;
  if(y) plot_circle(x, y, x_center, y_center, color);
}

/* Plot_circle() actually prints the points that
   define the circle.
*/
void plot_circle(int x, int y, /* point to plot */
                 int x_center, int y_center, /* center */
                 int color) /* color */
{
  int startx, endx, x1, starty, endy, y1;

  starty = y*asp_ratio;
  endy = (y+1)*asp_ratio;
  startx = x*asp_ratio;
  endx = (x+1)*asp_ratio;

  for (x1=startx; x1<endx; ++x1) {
    mempoint(x1+x_center, y+y_center, color);
    mempoint(x1+x_center, y_center-y, color);
    mempoint(x_center-x1, y_center-y, color);
    mempoint(x_center-x1, y+y_center, color);
  }

  for (y1=starty; y1<endy; ++y1) {
    mempoint(y1+x_center, x+y_center, color);
    mempoint(y1+x_center, y_center-x, color);
    mempoint(x_center-y1, y_center-x, color);
    mempoint(x_center-y1, x+y_center, color);
  }
```

```
}

/* Fill a circle by repeatedly calling circle()
   with smaller radius.
*/
void fill_circle(int x_center, int y_center,
                 int radius, int color)
{
  while(radius) {
    circle(x_center, y_center, radius, color);
    radius--;
  }
}

/* Write a point directly to mode 4 graphics RAM. */
void mempoint(int x, int y, /* coordinate of point */
              int color) /* color */
{
  union mask {
    char c[2];
    int i;
  } bit_mask;
  int index, bit_position;
  unsigned char t;
  char xor; /* xor color in or overwrite */

  /* pointer to mode 4 graphics RAM */
  char far *ptr = (char far *) 0xB8000000;

  bit_mask.i = 0xFF3F; /* 11111111 00111111 in binary */

  /* check range */
  if(x<0 || x>XMAX || y<0 || y>YMAX) return;

  xor = color & 128; /* see if xor mode is set */
  color = color & 127; /* mask off high bit */

  /* set bit_mask and color bits to the right location */
  bit_position = x%4;
  color <<= 2*(3-bit_position);
  bit_mask.i >>= 2*bit_position;

  /* find the correct byte in screen memory */
  index = y*40 + (x >> 2);
```

```
if(y % 2) index += 8152; /* if odd use 2nd bank */

/* write the color */
if(!xor) { /* overwrite mode */
  t = *(ptr+index) & bit_mask.c[0];
  *(ptr+index) = t | color;
}
else { /* xor mode */
  t = *(ptr+index) | (char) 0;
  *(ptr+index) = t ^ color;
}
}
```

SAVING AND LOADING A GRAPHICS IMAGE

It is a simple matter to save or load a graphics image. Since what is displayed on the screen is held in the video RAM, the contents of that RAM are easily copied to a disk file, or vice versa. The biggest problem is

Figure 4-1

Sample output from the simple graphics test program

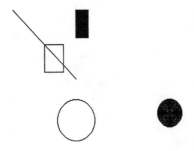

to let the user enter a file name because both the prompting message and the file name entered by the user cause part of the image to be overwritten. To avoid this, the functions **save_pic()** and **load_pic()**, shown here, save the top 14 rows of the image, clear that area, prompt for the file name, and then restore the image after the file name has been entered:

```c
/* Save the video graphics display. */
void save_pic(void)
{
  char fname[80];
  FILE *fp;
  register int i, j;
  int e=0;

  /* pointer to mode 4 graphics RAM */
  char far *ptr = (char far *) 0xB8000000;

  char far *temp;
  unsigned char buf[14][80]; /* hold the contents of screen */

  temp = ptr;
  /* save the top of the current screen */
  for(i=0; i<14; i++)
    for(j=0; j<80; j+=2) {
      buf[i][j] = *temp; /* even byte */
      buf[i][j+1] = *(temp+8152); /* odd byte */
      *temp = 0; *(temp+8152) = 0; /* clear top of screen */
      temp++;
    }

  goto_xy(0, 0);
  printf("Filename: ");
  gets(fname);
  if(!(fp=fopen(fname, "wb"))) {
    goto_xy(0, 0);
    printf("cannot open file - press a key ");
    getch();
    e = 1; /* flag error */
  }

  temp = ptr;
  /* restore the top of the current screen */
  for(i=0; i<14; i++)
    for(j=0; j<80; j+=2) {
      *temp = buf[i][j];
```

```
        *(temp+8152) = buf[i][j+1];
        temp++;
      }

  if(e) return; /* if file could not be opened, exit */

  /* save image to file */
  for(i=0; i<8152; i++) {
    putc(*ptr, fp); /* even byte */
    putc(*(ptr+8152), fp); /* odd byte */
    ptr++;
    }

  fclose(fp);
}

/* Load the video graphics display. */
void load_pic(void)
{
  char fname[80];
  FILE *fp;
  register int i, j;

  /* pointer to mode 4 graphics RAM */
  char far *ptr = (char far *) 0xB8000000;

  char far *temp;
  unsigned char buf[14][80]; /* hold the contents of screen */

  temp = ptr;
  /* save the top of the current screen */
  for(i=0; i<14; i++)
    for(j=0; j<80; j+=2) {
      buf[i][j] = *temp;
      buf[i][j+1] = *(temp+8152);
      *temp = 0; *(temp+8152) = 0; /* clear the top of the screen */
      temp++;
    }

  goto_xy(0, 0);
  printf("Filename: ");
  gets(fname);
  if(!(fp=fopen(fname, "rb"))) {
    goto_xy(0, 0);
    printf("cannot open file\n");
```

```
    temp = ptr;
    /* restore the top of the current screen */
    for(i=0; i<14; i++)
      for(j=0; j<80; j+=2) {
        *temp = buf[i][j];
        *(temp+8152) = buf[i][j+1];
        temp++;
      }
    return;
}

/* load image from file */
for(i=0; i<8152; i++) {
  *ptr = getc(fp); /* even byte */
  *(ptr+8152) = getc(fp); /* odd byte */
  ptr++;
}

fclose(fp);
}
```

The routines operate by assigning a pointer to the starting address of the video RAM and then by writing or reading each even and odd byte in ascending order. This allows the image to be loaded into RAM in a natural, visually pleasing way. If the video memory were accessed in a strictly ascending fashion, the even pixels would be displayed first, followed by the odd ones. Although an interesting effect, it is a bit unsettling for general use.

DUPLICATING PART OF THE SCREEN

It is sometimes useful to be able to copy the graphics image in one part of the screen to another location. This is easily accomplished by using the **copy()** function shown here:

```
/* Copy one region to another location. */
void copy(int startx, int starty, /* upper-left coordinate */
  int endx, int endy, /* lower-right coordinate */
  int x, int y) /* upper-left of region receiving the image */
{
  int i, j;
  unsigned char c;
```

```
for(; startx<=endx; startx++, x++)
  for(i=starty, j=y; i<=endy; i++, j++) {
    c = read_point(startx, i); /* read point */
    mempoint(x, j, c); /* write it to new location */
  }
}
```

As you can see, it is called with the upper-left and lower-right corner coordinates of the region to be copied and the upper-left coordinates of the location to which it is being copied. The function uses the **read_point()** function to return the value of the specified pixel. The **read_point()** function is shown here:

```
/* Read byte directly from the video RAM in mode 4. */
unsigned char read_point(int x, int y)
{
  union mask {
    char c[2];
    int i;
  } bit_mask;
  int index, bit_position;
  unsigned char t;

  /* pointer to mode 4 graphics RAM */
  char far *ptr = (char far *) 0xB8000000;

  bit_mask.i = 3;     /* 11111111 00111111 in binary */

  /* check range for mode 4 */
  if(x<0 || x>XMAX || y<0 || y>YMAX) return 0;

  /* set bit_mask and color_code bits to the right location */
  bit_position = x%4;
  bit_mask.i <<= 2*(3-bit_position);
  /* find the correct byte in screen memory */
  index = y*40 +(x >> 2);
  if(y % 2) index += 8152; /* if odd use 2nd bank */

  /* read the color */
  t = *(ptr+index) & bit_mask.c[0];
  t >>= 2*(3-bit_position);
  return t;
}
```

This function works just like **mempoint()** except that instead of writing a pixel, it returns the pixel's current setting.

As you might surmise, with only a slight change it is possible to transform **copy()** into **move()**. The **move()** function moves a region to another place and erases the original as it does so. The **move()** function is shown here:

```
/* Move one region to another location. */
void move(int startx, int starty, /* upper-left coordinate */
  int endx, int endy, /* lower-right coordinate */
  int x, int y) /* upper left of region receiving the image */
{
  int i, j;
  unsigned char c;

  for(; startx<=endx; startx++, x++)
    for(i=starty, j=y; i<=endy; i++, j++) {
      c = read_point(startx, i); /* read point */
      mempoint(startx, i, 0); /* erase old image */
      mempoint(x, j, c); /* write it to new location */
    }
}
```

TWO-DIMENSIONAL ROTATION

The rotation of an object in two-dimensional space is actually quite easy in the Cartesian coordinate system. You might recall from your high school analytic geometry class that the rotation of a point through an angle *theta* around the origin is described by these equations:

new_x = old_x * cos(theta) − old_y * sin(theta)
new_y = old_x * sin(theta) + old_y * cos(theta)

The only problem when you apply these formulas to the graphics display is that the screen is not technically a Cartesian space. A Cartesian axis defines four quadrants, as shown in Figure 4-2. However, the graphics screen defines only one quadrant—and the direction of the Y axis is inverted. To solve this problem, it is necessary to establish a new origin and to normalize the screen X,Y coordinates to it. Any point on the screen can be used as an origin, but generally you want to define an origin that is near (or at) the center of the object that you wish to rotate. The function

---

Figure 4-2

Cartesian axis versus the graphics screen

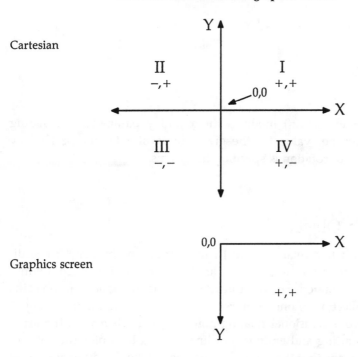

rotate _ point(), shown here, computes the proper new X,Y value for a specified angle of rotation:

```
/* Rotate a point around the origin, specified by
   x_org and y_org, by angle theta.
*/
void rotate_point(double theta, /* angle of rotation */
                  double *x, double *y, /* point to rotate */
                  int x_org, int y_org) /* origin */
{
  double tx, ty;

  /* normalize x and y */
  tx = *x - x_org;
  ty = *y - y_org;
```

```
/* rotate */
*x = tx * cos(theta) - ty * sin(theta);
*y = tx * sin(theta) + ty * cos(theta);

/* return coordinate values */
*x += x_org;
*y += y_org;

}
```

Notice that **rotate_point()** modifies the **x** and **y** parameters by setting them to their proper value for the given angle of rotation specified by **theta**. The angle of rotation is specified in radians.

Rotating an Object

Although the function **rotate_point()** will compute the proper X,Y coordinates that a rotated point will occupy, another function is needed if entire objects are to be rotated. For the purposes of this discussion, an object is defined as a collection of one or more straight lines. Each line in the object is held in a two-dimensional floating-point array. Each row in the array will hold the starting and ending coordinates for a line, plus the color of the line. This means that the array dimensions will be the number of lines making up the object by 5. For example, this array can define an object with up to ten sides:

```
double object[10][5];
```

The array will be organized as shown in Figure 4-3.

To define an object, place the beginning and ending points of each line of the object into the array and give each line a color. For example, if the object is the box shown here

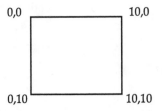

Figure 4-3

Conventional organization of an array

First index → Second index →	0	1	2	3	4
0	start_X1	start_Y1	end_X1	end_Y1	color
1	start_X2	start_Y2	end_X2	end_Y2	color
2	start_X3	start_Y3	end_X3	end_Y3	color
3	start_X4	start_Y4	end_X4	end_Y4	color
.	.				
.	.				
.	.				
n	start_Xn	start_Yn	end_Xn	end_Yn	color

---

and each line is green, the following code creates an array that defines that box:

```
object[0][0] = 0; object[0][1] = 0;
object[0][0] = 0; object[0][3] = 10;
object[0][4] = 1;

object[1][0] = 0; object[1][1] = 10;
object[1][0] = 10; object[1][3] = 10;
object[1][4] = 1;

object[2][0] = 10; object[2][1] = 10;
object[2][0] = 10; object[2][3] = 0;
object[2][4] = 1;

object[3][0] = 10; object[3][1] = 0;
object[3][0] = 0; object[3][3] = 0;
object[3][4] = 1;
```

Once you have defined an object, you can use the function **rotate_object()**, shown here, to rotate it in either a clockwise or counter-clockwise direction by pressing the R or L key, respectively:

```
/* Rotate the specified object. */
void rotate_object(double ob[][5], /* object definition */
```

```
        double theta, /* angle of rotation in radians */
        int x, int y, /* location of origin */
        int lines) /* number of lines in image */
{
  register int j;
  char ch;

  for(;;) {
    ch = getch(); /* see which direction to rotate */
    switch(tolower(ch)) {
      case 'l': /* counterclockwise */
        theta = theta < 0 ? -theta : theta;
        break;
      case 'r': /* clockwise */
        theta = theta > 0 ? -theta : theta;
        break;
      default: return;
    }

    for(j=0; j<lines; j++) {
      /* erase old line */
      line((int) ob[j][0], (int) ob[j][1],
        (int) ob[j][2], (int) ob[j][3], 0);

      rotate_point(theta, &ob[j][0],
        &ob[j][1], x, y);

      rotate_point(theta, &ob[j][2],
        &ob[j][3], x, y);

      line((int) ob[j][0], (int) ob[j][1],
        (int) ob[j][2], (int) ob[j][3], (int) ob[j][4]);
    }
  }
}
```

As indicated by the function parameter declarations, **rotate_object()** will rotate the object about the origin specified in **x** and **y** by the angle **theta**. Remember, **theta** must be specified in radians. The smallest practical value of **theta** is 0.01. Notice that the object is erased from its previous position and then moved to its new position. If this were not done, the screen would quickly become just a blur of color. You must be sure to specify the number of sides that an object has in the parameter **sides**.

Although it is not technically part of the rotation functions, **display_object()**, shown here, is useful when working with objects. It will display the object defined in **ob**:

```
/* Display an object. */
void display_object(double ob[][5], int lines)
{
  register int i;

  for(i=0; i<lines; i++)
    line((int) ob[i][0], (int) ob[i][1],
      (int) ob[i][2], (int) ob[i][3], (int) ob[i][4]);
}
```

To illustrate the usefulness of the rotation functions, the following program uses them to rotate a house about its center. A series of screen images taken at different points in the rotation is shown in Figure 4-4. The box around the house helps define the perspective.

```
/* An example of object rotation. */

#include "dos.h"
#include "stdio.h"
#include "math.h"
#include "conio.h"
#include "ctype.h"

#define XMAX 319
#define YMAX 199

void line(int startx, int starty, int endx, int endy,
        int color);
void mempoint(int x, int y, int color);
void palette(int pnum);
void mode(int mode_code);
void rotate_point(double theta, double *x, double *y,
                int x_org, int y_org);
void display_object(double ob[][5], int lines);
void rotate_object(double ob[][5], double theta,
                int x, int y, int lines);

/* house array */
double house[][5] = {
```

```
/* startx, starty, endx, endy, color */
   120, 120, 200, 120, 2, /* house */
   200, 120, 200, 80, 2,
   120, 80, 200, 80, 2,
   120, 80, 120, 120, 2,
   160, 60, 120, 80, 2, /* roof */
   160, 60, 200, 80, 2,
   155, 120, 155, 100, 2, /* door */
   155, 100, 165, 100, 2,
   165, 100, 165, 120, 2,
   130, 90, 130, 100, 2, /* windows */
   130, 90, 140, 90, 2,
   130, 100, 140, 100, 2,
   140, 90, 140, 100, 2,
   180, 90, 180, 100, 2,
   180, 90, 190, 90, 2,
   180, 100, 190, 100, 2,
   190, 90, 190, 100, 2
};

main(void)
{
   mode(4); /* mode 4 graphics, palette 0 */
   palette(0);

   /* draw a box around the house to give perspective */
   line(70, 30, 260, 30, 1);
   line(70, 160, 260, 160, 1);
   line(70, 30, 70, 160, 1);
   line(260, 30, 260, 160, 1);

   display_object(house, 17);
   rotate_object(house, 0.025, 160, 90, 17);
   mode(3);

   return 0;
}

/* Set the palette. */
void palette(int pnum)
{
   union REGS r;

   r.h.bh = 1; /* code for palette select */
   r.h.bl = pnum;
```

```
    r.h.ah = 11; /* set palette function */
    int86(0x10, &r, &r);
}

/* Set the video mode. */
void mode(int mode_code)
{
  union REGS r;

  r.h.al = mode_code;
  r.h.ah = 0;
  int86(0x10, &r, &r);
}

/* Draw a line in the specified color
   using Bresenham's integer-based algorithm.
*/
void line(int startx, int starty, /* beginning of line */
          int endx, int endy, /* end of line */
          int color) /* color */
{
  register int t, distance;
  int x=0, y=0, delta_x, delta_y;
  int incx, incy;

  /* Compute the distances in both directions. */
  delta_x = endx-startx;
  delta_y = endy-starty;

  /* Compute the direction of the increment.
     An increment of 0 means either a vertical
     or horizontal line.
  */
  if(delta_x>0) incx = 1;
  else if(delta_x==0) incx = 0;
  else incx = -1;

  if(delta_y>0) incy = 1;
  else if(delta_y==0) incy = 0;
  else incy = -1;

  /* determine which distance is greater */
  delta_x = abs(delta_x);
  delta_y = abs(delta_y);
  if(delta_x>delta_y) distance = delta_x;
```

```
      else distance = delta_y;

      /* draw the line */
      for(t=0; t<=distance+1; t++) {
        mempoint(startx, starty, color);
        x += delta_x;
        y += delta_y;
        if(x>distance) {
          x -= distance;
          startx += incx;
        }
        if(y>distance) {
          y -= distance;
          starty += incy;
        }
      }
   }
}

/* Write a point directly to mode 4 graphics RAM. */
void mempoint(int x, int y, /* coordinate of point */
              int color) /* color */
{
  union mask {
    char c[2];
    int i;
  } bit_mask;
  int index, bit_position;
  unsigned char t;
  char xor; /* xor color in or overwrite */

  /* pointer to mode 4 graphics RAM */
  char far *ptr = (char far *) 0xB8000000;

  bit_mask.i = 0xFF3F; /* 11111111 00111111 in binary */

  /* check range for mode 4 */
  if(x<0 || x>XMAX || y<0 || y>YMAX) return;

  xor = color & 128; /* see if xor mode is set */
  color = color & 127; /* mask off high bit */

  /* set bit_mask and color bits to the right location */
  bit_position = x%4;
  color <<= 2*(3-bit_position);
  bit_mask.i >>= 2*bit_position;
```

```
  /* find the correct byte in screen memory */
  index = y*40 + (x >> 2);
  if(y % 2) index += 8152; /* if odd use 2nd bank */

  /* write the color */
  if(!xor) { /* overwrite mode */
    t = *(ptr+index) & bit_mask.c[0];
    *(ptr+index) = t | color;
  }
  else { /* xor mode */
    t = *(ptr+index) | (char) 0;
    *(ptr+index) = t ^ color;
  }
}

/* Rotate a point around the origin, specified by
   x_org and y_org, by angle theta.
*/
void rotate_point(double theta, /* angle of rotation */
                  double *x, double *y, /* point to rotate */
                  int x_org, int y_org) /* origin */
{
  double tx, ty;

  /* normalize x and y */
  tx = *x - x_org;
  ty = *y - y_org;

  /* rotate */
  *x = tx * cos(theta) - ty * sin(theta);
  *y = tx * sin(theta) + ty * cos(theta);

  /* return to PC coordinate values */
  *x += x_org;
  *y += y_org;

}

/* Rotate the specified object. */
void rotate_object(double ob[][5], /* object definition */
           double theta, /* angle of rotation in radians */
           int x, int y, /* location of origin */
           int lines) /* number of lines in image */
{
```

```
   register int j;
   char ch;

   for(;;) {
     ch = getch(); /* see which direction to rotate */
     switch(tolower(ch)) {
       case 'l': /* counterclockwise */
         theta = theta < 0 ? -theta : theta;
         break;
       case 'r': /* clockwise */
         theta = theta > 0 ? -theta : theta;
         break;
       default: return;
     }

     for(j=0; j<lines; j++) {
       /* erase old line */
       line((int) ob[j][0], (int) ob[j][1],
         (int) ob[j][2], (int) ob[j][3], 0);

       rotate_point(theta, &ob[j][0],
         &ob[j][1], x, y);

       rotate_point(theta, &ob[j][2],
         &ob[j][3], x, y);

       line((int) ob[j][0], (int) ob[j][1],
         (int) ob[j][2], (int) ob[j][3], (int) ob[j][4]);
     }
   }
}

/* Display an object. */
void display_object(double ob[][5], int lines)
{
   register int i;

   for(i=0; i<lines; i++)
     line((int) ob[i][0], (int) ob[i][1],
       (int) ob[i][2], (int) ob[i][3], (int) ob[i][4]);
}
```

Figure 4-4

Rotating an object

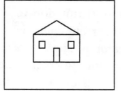

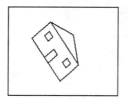

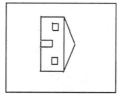

COMBINING THE ROUTINES

This final section presents a simple paint program that uses the graphic routines developed in this chapter. You are probably familiar with some of the popular paint-type programs that are available. A paint program generally uses a mouse to allow the user to "brush" lines onto the screen. However, mouse support will be added to the paint program in Chapter 9. Since not everyone has a mouse, the paint program developed here will rely on the cursor keys for its operation.

In a paint program, you must be able to see where the current X,Y position is. (In graphics mode, there is no cursor.) Doing this requires the use of a locator that resembles the crosshairs of a rifle scope. The function **xhairs()**, shown here, places a small crosshairs locator on the screen at the current X,Y position. Notice that the color code is ORed with 128, causing bit 7 to be set to 1. This tells the **mempoint()** function to XOR the color onto the screen instead of overwriting the current color. This achieves two very important objectives. First, the locator is always visible because it always has a color different than the surrounding color. Second, it makes it easy to return the pixels occupied by the locator to their former color by simply calling the function a second time. (Recall that a sequence of two XOR operations always produces the original value.)

```
/* display crosshair locator */
void xhairs(x,y)
int x,y;
{
   line(x-4, y, x+3, y, 1 | 128);
   line(x, y+4, x, y-3, 1 | 128);
}
```

The paint program shown here lets you do the following:

- Draw lines
- Draw boxes
- Fill boxes
- Draw circles
- Fill circles
- Select color
- Select palette
- Turn the brush on and off
- Set a speed of motion parameter
- Save a graphics image
- Load a graphics image
- Rotate an object around any point of origin
- Copy and move graphics images

The main loop of the program is shown here:

```
main(void)
{
   union k{
```

```
    char c[2];
    int i;
} key;

int x = 10, y = 10; /* current screen position */
int cc = 2; /* current color */
int on_flag = 1; /* pen on or off */
int pal_num = 1; /* palette number */

/* the end points of a defined line, circle, or box */
int startx = 0, starty = 0, endx = 0, endy = 0, first_point = 1;

int inc = 1; /* movement increment */
int sides = 0; /* number of sides of a defined object */

mode(4); /* switch to mode 4 CGA/EGA graphics */
palette(0); /* palette 0 */

xhairs(x, y); /* show the crosshairs */
do {
  key.i = readkey();
  xhairs(x, y);  /* plot the crosshairs */
  if(!key.c[0]) switch(key.c[1]) {
    case 72: /* up */
      if(on_flag) line(x, y, x, y-inc, cc);
      y -= inc;
      break;
    case 80: /* down */
      if(on_flag) line(x, y, x, y+inc, cc);
      y += inc;
      break;
    case 75: /* left */
      if(on_flag) line(x, y, x-inc, y, cc);
      x -= inc;
      break;
    case 77: /* right */
      if(on_flag) line(x, y, x+inc, y, cc);
      x += inc;
      break;
    case 71: /* up left */
      if(on_flag) line(x, y, x-inc, y-inc, cc);
      x -= inc; y -= inc;
      break;
    case 73: /* up right */
      if(on_flag) line(x, y, x+inc, y-inc, cc);
```

```
        x += inc; y -= inc;
        break;
    case 79: /* down left */
        if(on_flag) line(x, y, x-inc, y+inc, cc);
        x -= inc; y += inc;
        break;
    case 81: /* down right */
        if(on_flag) line(x, y, x+inc, y+inc, cc);
        x += inc; y += inc;
        break;
    case 59: inc = 1; /* F1 - slow speed */
        break;
    case 60: inc = 5; /* F2 - fast speed */
        break;
}
else switch(tolower(key.c[0])) {
    case 'o': on_flag = !on_flag; /* toggle brush */
        break;
    case '1': cc = 1; /* color 1 */
        break;
    case '2': cc = 2; /* color 2 */
        break;
    case '3': cc = 3; /* color 3 */
        break;
    case '0': cc = 0; /* color 0 */
        break;
    case 'b': box(startx, starty, endx, endy, cc);
        break;
    case 'f': fill_box(startx, starty, endx, endy, cc);
        break;
    case 'l': line(startx, starty, endx, endy, cc);
        break;
    case 'c': circle(startx, starty, endy-starty, cc);
        break;
    case 'h': fill_circle(startx, starty, endy-starty, cc);
        break;
    case 's': save_pic();
        break;
    case 'r': load_pic();
        break;
    case 'm': /* move a region */
        move(startx, starty, endx, endy, x, y);
        break;
    case 'x': /* copy a region */
```

```
      copy(startx, starty, endx, endy, x, y);
      break;
    case 'd': /* define an object to rotate */
      sides = define_object(object, x, y);
      break;
    case 'a': /* rotate the object */
      rotate_object(object, 0.05, x, y, sides);
      break;
    case '\r': /* set endpoints for line, circle, or box */
      if(first_point) {
        startx = x, starty = y;
      }
      else {
        endx = x; endy = y;
      }
      first_point = !first_point;
      break;
    case 'p': pal_num = pal_num==1 ? 2:1;
      palette(pal_num);
  }
  xhairs(x, y);
} while (key.c[0]!='q');
mode(3);

return 0;
}
```

The paint program works like this. The screen is first set to graphics mode 4. Palette 0 is selected and the locator is displayed in the upper-left corner. The brush is on with a default color of 2 (red in palette 0). Therefore, moving the cursor leaves a trail of pixels. This is the way color is "brushed" onto the screen. Each time a cursor key is pressed, the locator moves one pixel in the indicated direction. This can be rather slow at times, so the program allows you to move five pixels at a time by pressing the F2 function key. To return to single pixel moves, press the F1 function key. Different colors may be selected by pressing the numbers 0 through 3 on the keyboard. In palette 0, 0 is blank, 1 is green, 2 is red, and 3 is yellow. The brush may be turned off and on by pressing the O key. The HOME, PGUP, PGDN, and END keys move the locator at 45-degree angles in the expected direction.

The program supports several special commands that draw boxes, fill boxes, draw lines, draw circles, fill circles, copy or move images, save or load the contents of the screen, and define and rotate an object. Let's see how these commands operate.

To draw lines, boxes, and circles automatically, you must first define two coordinates. For boxes and filled boxes, you must specify the location of two opposing corners. For lines, you select the beginning and ending points. For circles and filled circles, you specify the center and a point on the circle directly below the center. You perform the selection process by pressing the ENTER key when the locator is over the desired spot. For example, to define the end points of a line, you move the locator to the point where the line will begin and press the ENTER key. Next, you position the locator at the place where the line will end and press the ENTER key again. Pressing the ENTER key loads the variables **startx**, **starty**, **endx**, and **endy**, which are then used as parameters to the appropriate function. Once the locations have been recorded, pressing a B draws a box, F draws a filled box, L draws a line, C draws a circle, and H fills a circle.

To move or copy a region of the screen, you must define the upper-left and lower-right corners of the region by pressing the ENTER key at the appropriate locations. Next, move the locator to the upper-left corner of the region where you want to move or copy the image. To move the image, press M, and to copy the image, press X. Remember, what was previously in the destination region will be overwritten.

To rotate an object, you must first define the object by pressing the D key. Next, using the ENTER key, define each line segment in the object. That is, trace the object, pressing the ENTER key at the beginning and ending point of each line in the object. When you have finished, press the FI key to stop the definition process. The definition process is performed by the **define _ object()** function, which is found in the complete program shown here. Once the object is defined, it can be rotated by pressing the A key and using the L or R key to rotate the object about an origin defined by the current position of the locator. To stop the rotate procedure, press any key other than L or R.

The program is terminated by pressing a Q.

The entire paint program is shown here. You might find it enjoyable to add other high-level commands or to interface it to a mouse (see Chapter 9). Sample output is shown in Figure 4-5.

```
/* A paint program that allows lines, boxes,
   and circles to be drawn. You may define
   an object and rotate it in either a clockwise
   or counterclockwise direction. Regions of the
   screen can be copied or moved. Also, the
   graphic image may be saved to disk and loaded
   at a later date.
*/
#include "dos.h"
```

```
#include "stdio.h"
#include "math.h"
#include "ctype.h"
#include "conio.h"

#define NUM_SIDES 20 /* Number of sides an object may
                         have. Enlarge as needed. */
#define XMAX 319
#define YMAX 199

void line(int startx, int starty, int endx, int endy,
        int color);
void box(int startx, int starty, int endx, int endy,
        int color);
void fill_box(int startx, int starty, int endx, int endy,
        int color);
void circle(int x_center, int y_center, int radius, int color);
void fill_circle(int x_center, int y_center, int radius,
                int color);
void plot_circle(int x, int y, int x_center, int y_center,
                int color);
void mempoint(int x, int y, int color);
void palette(int pnum);
void mode(int mode_code);
void rotate_point(double theta, double *x, double *y,
                int x_org, int y_org);
void display_object(double ob[][5], int lines);
void rotate_object(double ob[][5], double theta,
                int x, int y, int lines);
int define_object(double ob[][5], int x, int y);
void move(int startx, int starty, int endx, int endy,
        int x, int y);
void copy(int startx, int starty, int endx, int endy,
        int x, int y);
void xhairs(int x, int y), goto_xy(int x, int y);
void save_pic(void), load_pic(void);
int readkey(void);

/* This array will hold the coordinates of an object
   that is defined dynamically.
*/
double object[NUM_SIDES][5];

double asp_ratio; /* holds aspect ratio for circles */

main(void)
{
```

```
union k{
  char c[2];
  int i;
} key;

int x = 10, y = 10; /* current screen position */
int cc = 2; /* current color */
int on_flag = 1; /* pen on or off */
int pal_num = 1; /* palette number */

/* the end points of a defined line, circle, or box */
int startx = 0, starty = 0, endx = 0, endy = 0, first_point = 1;

int inc = 1; /* movement increment */
int  sides = 0; /* number of sides of a defined object */

mode(4); /* switch to mode 4 CGA/EGA graphics */
palette(0); /* palette 0 */

xhairs(x, y); /* show the crosshairs */
do {
  key.i = readkey();
  xhairs(x, y);  /* plot the crosshairs */
  if(!key.c[0]) switch(key.c[1]) {
    case 72: /* up */
      if(on_flag) line(x, y, x, y-inc, cc);
      y -= inc;
      break;
    case 80: /* down */
      if(on_flag) line(x, y, x, y+inc, cc);
      y += inc;
      break;
    case 75: /* left */
      if(on_flag) line(x, y, x-inc, y, cc);
      x -= inc;
      break;
    case 77: /* right */
      if(on_flag) line(x, y, x+inc, y, cc);
      x += inc;
      break;
    case 71: /* up left */
      if(on_flag) line(x, y, x-inc, y-inc, cc);
      x -= inc; y -= inc;
      break;
    case 73: /* up right */
```

```
      if(on_flag) line(x, y, x+inc, y-inc, cc);
      x += inc; y -= inc;
      break;
    case 79: /* down left */
      if(on_flag) line(x, y, x-inc, y+inc, cc);
      x -= inc; y += inc;
      break;
    case 81: /* down right */
      if(on_flag) line(x, y, x+inc, y+inc, cc);
      x += inc; y += inc;
      break;
    case 59: inc = 1; /* F1 - slow speed */
      break;
    case 60: inc = 5; /* F2 - fast speed */
      break;
  }
  else switch(tolower(key.c[0])) {
    case 'o': on_flag = !on_flag; /* toggle brush */
      break;
    case '1': cc = 1; /* color 1 */
      break;
    case '2': cc = 2; /* color 2 */
      break;
    case '3': cc = 3; /* color 3 */
      break;
    case '0': cc = 0; /* color 0 */
      break;
    case 'b': box(startx, starty, endx, endy, cc);
      break;
    case 'f': fill_box(startx, starty, endx, endy, cc);
      break;
    case 'l': line(startx, starty, endx, endy, cc);
      break;
    case 'c': circle(startx, starty, endy-starty, cc);
      break;
    case 'h': fill_circle(startx, starty, endy-starty, cc);
      break;
    case 's': save_pic();
      break;
    case 'r': load_pic();
      break;
    case 'm': /* move a region */
      move(startx, starty, endx, endy, x, y);
      break;
    case 'x': /* copy a region */
```

```
            copy(startx, starty, endx, endy, x, y);
            break;
        case 'd': /* define an object to rotate */
            sides = define_object(object, x, y);
            break;
        case 'a': /* rotate the object */
            rotate_object(object, 0.05, x, y, sides);
            break;
        case '\r': /* set endpoints for line, circle, or box */
            if(first_point) {
                startx = x, starty = y;
            }
            else {
                endx = x; endy = y;
            }
            first_point = !first_point;
            break;
        case 'p': pal_num = pal_num==1 ? 2:1;
            palette(pal_num);
        }
        xhairs(x, y);
    } while (key.c[0]!='q');
    mode(3);

    return 0;
}
/* Set the palette. */
void palette(int pnum)
{
    union REGS r;

    r.h.bh = 1;  /* code for palette select */
    r.h.bl = pnum;
    r.h.ah = 11; /* set palette function */
    int86(0x10, &r, &r);
}

/* Set the video mode. */
void mode(int mode_code)
{
    union REGS r;

    r.h.al = mode_code;
    r.h.ah = 0;
    int86(0x10, &r, &r);
```

```
}

/* Draw a box. */
void box(int startx, int starty, /* upper-left corner */
         int endx, int endy, /* lower-right corner */
         int color) /* color */
{
  line(startx, starty, endx, starty, color);
  line(startx, starty, startx, endy, color);
  line(startx, endy, endx, endy, color);
  line(endx, starty, endx, endy, color);
}


/* Draw a line in specified color
   using Bresenham's integer-based algorithm.
*/
void line(int startx, int starty, /* upper-left corner */
          int endx, int endy, /* lower-right corner */
          int color) /* color */
{
  register int t, distance;
  int x=0, y=0, delta_x, delta_y;
  int incx, incy;

  /* Compute the distances in both directions. */
  delta_x = endx-startx;
  delta_y = endy-starty;

  /* Compute the direction of the increment.
     An increment of 0 means either a vertical
     or horizontal line.
  */
  if(delta_x>0) incx = 1;
  else if(delta_x==0) incx = 0;
  else incx = -1;

  if(delta_y>0) incy = 1;
  else if(delta_y==0) incy = 0;
  else incy = -1;

  /* determine which distance is greater */
  delta_x = abs(delta_x);
  delta_y = abs(delta_y);
  if(delta_x>delta_y) distance = delta_x;
```

```
  else distance = delta_y;

  /* draw the line */
  for(t=0; t<=distance+1; t++) {
    mempoint(startx, starty, color);
    x += delta_x;
    y += delta_y;
    if(x>distance) {
      x -= distance;
      startx += incx;
    }
    if(y>distance) {
      y -= distance;
      starty += incy;
    }
  }
}

/* Fill box with specified color. */
void fill_box(int startx, int starty, /* upper-left corner */
          int endx, int endy, /* lower-right corner */
          int color) /* color */
{
  register int i, begin, end;

  begin = startx<endx ? startx : endx;
  end = startx>endx ? startx : endx;

  for(i=begin; i<=end;i++)
    line(i, starty, i, endy, color);
}

/* Draw a circle using Bresenham's integer-based algorithm. */
void circle(int x_center, int y_center, /* center */
          int radius, /* radius */
          int color) /* color */
{
  register int x, y, delta;

  asp_ratio = 1.0; /* for different aspect ratios, alter
                this number */

  y = radius;
  delta = 3 - 2 * radius;
```

```
    for(x=0; x<y; ) {
      plot_circle(x, y, x_center, y_center, color);

      if (delta < 0)
        delta += 4*x+6;
      else {
        delta += 4*(x-y)+10;
        y--;
      }
      x++;
    }
    x = y;
    if(y) plot_circle(x, y, x_center, y_center, color);
}

/* Plot_circle actually prints the points that
   define the circle.
*/
void plot_circle(int x, int y,
                 int x_center, int y_center,
                 int color)
{
  int startx, endx, x1, starty, endy, y1;

  starty = y*asp_ratio;
  endy = (y+1)*asp_ratio;
  startx = x*asp_ratio;
  endx = (x+1)*asp_ratio;

  for (x1=startx; x1<endx; ++x1) {
    mempoint(x1+x_center, y+y_center, color);
    mempoint(x1+x_center, y_center-y, color);
    mempoint(x_center-x1, y_center-y, color);
    mempoint(x_center-x1, y+y_center, color);
  }

  for (y1=starty; y1<endy; ++y1) {
    mempoint(y1+x_center, x+y_center, color);
    mempoint(y1+x_center, y_center-x, color);
    mempoint(x_center-y1, y_center-x, color);
    mempoint(x_center-y1, x+y_center, color);
  }
}

/* Fill a circle by repeatedly calling circle()
```

```
      with smaller radius.
*/
void fill_circle(int x_center, int y_center,
                 int radius, int color)
{
  while(radius) {
    circle(x_center, y_center, radius, color);
    radius--;
  }
}

/* Write a point directly to mode 4 graphics RAM. */
void mempoint(int x, int y, /* coordinate of point */
              int color) /* color */
{
  union mask {
    char c[2];
    int i;
  } bit_mask;
  int index, bit_position;
  unsigned char t;
  char xor; /* xor color in or overwrite */

  /* pointer to mode 4 graphics RAM */
  char far *ptr = (char far *) 0xB8000000;

  bit_mask.i = 0xFF3F; /* 11111111 00111111 in binary */

  /* check range */
  if(x<0 || x>XMAX || y<0 || y>YMAX) return;

  xor = color & 128; /* see if xor mode is set */
  color = color & 127; /* mask off high bit */

  /* set bit_mask and color bits to the right location */
  bit_position = x%4;
  color <<= 2*(3-bit_position);
  bit_mask.i >>= 2*bit_position;

  /* find the correct byte in screen memory */
  index = y*40 + (x >> 2);
  if(y % 2) index += 8152; /* if odd use 2nd bank */

  /* write the color */
  if(!xor) { /* overwrite mode */
```

```
    t = *(ptr+index) & bit_mask.c[0];
    *(ptr+index) = t ¦ color;
  }
  else { /* xor mode */
    t = *(ptr+index) ¦ (char) 0;
    *(ptr+index) = t ^ color;
  }
}

/* Display crosshair locator. */
void xhairs(int x, int y)
{
  line(x-4, y, x+3, y, 1 ¦ 128);
  line(x, y+4, x, y-3, 1 ¦ 128);
}

/* Read byte directly from the video RAM in mode 4. */
unsigned char read_point(int x, int y)
{
  union mask {
    char c[2];
    int i;
  } bit_mask;
  int index, bit_position;
  unsigned char t;

  /* pointer to mode 4 graphics RAM */
  char far *ptr = (char far *) 0xB8000000;

  bit_mask.i = 3;        /* 11111111 00111111 in binary */

  /* check range for mode 4 */
  if(x<0 ¦¦ x>XMAX ¦¦ y<0 ¦¦ y>YMAX) return 0;

  /* set bit_mask and color_code bits to the right location */
  bit_position = x%4;
  bit_mask.i <<= 2*(3-bit_position);
  /* find the correct byte in screen memory */
  index = y*40 +(x >> 2);
  if(y % 2) index += 8152; /* if odd use 2nd bank */

  /* read the color */
  t = *(ptr+index) & bit_mask.c[0];
  t >>= 2*(3-bit_position);
  return t;
}
```

```
/* Save the video graphics display. */
void save_pic(void)
{
  char fname[80];
  FILE *fp;
  register int i, j;
  int e=0;

  /* pointer to mode 4 graphics RAM */
  char far *ptr = (char far *) 0xB8000000;

  char far *temp;
  unsigned char buf[14][80]; /* hold the contents of screen */

  temp = ptr;
  /* save the top of the current screen */
  for(i=0; i<14; i++)
    for(j=0; j<80; j+=2) {
      buf[i][j] = *temp; /* even byte */
      buf[i][j+1] = *(temp+8152); /* odd byte */
      *temp = 0; *(temp+8152) = 0; /* clear top of screen */
      temp++;
    }

  goto_xy(0, 0);
  printf("Filename: ");
  gets(fname);
  if(!(fp=fopen(fname, "wb"))) {
    goto_xy(0, 0);
    printf("cannot open file - press a key ");
    getch();
    e = 1; /* flag error */
  }

  temp = ptr;
  /* restore the top of the current screen */
  for(i=0; i<14; i++)
    for(j=0; j<80; j+=2) {
      *temp = buf[i][j];
      *(temp+8152) = buf[i][j+1];
      temp++;
    }

  if(e) return; /* if file could not be opened, exit */
```

```
/* save image to file */
for(i=0; i<8152; i++) {
   putc(*ptr, fp); /* even byte */
   putc(*(ptr+8152), fp); /* odd byte */
   ptr++;
 }

 fclose(fp);
}

/* Load the video graphics display. */
void load_pic(void)
{
  char fname[80];
  FILE *fp;
  register int i, j;

  /* pointer to mode 4 graphics RAM */
  char far *ptr = (char far *) 0xB8000000;

  char far *temp;
  unsigned char buf[14][80]; /* hold the contents of screen */

  temp = ptr;
  /* save the top of the current screen */
  for(i=0; i<14; i++)
    for(j=0; j<80; j+=2) {
      buf[i][j] = *temp;
      buf[i][j+1] = *(temp+8152);
      *temp = 0; *(temp+8152) = 0; /* clear the top of the screen */
      temp++;
    }

  goto_xy(0, 0);
  printf("Filename: ");
  gets(fname);
  if(!(fp=fopen(fname, "rb"))) {
    goto_xy(0, 0);
    printf("cannot open file\n");
    temp = ptr;
    /* restore the top of the current screen */
    for(i=0; i<14; i++)
      for(j=0; j<80; j+=2) {
        *temp = buf[i][j];
```

```
        *(temp+8152) = buf[i][j+1];
        temp++;
      }
    return;
  }

  /* load image from file */
  for(i=0; i<8152; i++) {
    *ptr = getc(fp); /* even byte */
    *(ptr+8152) = getc(fp); /* odd byte */
    ptr++;
  }

  fclose(fp);
}

/* Send the cursor to the specified X,Y position. */
void goto_xy(int x, int y)
{
  union REGS r;

  r.h.ah = 2; /* cursor addressing function */
  r.h.dl = x; /* column coordinate */
  r.h.dh = y; /* row coordinate */
  r.h.bh = 0; /* video page */
  int86(0x10, &r, &r);
}

/* Move one region to another location. */
void move(int startx, int starty, /* upper-left coordinate */
  int endx, int endy, /* lower-right coordinate */
  int x, int y) /* upper-left of region receiving the image */
{
  int i, j;
  unsigned char c;

  for(; startx<=endx; startx++, x++)
    for(i=starty, j=y; i<=endy; i++, j++) {
      c = read_point(startx, i); /* read point */
      mempoint(startx, i, 0); /* erase old image */
      mempoint(x, j, c); /* write it to new location */
    }
}

/* Copy one region to another location. */
```

```
void copy(int startx, int starty, /* upper-left coordinate */
   int endx, int endy, /* lower-right coordinate */
   int x, int y) /* upper left of region receiving the image */
{
  int i, j;
  unsigned char c;

  for(; startx<=endx; startx++, x++)
    for(i=starty, j=y; i<=endy; i++, j++) {
      c = read_point(startx, i); /* read point */
      mempoint(x, j, c); /* write it to new location */
    }
}


/* Rotate a point around the origin, specified by
   x_org and y_org, by angle theta.
*/
void rotate_point(double theta, /* angle of rotation */
                  double *x, double *y, /* point to rotate */
                  int x_org, int y_org) /* origin */
{
  double tx, ty;

  /* normalize x and y */
  tx = *x - x_org;
  ty = *y - y_org;

  /* rotate */
  *x = tx * cos(theta) - ty * sin(theta);
  *y = tx * sin(theta) + ty * cos(theta);

  /* return to PC coordinate values */
  *x += x_org;
  *y += y_org;

}

/* Rotate the specified object. */
void rotate_object(double ob[][5], /* object definition */
          double theta, /* angle of rotation in radians */
          int x, int y, /* location of origin */
          int lines) /* number of lines in image */
{
  register int j;
  char ch;
```

```
    for(;;) {
      ch = getch(); /* see which direction to rotate */
      switch(tolower(ch)) {
        case 'l': /* counterclockwise */
          theta = theta < 0 ? -theta : theta;
          break;
        case 'r': /* clockwise */
          theta = theta > 0 ? -theta : theta;
          break;
        default: return;
      }

      for(j=0; j<lines; j++) {
        /* erase old line */
        line((int) ob[j][0], (int) ob[j][1],
          (int) ob[j][2], (int) ob[j][3], 0);

        rotate_point(theta, &ob[j][0],
          &ob[j][1], x, y);

        rotate_point(theta, &ob[j][2],
          &ob[j][3], x, y);

        line((int) ob[j][0], (int) ob[j][1],
          (int) ob[j][2], (int) ob[j][3], (int) ob[j][4]);
      }
    }
}

/* Display an object. */
void display_object(double ob[][5], int lines)
{
  register int i;

  for(i=0; i<lines; i++)
    line((int) ob[i][0], (int) ob[i][1],
      (int) ob[i][2], (int) ob[i][3], (int) ob[i][4]);
}

/* Define an object by specifying its endpoints */
define_object(double ob[][5], int x, int y)
{

  union k{
```

```
    char c[2];
    int i;
} key;
register int i, j;

/* pointer to mode 4 graphics RAM */
char far *ptr = (char far *) 0xB8000000;

char far *temp;
unsigned char buf[14][80]; /* hold the contents of screen */
int sides = 0;

temp = ptr;
/* save the top of the current screen */
for(i=0; i<14; i++)
  for(j=0; j<80; j+=2) {
    buf[i][j] = *temp;
    buf[i][j+1] = *(temp+8152);
    *temp = 0; *(temp+8152) = 0; /* clear the top of the screen */
    temp++;
  }

i = 0;
xhairs(x, y);
do {
  goto_xy(0, 0);
  printf("Define side %d,", sides+1);
  if(i==0) printf(" enter first endpoint");
  else printf(" enter second endpoint");

  key.i = readkey();
  xhairs(x, y);  /* plot the crosshairs */
  if(key.c[0]=='\r') {
    ob[sides][i++] = (double) x;
    ob[sides][i++] = (double) y;
    if(i==4) {
      ob[sides][4] = read_point(x, y); /* get color */
      i = 0;
      sides++;
    }
  }
}

  /* if arrow key, move the crosshairs */
  if(!key.c[0]) switch(key.c[1]) {
    case 75: /* left */
```

```
        x -= 1;
        break;
      case 77: /* right */
        x += 1;
        break;
      case 72: /* up */
        y -= 1;
        break;
      case 80: /* down */
        y += 1;
        break;
      case 71: /* up left */
        x -= 1; y -= 1;
        break;
      case 73: /* up right */
        x += 1; y -= 1;
        break;
      case 79: /* down left*/
        x -= 1; y+=1;
        break;
      case 81: /* down right */
        x += 1; y += 1;
        break;
      }
    if(key.c[1]!=59) xhairs(x, y);
  } while(key.c[1]!=59); /* F1 to stop */

  temp = ptr;
  /* restore the top of the current screen */
  for(i=0; i<14; i++)
    for(j=0; j<80; j+=2) {
      *temp = buf[i][j];
      *(temp+8152) = buf[i][j+1];
      temp++;
    }
  return sides;
}

/* Return the 16-bit scan code from the keyboard. */
readkey(void)
{
  union REGS r;

  r.h.ah = 0;
  return int86(0x16, &r, &r);
}
```

Figure 4-5

Sample output from the paint program

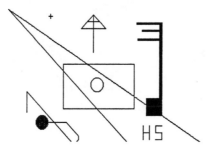

Even though the paint program requires a lot of code, you should enter it into your computer because it is really fun to use. Also, it gives you a powerful graphics toolbox that you can draw upon at any time.

CHAPTER FIVE

Video Games

Video games are either a blessing or a curse, depending upon your point of view. However, the art of video game programming is an exciting and rewarding pursuit. (In fact, one good way to get rich quick is to write the next hit video game!) A good video game combines animated graphics with some often very complex logic to produce an enjoyable challenge to the player. Some of the best games even apply artificial intelligence techniques to allow the computer's strategy to respond to user input.

In this chapter, you will learn some basic programming techniques that you can use to develop your own video games. In the process, you will learn how to animate objects on the screen. Also, a complete video game is developed for you to use as a starting point. Many of the principles used to create video games can be applied to your application programs to add excitement or interest.

The code examples developed in this chapter require an IBM PC or compatible with a CGA, EGA, or VGA color graphics adapter. Many of the graphics functions used in this chapter are developed in Chapter 4. If you haven't read Chapter 4, you might want to do so at this time.

RANDALL MERILATT

Co-creator of the db_VISTA database management system and co-founder of Raima Corporation, Randall Merilatt's programming career has been richly varied. He was a programmer for the Colorado Bureau of Investigation, working on their statewide crime management system. After that, he moved to Boeing Computer Services. He was project manager and technical lead on a project to develop the Integrated Verification and Testing System (IVTS) for NASA's HAL/S programming language. While at Boeing, he met Wayne Warren, the other co-founder of Raima Corporation. In 1983, they both left Boeing and began work on db_VISTA.

I asked Randy what qualities about C made it stand out as a programming language. He responded, "C is one of the easiest languages in which to write code. There is little in the language that inhibits the efficient expression of an algorithm. In other languages, a programmer often has to code around some limitation imposed by the programming language. For example, the fact that the assignment statement in C returns a value that can be used in a conditional statement allows very efficient implementation of many types of loops. Also, consider the fact that in a conditional statement, true is defined as any non-zero value. This feature simplifies the coding of several types of algorithms."

Randy's design philosophy is similar to my own and is based on incremental development. Randy explains, "I personally prefer an incremental development approach in which a system's capabilities are incrementally developed and tested. I'm motivated by the desire to see something work. Incremental development does carry with it the risk that some design flaws will be uncovered that will require reprogramming some of the earlier developed code. Well, so be it. As Fred Brooks states in *The Mythical Man-Month*, the first version of a program will usually be thrown away. Thus, by the time the project is done using incremental development, the first version may actually be the second version and may not have to be thrown away after all."

Given the quality of Randy's work, I asked what advice he had for beginning programmers. He said, "Learn from other master programmers. Study others' programs. Ask them why they did things a certain way. Have them critique your code. For example, as a young programmer at the Colorado Bureau of Investigation in the 1970s I learned assembler programming from two outstanding Univac systems programmers. Finally, study books on programming." This sounds like excellent advice to me!

Randall Merilatt holds a BS in Applied Mathematics from the University of Colorado. He currently lives with his wife and four children in Bellevue, Washington.

SPRITES

Many arcade-style video games consist of two main components: the environment (hereafter referred to as the "game board") and sprites. A *sprite* is a small, animated object that moves about the game board according to certain rules and for some purpose. For example, when a rocket ship fires a photon torpedo, the image of the fast-moving "torpedo" is accomplished by animating a sprite across the screen.

For the purposes of this chapter, a sprite is assumed to consist solely of straight-line segments. However, it is possible to create sprites based on circular patterns. A sprite's definition will be held in a two-dimensional integer array, such as the one shown here:

```
int sprite[4][5];
```

The first dimension specifies a particular line, and the second dimension specifies the beginning and ending coordinates of that line, plus the color of the line. (This is similar to an object's definition, as described in Chapter 4.) In other words, each second dimension will be, by convention, organized like this:

start_x, start_y, end_x, end_y, color

Therefore, if the first line segment of a sprite begins at location 0,0, ends at 0,10, and is green, you would define it as shown here in the **sprite** array:

```
sprite[0][0] = 0;   /* start_x */
sprite[0][1] = 0;   /* start_y */
sprite[0][2] = 0;   /* end_x */
sprite[0][3] = 10;  /* end_y */
sprite[0][4] = 1;   /* green */
```

THE GAME BOARD

In most video games, the *game board* consists of a graphics image inside of which the action of the game takes place. The game board may be stationary or in motion. The example video game developed in this chapter uses a stationary game board for simplicity. The actual layout of the game board can be created by another program and simply loaded by the video game at startup. In this way, the video game need not actually contain all the overhead necessary to dynamically create the game board. This is the approach taken in this chapter. The paint program developed in Chapter 4 is used to create a graphics image, which is then saved to disk. The video game then loads this image and begins play.

SCREEN-LEVEL ANIMATION

The key to (and excitement of) video games is their animation. Indeed, the animated graphic images set a video game apart from a noncomputerized board game. The general method of animation is quite easy: erase the part of the screen that currently displays the object and redisplay the object in its new position, which must be very close to its old position. The catch is that the process must be accomplished very fast. For this reason, it is again necessary to bypass the BIOS video service interrupts in favor of the direct video RAM accessing routines shown in Chapter 4.

By far the best approach to displaying, erasing, and redisplaying an object is to XOR each point in the object onto the screen. In this way, the first time an object is written to the screen, it is displayed, and the second time it is written to the same location, the previous contents of the screen are restored. In this way, it is possible to create sprites that move across the entire game board, no matter what color is currently in a specific location, without destroying what is already there.

The routine that actually displays a sprite is a slightly modified version of **display_object()**, developed in Chapter 4. The modified version is shown here:

```
/* Display an object. */
void display_object(int ob[][5], int lines)
{
  register int i;

  for(i=0; i<lines; i++)
    line(ob[i][0], ob[i][1],
         ob[i][2], ob[i][3], ob[i][4] | 128);
}
```

As you can see, this function draws all the lines in the object by using the **line()** function (also from Chapter 4). Notice, however, that the color parameter is ORed with 128 in order to set the high-order bit. This causes the **mempoint()** function (used by **line()** to actually write each pixel) to XOR the color with what is already there and allows the sprite to be visible no matter what the background color.

To see how the animation process works, enter the following program into your computer at this time. The program allows you to move a sprite around the screen by using the cursor keys. The sprite is a small 6-pixel by 6-pixel + (plus) sign.

```
/* Animated sprite example. */

#include "dos.h"
#include "stdio.h"
#include "stdlib.h"

#define XMAX 319
#define YMAX 199

void mempoint(int x, int y, int color);
void palette(int pnum);
void mode(int mode_code);
void display_object(int ob[][5], int lines);
void line(int startx, int starty, int endx, int endy,
          int color);
void update_object(int ob[][5], int x, int y,
                   register int sides);
int is_legal(int ob[][5], int x, int y, int sides);
int readkey(void);

int sprite[2][5] = {
  3, 0, 3, 5, 1,
  0, 3, 5, 3, 1
};

main(void)
{
  union k{
    char c[2];
    int i;
  } key;

  int deltax = 0, deltay = 0; /* direction of movement */
```

```
mode(4);  /* switch to mode 4 graphics */
palette(0); /* palette 0 */

display_object(sprite, 2);
do {
  deltay = deltax = 0;
  key.i = readkey();
  if(!key.c[0]) switch(key.c[1]) {
    case 75: /* left */
      deltax = -1;
      break;
    case 77: /* right */
      deltax = 1;
      break;
    case 72: /* up */
      deltay = -1;
      break;
    case 80: /* down */
      deltay = 1;
      break;
    case 71: /* up left */
      deltax = -1; deltay = -1;
      break;
    case 73: /* up right */
      deltay = -1; deltax = 1;
      break;
    case 79: /* down left*/
      deltay = 1; deltax = -1;
      break;
    case 81: /* down right */
      deltax = 1; deltay = 1;
      break;
  }
  /* erase sprite's current position */
  display_object(sprite, 2);

  /* if move is legal, update object definition */
  if(is_legal(sprite, deltax, deltay, 2))
    update_object(sprite, deltax, deltay, 2);

  /* redisplay sprite in new position */
  display_object(sprite, 2);
} while (key.c[0] != 'q');
```

```
    mode(3);
    return 0;
}

/* Set the palette. */
void palette(int pnum)
{
  union REGS r;

  r.h.bh = 1;    /* code for palette select */
  r.h.bl = pnum;
  r.h.ah = 11;   /* set palette function */
  int86(0x10, &r, &r);
}

/* Set the video mode. */
void mode(int mode_code)
{
  union REGS r;

  r.h.al = mode_code;
  r.h.ah = 0;
  int86(0x10, &r, &r);
}

/* Draw a line in specified color
   using Bresenham's integer-based algorithm.
*/
void line(int startx, int starty, /* upper-left corner */
          int endx, int endy, /* lower-right corner */
          int color) /* color */
{
  register int t, distance;
  int x=0, y=0, delta_x, delta_y;
  int incx, incy;

  /* Compute the distances in both directions. */
  delta_x = endx-startx;
  delta_y = endy-starty;

  /* Compute the direction of the increment.
     An increment of 0 means either a vertical
     or horizontal line.
  */
```

```
    if(delta_x>0) incx = 1;
    else if(delta_x==0) incx = 0;
    else incx = -1;

    if(delta_y>0) incy = 1;
    else if(delta_y==0) incy = 0;
    else incy = -1;

    /* determine which distance is greater */
    delta_x = abs(delta_x);
    delta_y = abs(delta_y);
    if(delta_x>delta_y) distance = delta_x;
    else distance = delta_y;

    /* draw the line */
    for(t=0; t<=distance+1; t++) {
      mempoint(startx, starty, color);
      x += delta_x;
      y += delta_y;
      if(x>distance) {
        x -= distance;
        startx += incx;
      }
      if(y>distance) {
        y -= distance;
        starty += incy;
      }
    }
  }
}

/* Write a point directly to mode 4 graphics RAM. */
void mempoint(int x, int y, /* coordinate of point */
              int color) /* color */
{
  union mask {
    char c[2];
    int i;
  } bit_mask;
  int index, bit_position;
  unsigned char t;
  char xor; /* xor color in or overwrite */

  /* pointer to mode 4 graphics RAM */
  char far *ptr = (char far *) 0xB8000000;
```

```
bit_mask.i = 0xFF3F;   /* 11111111 00111111 in binary */

/* check range */
if(x<0 || x>XMAX || y<0 || y>YMAX) return;

xor = color & 128; /* see if xor mode is set */
color = color & 127; /* mask off high bit */

/* set bit_mask and color bits to the right location */
bit_position = x%4;
color <<= 2*(3-bit_position);
bit_mask.i >>= 2*bit_position;

/* find the correct byte in screen memory */
index = y*40 + (x >> 2);
if(y % 2) index += 8152; /* if odd use 2nd bank */

/* write the color */
if(!xor) { /* overwrite mode */
  t = *(ptr+index) & bit_mask.c[0];
  *(ptr+index) = t | color;
}
else { /* xor mode */
  t = *(ptr+index) | (char) 0;
  *(ptr+index) = t ^ color;
}
}

/* Read byte directly from the video RAM in mode 4. */
unsigned char read_point(int x, int y)
{
  union mask {
    char c[2];
    int i;
  } bit_mask;
  int index, bit_position;
  unsigned char t;

  /* pointer to mode 4 graphics RAM */
  char far *ptr = (char far *) 0xB8000000;

  bit_mask.i = 3;      /* 11111111 00111111 in binary */

  /* check range for mode 4 */
  if(x<0 || x>XMAX || y<0 || y>YMAX) return 0;
```

```
  /* set bit_mask and color_code bits to the right location */
  bit_position = x%4;
  bit_mask.i <<= 2*(3-bit_position);
  /* find the correct byte in screen memory */
  index = y*40 +(x >> 2);
  if(y % 2) index += 8152; /* if odd use 2nd bank */

  /* read the color */
  t = *(ptr+index) & bit_mask.c[0];
  t >>= 2*(3-bit_position);
  return t;
}


/* Display an object. */
void display_object(int ob[][5], int lines)
{
  register int i;

  for(i=0; i<lines; i++)
    line(ob[i][0], ob[i][1],
         ob[i][2], ob[i][3], ob[i][4] | 128);
}

/* Update an object's position as specified in X,Y. */
void update_object(int ob[][5], /* object */
  int x, int y, /* amount to update */
  register int sides) /* number of sides */
{
  sides--;
  for( ; sides>=0; sides--) {
    ob[sides][0] += x;
    ob[sides][1] += y;
    ob[sides][2] += x;
    ob[sides][3] += y;
  }
}

/* See if a prospective move is legal.
   Returns 1 if legal; 0 otherwise.
*/
is_legal(int ob[][5], /* object */
  int x, int y, /* increment to move */
  int sides) /* number of sides the object has */
{
```

```
   if(x==0 && y==0) return 1;
   sides--;
   for( ; sides>=0; sides--) {
     /* check for out of range */
     if(ob[sides][0]+x>XMAX ¦¦ ob[sides][1]+y >YMAX) return 0;
     if(ob[sides][2]+x<0 ¦¦ ob[sides][3]+y<0) return 0;
     /* check for obstacle */
     if(read_point(ob[sides][0]+x, ob[sides][1] + y)==2) return 0;
     if(read_point(ob[sides][2]+x, ob[sides][3] + y)==2) return 0;
   }
   return 1;
}

/* Return the 16-bit scan code from the keyboard. */
readkey(void)
{
  union REGS r;

  r.h.ah = 0;
  return int86(0x16, &r, &r);
}
```

The program works as follows. The arrow keys plus the HOME, PGUP, END, and PGDN keys control the position of the sprite. Each time a key is pressed, the sprite moves one pixel in the desired direction. The arrow keys control horizontal and vertical movement, and the others control diagonal motion. The **is_legal()** function determines whether a prospective move is legal. If the move would take the sprite off the screen, the move is not allowed. All the other functions in the program work as described in Chapter 4.

It is usually necessary to keep the size of the object that you animate fairly small so it can be redrawn quickly enough to appear to move smoothly. If the object is too big, it will seem to move in a jerky fashion. Keep in mind that the faster the computer or the graphics adapter, the larger the animated object can be.

SPRITE-LEVEL ANIMATION

The ability to move the sprite about the screen takes you only halfway to professional-quality animation. Generally, the sprite should appear to be doing something that helps create the illusion of motion. For example, a sprite that looks like a person may move its legs so as to appear to be walking. This type of animation is best (and most easily) accomplished by creating object definitions for two (or more) variations of the same sprite. The only differences between the variations are in the part of the sprite that will move. The program will then switch between the variations, in sequence, as the sprite is moved across the screen.

For example, add the second sprite and substitute this **main()** function in the previously shown program. The second sprite displays a + rotated by 45 degrees. If you run this program, the + seems to turn around as it moves across the screen. The **swap** variable is used to select which sprite is used.

```c
int sprite2[2][5] = {
  0, 0, 5, 5, 1,
  0, 5, 5, 0, 1
};

main(void)
{
  union k{ /* holds both scan and key codes */
    char c[2];
    int i;
  } key;

  int deltax = 0, deltay = 0; /* direction of movement */
  int swap = 0; /* controls which sprite is used. */

  mode(4);  /* switch to mode 4 graphics */
  palette(0); /* palette 0 */


  display_object(sprite, 2);
  do {
    deltay = deltax = 0;
    key.i = readkey();
    if(!key.c[0]) switch(key.c[1]) {
      case 75: /* left */
        deltax = -1;
        break;
      case 77: /* right */
        deltax = 1;
        break;
      case 72: /* up */
```

```
        deltay = -1;
        break;
      case 80: /* down */
        deltay = 1;
        break;
      case 71: /* up left */
        deltax = -1; deltay = -1;
        break;
      case 73: /* up right */
        deltay = -1; deltax = 1;
        break;
      case 79: /* down left*/
        deltay = 1; deltax = -1;
        break;
      case 81: /* down right */
        deltay = 1; deltax = 1;
        break;
    }
    /* erase sprite's current position */
    if(swap<1) display_object(sprite, 2);
    else display_object(sprite2, 2);

    /* change the object database if move is legal */
    if(is_legal(sprite, deltax, deltay, 2)) {
      update_object(sprite, deltax, deltay, 2);
      update_object(sprite2, deltax, deltay, 2);
    }

    swap++;
    if(swap==2) swap = 0;
    /* redisplay sprite in new location */
    if(swap<1) display_object(sprite, 2);
    else display_object(sprite2, 2);
  } while (key.c[0] != 'q');

  mode(3);
  return 0;
}
```

ORGANIZING THE VIDEO GAME DATA

Like most programs, video games involve both code and data. Aside from
the current score and the status of various consumable game resources

(for example, how many photon torpedos remain), most of the data related to a video game consists of the screen positions of the various objects. Generally, the screen position of an object that moves must be stored explicitly in a set of variables. However, most often the information about fixed objects on the game board is implicitly stored in the video RAM. Therefore, if your game needs information about the game board (as most do), you can access the video RAM as a large array to see what is there.

Recognizing Boundaries

Most video games have a sprite that is under the player's control. Generally, however, you are not allowed to move the sprite through certain environmental objects on the game board or through another sprite. There are two ways to restrict the destination of the sprite. The first is to keep a set of variables that hold the end points to various boundaries and check those coordinates against the location into which the sprite will move in order to determine if a boundary will be violated. This method is fairly tedious, and in games with a large number of objects, it can be very slow. The better solution is simply to see if an intended screen location already contains something by checking its corresponding location in the video RAM. Since all the information about the game board is already in the video RAM, it seems senseless to duplicate the information elsewhere.

A second advantage of using the screen image in the video RAM as the only (or at least main) source of information about the game is that it allows new game boards to be loaded dynamically during play without having to reset—or worse, compute—new settings for several variables.

Color Counts

Often, you will want different colors to have different meanings. For example, you might use red to indicate noncrossable boundaries, green for your sprite, and yellow for the opponent's sprite. Though it is possible to use a set of variables to specify which objects are what, it is often possible (and much easier) to let objects be defined by their color. Not only does this make the game code easier, it also makes it faster. For example, if purple indicates the color of a mine, to determine if your sprite has hit a mine, check if the color of one of the pixels next to it is purple.

The use of color-coding for different objects has a long history in video games. For example, the first "ping-pong" video game used the simplest approach conceivable: black and white. In the old "ping-pong" game, white repelled white, but white could move through black. Therefore, the white ball could move through the black playing space unless it either was struck by the white paddle or hit the white wall behind the paddle. The same basic principles are expanded when other colors are used. When the objects in the game are color coded, the routines that must determine what is happening in the game become much easier to write and run faster.

SCOREKEEPER VERSUS ACTIVE PARTICIPANT

The computer's role in a video game depends to a great extent on whether the game is a two-player game or a single-player game. If two players are involved, the computer's role is largely that of scorekeeper and referee. However, in a single-player game, the computer also becomes an active participant. From a programming point of view, the computer-as-participant type of game is of the most interest.

DEVELOPING A VIDEO GAME

This section develops a complete video game that illustrates many of the principles discussed in this chapter.

Defining the Game

The first step in creating a video game is deciding the nature of the game and how it will be played. The game developed here is a computerized version of the traditional childhood game of tag. The player and the computer each control one "person." Whoever is "it" chases the other until contact is made, in which case the other person becomes "it." The winner of the game is the person who is not "it" for the longest period of time.

The score is kept by monitoring the system time: for each second that passes, 1 is added to the score of the person who is not "it." The score is displayed continuously at the bottom of the screen. The game ends when one player reaches 999 seconds. For convenience, the game can also be terminated by pressing Q.

The player controls the sprite with the arrow keys.

The game board is not created by the game itself. Rather, it is created with the paint program developed in Chapter 4; the board is loaded by the game. In this way, you can create several different playing environments.

Color-coding the Game

Tag lends itself to a color-coded approach for identifying objects. For example, you can make the player's sprite green, the computer's sprite yellow, and boundaries and objects red. With this approach, it is not necessary to keep a separate database on the location of obstacles—the routines simply check to see what is in the video RAM. It then becomes a simple matter to restrict a sprite from moving into a red region by making a small addition to the **is_legal()** function developed earlier, as shown here:

```
/* See if a prospective move is legal.
   Returns 1 if legal; 0 otherwise.
*/
is_legal(int ob[][5], /* object */
  int x, int y, /* increment to move */
  int sides) /* number of sides the object has */
{
  if(x==0 && y==0) return 1;
  sides--;
  for( ; sides>=0; sides--) {
    /* check for out of range */
    if(ob[sides][0]+x>XMAX ¦¦ ob[sides][1]+y >YMAX) return 0;
    if(ob[sides][2]+x<0 ¦¦ ob[sides][3]+y<0) return 0;
    /* check for obstacle */
    if(read_point(ob[sides][0]+x, ob[sides][1] + y)==2) return 0;
    if(read_point(ob[sides][2]+x, ob[sides][3] + y)==2) return 0;
  }
  return 1;
}
```

Remember, in palette 0, the color code for yellow is 1, red is 2, green is 3, and black (background) is 0.

Defining the Sprites

The sprites used in the game must be designed to resemble people running. The sprites are defined by four lines and look like this:

The program creates two versions of the sprite. In the second version, the legs are slightly closer together. Quickly alternating between the two makes the "person" seem to run.

The player's sprite begins near the upper-left corner, and the computer's sprite starts near the lower-left corner. Their object definitions are shown here:

```
int human[4][5] = { /* your sprites */
    6, 1, 6, 6, 1,
    2, 4, 9, 3, 1,
    1, 9, 6, 6, 1,
    11, 9, 6, 6, 1
};

int human2[4][5] = {
    6, 1, 6, 6, 1,
```

```
   2, 4, 9, 3, 1,
   3, 9, 6, 6, 1,
   9, 9, 6, 6, 1
};

int computer[4][5] = { /* computer's sprites */
   6, 180, 6, 185, 3,
   2, 183, 9, 182, 3,
   1, 188, 6, 185, 3,
   11, 188, 6, 185, 3
};

int computer2[4][5] = {
   6, 180, 6, 185, 3,
   2, 183, 9, 182, 3,
   3, 188, 6, 185, 3,
   9, 188, 6, 185, 3
};
```

The Main Loop

As you create your own video games, you quickly discover that they all
have one thing in common—a fairly complex main loop that drives the
game. This is because the program must continuously update the display,
watch for keyboard input, check for illegal moves, display the score, and
generate its own moves. The tag game's main loop, inside the **main()**
function, is shown here:

```
int directx, directy; /* direction of human */

main(void)
{
  union k { /* holds both scan and key codes */
    char c[2];
    int i;
  } key;

  int deltax = 0, deltay = 0; /* direction of movement */
  int swaph = 0, swapc = 0; /* select sprites */
  int it = COMPUTER; /* who's "it" */
  long htime, ctime, starttime, curtime;
  int count; /* used to let the players separate slightly
```

```
                after a tag */

mode(4);  /* switch to mode 4 graphics */
palette(0); /* palette 0 */

load_pic(); /* get the game board */

time(&starttime); /* set up the clocks */
htime = ctime = 0;

display_object(human, 4);
display_object(computer, 4);
count = 0;

/* main game loop */
do {
  /* update the score counters */
  time(&curtime);
  if(it==COMPUTER) htime += curtime-starttime;
  else ctime += curtime-starttime;
  time(&starttime);
  show_score(it, htime, ctime);

  if(kbhit()) { /* if key pressed */
    directx = directy = IDLE; /* reset direction for each move */
    key.i = readkey(); /* read the key */
    deltax = 0; deltay = 0;
    if(!key.c[0]) switch(key.c[1]) {
      case 75: /* left */
        deltax = -1;
        directx = LEFT;
        break;
      case 77: /* right */
        deltax = 1;
        directx = RIGHT;
        break;
      case 72: /* up */
        deltay = -1;
        directy = UP;
        break;
      case 80: /* down */
        deltay = 1;
        directy = DOWN;
        break;
      case 71: /* up left */
```

```
        deltax = -1; deltay = -1;
        directy = UP; directx = LEFT;
        break;
      case 73: /* up right */
        deltay = -1; deltax = 1;
        directy = UP; directx = RIGHT;
        break;
      case 79: /* down left*/
        deltay = 1; deltax = -1;
        directy = DOWN; directx = LEFT;
        break;
      case 81: /* down right */
        deltay = 1; deltax = 1;
        directy = DOWN; directx = RIGHT;
        break;
  }
}
/* turn off player's person */
if(swaph<5) display_object(human, 4);
else display_object(human2, 4);

/* see if move is legal */
if(is_legal(human, deltax, deltay, 4)) {
  update_object(human, deltax, deltay, 4);
  update_object(human2, deltax, deltay, 4);
}

/* see if a tag has occurred */
if(!count && tag(human, computer)) {
  it = !it;  /* switch who is "it" */
  count = 6; /* don't allow an instant retag */
}

swaph++;
if(swaph==10) swaph = 0;
/* redisplay person in new position */
if(swaph<5) display_object(human, 4);
else display_object(human2, 4);

/* turn off computer's person */
if(swapc<5) display_object(computer, 4);
else display_object(computer2, 4);

/* generate the computer's move */
if(it==COMPUTER) it_comp_move(computer, computer2, human, 4);
```

```
   else not_it_comp_move(computer, computer2, directx, directy, 4);
   if(!count && tag(human, computer)) {
     it = !it; /* switch who is "it" */
     count = 6; /* don't allow an instant retag */
     /* if computer tag's person, shift computer's  X
        position by 2 so that it is not trivial to retag.
     */
     if(is_legal(computer, 2, 0, 4)) {
       update_object(computer, 2, 0, 4);
       update_object(computer2, 2, 0, 4);
     }
     else {
       update_object(computer, -2, 0, 4);
       update_object(computer2, -2, 0, 4);
     }

   }
   swapc++;
   if(swapc==10) swapc = 0;
   /* display computer's person */
   if(swapc<5) display_object(computer, 4);
   else display_object(computer2, 4);

   if(count) count--;
} while (key.c[0]!='q' && htime<999 && ctime<999);
mode(3);

if(ctime>htime) printf("Computer wins!");
else printf("You win!");

return 0;
}
```

Before filling in all the functions, let's examine the main loop to see how the game operates. In the **main()** function, prior to the main loop, the screen is switched to mode 4 graphics, palette 0, the score timer variables are initialized, and the game board is loaded. Also, the two sprites are displayed in their starting positions.

The variable **htime** holds the score of the human player, and **ctime** holds the computer's score. The variables **swapc** and **swaph** switch between the two versions of the sprites. The variables **deltax** and **deltay** hold the direction of the player's last keypress. The global variables **directx** and **directy** hold the direction the player's sprite travels. This information is used by the computer to generate its own defensive moves. The **it** variable contains the current "it" of the game. It will have either the value **COMPUTER** or **HUMAN**, which are macros defined near the start of the program. The function of the **count** variable will be explained shortly.

When the loop begins, it updates and displays the current scores. Next, it checks to see if there has been a keypress, using **kbhit()**. This function is not defined by the ANSI C standard, but it is found in one form or another in all C compilers. It returns true if a key is pressed, false otherwise. If a key has been pressed, it is read, and the appropriate action is taken. Keep in mind that the loop does not pause, waiting for a keypress, but rather continues to run. Next, the player's sprite is moved in the direction indicated by the last keypress, if possible, and a check for tag is made. It is important to understand that the player's sprite continues to move in the direction indicated by the last keypress even if no key is held down. For example, if the RIGHT ARROW key is pressed and released, the sprite will move from its current position to the far right side of the screen if no other directional key is pressed. Thus, the sprite is always moving, making for a very fast and exciting game.

After the player's move has been processed, the computer's move is generated and its sprite is moved, if possible. Notice that different functions are called when the computer is "it" and when it isn't because different strategies are used.

After each move, a check for a tag must be made. If a tag has occurred, the variable **count** is set to 6. This variable is decremented each time the main loop iterates until it becomes 0. This variable is used to prevent an instant retag by allowing the two sprites to separate slightly.

Now, let's look at some of the support routines.

Generating the Computer's Move

If the computer is "it," its next move is generated by the function **it_comp_move()**. The computer's general, if somewhat simplistic, strategy is to move its sprite in the direction of the player's sprite. It will try to go around objects that stand between it and the player's sprite. However, as the function stands, it cannot go around all types of objects, an intentional feature that helps balance the skill level of the game. In designing video games, it is sometimes hard to "hold the computer back." The human player should have a reasonable chance of winning the game without the game being boring.

The function **it _ comp _ move()** is shown here:

```
/* Generate the computer's move when it is "it". */
void it_comp_move(int ob1[][5], int ob2[][5],
  int human[][5],
  int sides)
{
  register int  x, y;
  static skip = 0;

  skip++;
  if(skip==3) {
    skip = 0;
    return;
  }
  x = 0; y = 0;

  /* move toward the human */
  if(human[0][0]<ob1[0][0]) x = -1;
  else if(human[0][0]>ob1[0][0]) x = 1;

  if(human[0][1]<ob1[0][1]) y = -1;
  else if(human[0][1]>ob1[0][1]) y = 1;

  if(is_legal(ob1, x, y, sides)) {
    update_object(ob1, x, y, sides);
    update_object(ob2, x, y, sides);
  }
  else { /* if not legal, try to go around */
    if(x && is_legal(ob1, x, 0, sides)) {
      update_object(ob1, x, 0, sides);
      update_object(ob2, x, 0, sides);
    }
    else if(is_legal(ob1, 0, y, sides)) {
      update_object(ob1, 0, y, sides);
      update_object(ob2, 0, y, sides);
    }
  }
}
```

Notice that the function changes the position of the computer's sprite only two-thirds of the time. This is necessary to slow the computer to a level a human player can deal with.

The function that generates the computer's moves when it is not "it" works by always moving the computer's sprite in the opposite direction of the player's sprite. Although this is not the most sophisticated approach, it actually presents a fairly challenging game that requires good timing on the player's part to "tag" the computer's sprite. The function is shown here:

```c
/* Generate the computer's move when it is not "it". */
void not_it_comp_move(int ob1[][5], int ob2[][5],
  int directx, int directy, /* direction of human's last move */
  int sides)
{
  register int  x, y;
  static skip = 1;

  skip++;
  if(skip==3) {
    skip = 0;
    return;
  }
  x = 0; y = 0;

  /* move in opposite direction as human */
  x = -directx;
  y = -directy;

  if(is_legal(ob1, x, y, sides)) {
    update_object(ob1, x, y, sides);
    update_object(ob2, x, y, sides);
  }
  else { /* if not legal, try to go around */
    if(x && is_legal(ob1, x, 0, sides)) {
      update_object(ob1, x, 0, sides);
      update_object(ob2, x, 0, sides);
    }
    else if(is_legal(ob1, 0, y, sides)) {
      update_object(ob1, 0, y, sides);
      update_object(ob2, 0, y, sides);
    }
  }
}
```

Again, notice that the function is delayed slightly and executes only two out of every three calls.

Check for Tag

In this game, a tag occurs when one sprite is within one pixel in any direction of being directly on top of the other sprite. (A tag can be defined as one sprite being exactly on top of the other, but for most players this constraint proves too difficult to be enjoyable.) The function **tag**, shown here, returns 1 if a tag has occurred and 0 otherwise:

```
/* See if a tag has taken place. */
tag(int ob1[][5], int ob2[][5])
{
  register int i;

  /* To tag, one figure must be within one pixel of being
     directly on top of the other.
  */
  for(i=-1; i<2; i++) {
    if(ob1[0][0]==ob2[0][0]+i && ob1[0][1]==ob2[0][1]+i) {
      return 1;
    }
  }
  return 0;
}
```

You may wish to modify this function's operation to suit your personal taste.

The Entire Tag Program

The entire tag game is shown here. You should enter it into your computer at this time. Remember that it does require a graphics adapter for operation.

```
/* A simple animated video game of TAG.

   The object of the game is for your "person" to
```

```
      tag the other "person" by running into him or her.

      Your person is green, the computer's is yellow. No
      red boundary may be crossed.

      For the tag to count, the two "people" must be within
      one pixel of being directly on top of one another.
*/

#include "dos.h"
#include "stdio.h"
#include "math.h"
#include "time.h"
#include "conio.h"

#define XMAX 319
#define YMAX 199

#define COMPUTER 0
#define HUMAN 1

#define IDLE 0
#define DOWN 1
#define UP -1
#define LEFT -1
#define RIGHT 1

void line(int startx, int starty, int endx, int endy,
          int color);
void mempoint(int x, int y, int color);
void palette(int pnum);
void mode(int mode_code);
void display_object(int ob[][5], int lines);
void xhairs(int x, int y), goto_xy(int x, int y);
void save_pic(void), load_pic(void);
void it_comp_move(int ob1[][5], int ob2[][5], int human[][5],
                  int sides);
void not_it_comp_move(int ob1[][5], int ob2[][5],
                      int directx, int directy, int sides);
void show_score(int it, long htime, long ctime);
void update_object(int ob[][5], int x, int y,
                   register int sides);
int readkey(void), kbhit(void);
int is_legal(int ob[][5], int x, int y, int sides);
int tag(int ob1[][5], int ob2[][5]);
```

```
int human[4][5] = { /* your sprites */
  6, 1, 6, 6, 1,
  2, 4, 9, 3, 1,
  1, 9, 6, 6, 1,
  11, 9, 6, 6, 1
};

int human2[4][5] = {
  6, 1, 6, 6, 1,
  2, 4, 9, 3, 1,
  3, 9, 6, 6, 1,
  9, 9, 6, 6, 1
};

int computer[4][5] = { /* computer's sprites */
  6, 180, 6, 185, 3,
  2, 183, 9, 182, 3,
  1, 188, 6, 185, 3,
  11, 188, 6, 185, 3
};

int computer2[4][5] = {
  6, 180, 6, 185, 3,
  2, 183, 9, 182, 3,
  3, 188, 6, 185, 3,
  9, 188, 6, 185, 3
};

int directx, directy; /* direction of human */

main(void)
{
  union k { /* holds both scan and key codes */
    char c[2];
    int i;
  } key;

  int deltax = 0, deltay = 0; /* direction of movement */
  int swaph = 0, swapc = 0; /* select sprites */
  int it = COMPUTER; /* who's "it" */
  long htime, ctime, starttime, curtime;
  int count; /* used to let the players separate slightly
              after a tag */

  mode(4);  /* switch to mode 4 graphics */
```

```
palette(0); /* palette 0 */

load_pic(); /* get the game board */

time(&starttime); /* set up the clocks */
htime = ctime = 0;

display_object(human, 4);
display_object(computer, 4);
count = 0;

/* main game loop */
do {
  /* update the score counters */
  time(&curtime);
  if(it==COMPUTER) htime += curtime-starttime;
  else ctime += curtime-starttime;
  time(&starttime);
  show_score(it, htime, ctime);

  if(kbhit()) { /* if key pressed */
    directx = directy = IDLE; /* reset direction for each move */
    key.i = readkey(); /* read the key */
    deltax = 0; deltay = 0;
    if(!key.c[0]) switch(key.c[1]) {
      case 75: /* left */
        deltax = -1;
        directx = LEFT;
        break;
      case 77: /* right */
        deltax = 1;
        directx = RIGHT;
        break;
      case 72: /* up */
        deltay = -1;
        directy = UP;
        break;
      case 80: /* down */
        deltay = 1;
        directy = DOWN;
        break;
      case 71: /* up left */
        deltax = -1; deltay = -1;
        directy = UP; directx = LEFT;
        break;
```

```
      case 73: /* up right */
        deltay = -1; deltax = 1;
        directy = UP; directx = RIGHT;
        break;
      case 79: /* down left*/
        deltay = 1; deltax = -1;
        directy = DOWN; directx = LEFT;
        break;
      case 81: /* down right */
        deltay = 1; deltax = 1;
        directy = DOWN; directx = RIGHT;
        break;
    }
  }
  /* turn off player's person */
  if(swaph<5) display_object(human, 4);
  else display_object(human2, 4);

  /* see if move is legal */
  if(is_legal(human, deltax, deltay, 4)) {
    update_object(human, deltax, deltay, 4);
    update_object(human2, deltax, deltay, 4);
  }

  /* see if a tag has occurred */
  if(!count && tag(human, computer)) {
    it = !it;  /* switch who is "it" */
    count = 6; /* don't allow an instant retag */
  }

  swaph++;
  if(swaph==10) swaph = 0;
  /* redisplay person in new position */
  if(swaph<5) display_object(human, 4);
  else display_object(human2, 4);

  /* turn off computer's person */
  if(swapc<5) display_object(computer, 4);
  else display_object(computer2, 4);

  /* generate the computer's move */
  if(it==COMPUTER) it_comp_move(computer, computer2, human, 4);
  else not_it_comp_move(computer, computer2, directx, directy, 4);
  if(!count && tag(human, computer)) {
    it = !it; /* switch who is "it" */
```

```
        count = 6; /* don't allow an instant retag */
        /* if computer tag's person, shift computer's  X
            position by 2 so that it is not trivial to retag.
        */
        if(is_legal(computer, 2, 0, 4)) {
          update_object(computer, 2, 0, 4);
          update_object(computer2, 2, 0, 4);
        }
        else {
          update_object(computer, -2, 0, 4);
          update_object(computer2, -2, 0, 4);
        }


      }
      swapc++;
      if(swapc==10) swapc = 0;
      /* display computer's person */
      if(swapc<5) display_object(computer, 4);
      else display_object(computer2, 4);

      if(count) count--;
    } while (key.c[0]!='q' && htime<999 && ctime<999);
    mode(3);

    if(ctime>htime) printf("Computer wins!");
    else printf("You win!");

    return 0;
}

/* Display the score.
   When the YOU or ME is in caps, points
   are scored.
*/
void show_score(int it, long htime, long ctime)
{
  goto_xy(6, 24);
  if(it==COMPUTER) printf("YOU:%ld", htime);
  else printf("you:%ld", htime);
  goto_xy(26, 24);
  if(it==HUMAN) printf("ME:%ld", ctime);
  else printf("me:%ld", ctime);
}

/* Set the palette. */
```

```
void palette(int pnum)
{
  union REGS r;

  r.h.bh = 1;    /* code for palette select */
  r.h.bl = pnum;
  r.h.ah = 11;  /* set palette function */
  int86(0x10, &r, &r);
}

/* Set the video mode. */
void mode(int mode_code)
{
  union REGS r;

  r.h.al = mode_code;
  r.h.ah = 0;
  int86(0x10, &r, &r);
}

/* Draw a line in specified color
   using Bresenham's integer-based algorithm.
*/
void line(int startx, int starty, /* upper-left corner */
          int endx, int endy, /* lower-right corner */
          int color) /* color */
{
  register int t, distance;
  int x=0, y=0, delta_x, delta_y;
  int incx, incy;

  /* Compute the distances in both directions. */
  delta_x = endx-startx;
  delta_y = endy-starty;

  /* Compute the direction of the increment.
     An increment of 0 means either a vertical
     or horizontal line.
  */
  if(delta_x>0) incx = 1;
  else if(delta_x==0) incx = 0;
  else incx = -1;
  if(delta_y>0) incy = 1;
  else if(delta_y==0) incy = 0;
  else incy = -1;
```

```
/* determine which distance is greater */
delta_x = abs(delta_x);
delta_y = abs(delta_y);
if(delta_x>delta_y) distance = delta_x;
else distance = delta_y;

/* draw the line */
for(t=0; t<=distance+1; t++) {
  mempoint(startx, starty, color);
  x += delta_x;
  y += delta_y;
  if(x>distance) {
    x -= distance;
    startx += incx;
  }
  if(y>distance) {
    y -= distance;
    starty += incy;
  }
}
}

/* Write a point directly to mode 4 graphics RAM. */
void mempoint(int x, int y, /* coordinate of point */
              int color) /* color */
{
  union mask {
    char c[2];
    int i;
  } bit_mask;
  int index, bit_position;
  unsigned char t;
  char xor; /* xor color in or overwrite */

  /* pointer to mode 4 graphics RAM */
  char far *ptr = (char far *) 0xB8000000;

  bit_mask.i = 0xFF3F;   /* 11111111 00111111 in binary */

  /* check range */
  if(x<0 || x>XMAX || y<0 || y>YMAX) return;

  xor = color & 128; /* see if xor mode is set */
  color = color & 127; /* mask off high bit */
```

```
    /* set bit_mask and color bits to the right location */
    bit_position = x%4;
    color <<= 2*(3-bit_position);
    bit_mask.i >>= 2*bit_position;

    /* find the correct byte in screen memory */
    index = y*40 + (x >> 2);
    if(y % 2) index += 8152; /* if odd use 2nd bank */

    /* write the color */
    if(!xor) { /* overwrite mode */
      t = *(ptr+index) & bit_mask.c[0];
      *(ptr+index) = t ¦ color;
    }
    else { /* xor mode */
      t = *(ptr+index) ¦ (char) 0;
      *(ptr+index) = t ^ color;
    }
}
/* Display crosshair locator. */
void xhairs(int x, int y)
{
  line(x-4, y, x+3, y, 1 ¦ 128);
  line(x, y+4, x, y-3, 1 ¦ 128);
}

/* Read byte directly from the video RAM in mode 4. */
unsigned char read_point(int x, int y)
{
  union mask {
    char c[2];
    int i;
  } bit_mask;
  int index, bit_position;
  unsigned char t;

  /* pointer to mode 4 graphics RAM */
  char far *ptr = (char far *) 0xB8000000;

  bit_mask.i = 3;        /* 11111111 00111111 in binary */

  /* check range for mode 4 */
  if(x<0 ¦¦ x>XMAX ¦¦ y<0 ¦¦ y>YMAX) return 0;

  /* set bit_mask and color_code bits to the right location */
```

```
   bit_position = x%4;
   bit_mask.i <<= 2*(3-bit_position);
   /* find the correct byte in screen memory */
   index = y*40 +(x >> 2);
   if(y % 2) index += 8152; /* if odd use 2nd bank */

   /* read the color */
   t = *(ptr+index) & bit_mask.c[0];
   t >>= 2*(3-bit_position);
   return t;
}

/* Save the video graphics display. */
void save_pic(void)
{
   char fname[80];
   FILE *fp;
   register int i, j;
   int e=0;

   /* pointer to mode 4 graphics RAM */
   char far *ptr = (char far *) 0xB8000000;

   char far *temp;
   unsigned char buf[14][80]; /* hold the contents of screen */

   temp = ptr;
   /* save the top of the current screen */
   for(i=0; i<14; i++)
     for(j=0; j<80; j+=2) {
       buf[i][j] = *temp; /* even byte */
       buf[i][j+1] = *(temp+8152); /* odd byte */
       *temp = 0; *(temp+8152) = 0;  /* clear top of screen */
       temp++;
     }

   goto_xy(0, 0);
   printf("Game board: ");
   gets(fname);
   if(!(fp=fopen(fname, "wb"))) {
     goto_xy(0, 0);
     printf("cannot open file - press a key ");
     getch();
     e = 1;  /* flag error */
   }
```

```
    temp = ptr;
   /* restore the top of the current screen */
   for(i=0; i<14; i++)
     for(j=0; j<80; j+=2) {
       *temp = buf[i][j];
       *(temp+8152) = buf[i][j+1];
       temp++;
     }

  if(e) return; /* if file could not be opened, exit */

  /* save image to file */
  for(i=0; i<8152; i++) {
     putc(*ptr, fp); /* even byte */
     putc(*(ptr+8152), fp); /* odd byte */
     ptr++;
  }

  fclose(fp);
}

/* Load the video graphics display. */
void load_pic(void)
{
  char fname[80];
  FILE *fp;
  register int i, j;

  /* pointer to mode 4 graphics RAM */
  char far *ptr = (char far *) 0xB8000000;

  char far *temp;
  unsigned char buf[14][80]; /* hold the contents of screen */

  temp = ptr;
  /* save the top of the current screen */
  for(i=0; i<14; i++)
    for(j=0; j<80; j+=2) {
      buf[i][j] = *temp;
      buf[i][j+1] = *(temp+8152);
      *temp = 0; *(temp+8152) = 0; /* clear the top of the screen */
      temp++;
    }

  goto_xy(0, 0);
```

```
   printf("Filename: ");
   gets(fname);
   if(!(fp=fopen(fname, "rb"))) {
     goto_xy(0, 0);
     printf("cannot open file\n");
     temp = ptr;
     /* restore the top of the current screen */
     for(i=0; i<14; i++)
       for(j=0; j<80; j+=2) {
         *temp = buf[i][j];
         *(temp+8152) = buf[i][j+1];
         temp++;
       }
     return;
   }

   /* load image from file */
   for(i=0; i<8152; i++) {
     *ptr = getc(fp); /* even byte */
     *(ptr+8152) = getc(fp); /* odd byte */
     ptr++;
   }

   fclose(fp);
}

/* Send the cursor to the specified X,Y position. */
void goto_xy(int x, int y)
{
   union REGS r;

   r.h.ah = 2; /* cursor addressing function */
   r.h.dl = x; /* column coordinate */
   r.h.dh = y; /* row coordinate */
   r.h.bh = 0; /* video page */
   int86(0x10, &r, &r);
}

/* Display an object. */
void display_object(int ob[][5], int lines)
{
   register int i;

   for(i=0; i<lines; i++)
     line(ob[i][0], ob[i][1],
```

```
        ob[i][2], ob[i][3], ob[i][4] ¦ 128);
}

/* Update an object's position as specified in X,Y. */
void update_object(int ob[][5], /* object */
  int x, int y, /* amount to update */
  register int sides) /* number of sides */
{
  sides--;
  for( ; sides>=0; sides--) {
    ob[sides][0] += x;
    ob[sides][1] += y;
    ob[sides][2] += x;
    ob[sides][3] += y;
  }
}

/* See if a prospective move is legal.
   Returns 1 if legal; 0 otherwise.
*/
is_legal(int ob[][5], /* object */
  int x, int y, /* increment to move */
  int sides) /* number of sides the object has */
{
  if(x==0 && y==0) return 1;
  sides--;
  for( ; sides>=0; sides--) {
    /* check for out of range */
    if(ob[sides][0]+x>XMAX ¦¦ ob[sides][1]+y >YMAX) return 0;
    if(ob[sides][2]+x<0 ¦¦ ob[sides][3]+y<0) return 0;
    /* check for obstacle */
    if(read_point(ob[sides][0]+x, ob[sides][1] + y)==2) return 0;
    if(read_point(ob[sides][2]+x, ob[sides][3] + y)==2) return 0;
  }
  return 1;
}

/* Generate the computer's move when it is "it". */
void it_comp_move(int ob1[][5], int ob2[][5],
  int human[][5],
  int sides)
{
  register int  x, y;
  static skip = 0;
```

```
    skip++;
    if(skip==3) {
      skip = 0;
      return;
    }
    x = 0; y = 0;

    /* move toward the human */
    if(human[0][0]<ob1[0][0]) x = -1;
    else if(human[0][0]>ob1[0][0]) x = 1;

    if(human[0][1]<ob1[0][1]) y = -1;
    else if(human[0][1]>ob1[0][1]) y = 1;

    if(is_legal(ob1, x, y, sides)) {
      update_object(ob1, x, y, sides);
      update_object(ob2, x, y, sides);
    }
    else { /* if not legal, try to go around */
      if(x && is_legal(ob1, x, 0, sides)) {
        update_object(ob1, x, 0, sides);
        update_object(ob2, x, 0, sides);
      }
      else if(is_legal(ob1, 0, y, sides)) {
        update_object(ob1, 0, y, sides);
        update_object(ob2, 0, y, sides);
      }
    }
}

/* Generate the computer's move when it is not "it". */
void not_it_comp_move(int ob1[][5], int ob2[][5],
    int directx, int directy, /* direction of human's last move */
    int sides)
{
    register int  x, y;
    static skip = 1;

    skip++;
    if(skip==3) {
      skip = 0;
      return;
    }
    x = 0; y = 0;
```

```
    /* move in opposite direction as human */
    x = -directx;
    y = -directy;

    if(is_legal(ob1, x, y, sides)) {
      update_object(ob1, x, y, sides);
      update_object(ob2, x, y, sides);
    }
    else { /* if not legal, try to go around */
      if(x && is_legal(ob1, x, 0, sides)) {
        update_object(ob1, x, 0, sides);
        update_object(ob2, x, 0, sides);
      }
      else if(is_legal(ob1, 0, y, sides)) {
        update_object(ob1, 0, y, sides);
        update_object(ob2, 0, y, sides);
      }
    }
}
/* See if a tag has taken place. */
tag(int ob1[][5], int ob2[][5])
{
  register int i;

  /* To tag, one figure must be within one pixel
     of being directly on top of the other.
  */
  for(i=-1; i<2; i++) {
    if(ob1[0][0]==ob2[0][0]+i && ob1[0][1]==ob2[0][1]+i) {
      return 1;
    }
  }
  return 0;
}

/* Return the 16-bit scan code from the keyboard. */
readkey(void)
{
  union REGS r;

  r.h.ah = 0;
  return int86(0x16, &r, &r);
}
```

Figure 5-1

The tag game with the first game board

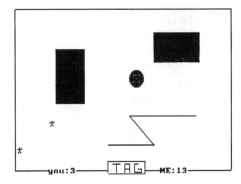

To use the program, you must first create one or more game boards by using the paint program from Chapter 4. (You can use a blank screen, but that is much less fun!) Use red for obstacles that cannot be penetrated by the sprites. You may use yellow and green for decoration, but they will have no effect on the game. Figures 5-1 and 5-2 show two game boards so you can see how the game looks on the screen.

Figure 5-2

The tag game with the second game board

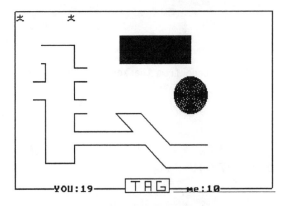

FOR FURTHER EXPLORATION

You will probably want to create your own video games, but you might want to try improving the tag game first. For example, the computer's ability to go around objects or follow a maze can be improved. The basic approach is to create a function that follows the side of an object. Although this task is not especially difficult, it does require a fair amount of code because a database of points visited must be maintained to prevent the computer from following the same object endlessly.

A second improvement would be to give the computer the ability to predict the player's moves so that it has a better chance of tagging.

You might want to add a third sprite that appears briefly and then disappears. If either the computer or the player tags this sprite, bonus points are earned.

One last piece of advice: When developing video games, it is best to start with a simple, well-designed skeleton of the game. Once you have played the game for a while you can begin adding enhancements.

CHAPTER SIX

Using the Serial Port: File Transfers and a Poor Man's LAN

Perhaps no other standard feature causes as much grief for the programmer as the asynchronous serial port. Unlike the much simpler parallel port, a serial port can experience several types of transmission errors. To complicate matters, the "handshaking" capabilities of the serial port, which help provide reliable communication, are often bypassed by the wiring in the cable that connects the serial port to the external device. Even with these problems, the serial port is widely used because it is the least expensive way to link two devices that are separated by more than a couple of feet.

The goal of this chapter is to explain the basics of the serial port's operation, including initialization, transmission, and reception of data, and to discuss some common errors that can occur. The chapter focuses on the asynchronous serial port as it is used with devices other than the modem. Once the operation of the serial port is covered, two separate applications that use the port are developed. The first is a file transfer program that you can use to transfer any type of file (including binary files) between two computers. The file transfer program is especially useful to those who have several different types of computers. The second

JAMES SINNAMON

If you have been involved with microcomputers since the early days, you've probably used one of Jim Sinnamon's creations. He wrote the TR880 Pascal and C compilers for Tandy Corporation. He then went on to write the Mix C and Power C compilers.

When I asked Jim how he became a C programmer, he responded with a playful sense of humor that is typical of many great programmers. "In 1983, I was writing a C compiler so it seemed like a good idea to learn the language," he said with a smile.

I asked Jim to describe the C language. He said, "Many people call C a low-level language. Some call it a high-level assembly language. C is actually a high-level language in the same sense as Pascal or FORTRAN. It's just that C restricts you less than other languages."

Jim went on to describe his personal design philosophy: "Keep it simple. The structure of the program should follow the structure of the problem. I usually concentrate on the data structure and flow of information as a first step. I try to keep the functions simple, straightforward, and reasonably small."

Jim is a programmer driven by a desire to produce the best. I asked him how one becomes a great programmer. "The best way to become a better programmer is to write programs," Jim commented. "As you become better through practice, you should also keep an open mind and try new approaches and techniques. Keep using the techniques that work and discard any that are clumsy or otherwise unsuccessful. Also, go back to your old programs. A well-written program is one that you can still understand and modify years later." These are sentiments that I could not agree with more!

James Sinnamon holds a BS in Chemistry from Trinity College and an MS in Computer Science from Indiana University. He currently lives with his wife in Richardson, Texas.

is the creation of a "poor man's" local area network (LAN), which includes a file server and two new commands that allow remote computers to load files from, or save them to, the server.

The examples in this chapter once again assume a DOS-based, PC environment running DOS. However, you should be able to generalize to other systems.

ASYNCHRONOUS SERIAL TRANSMISSION OF DATA

Before learning about the asynchronous serial port itself, it's important to understand asynchronous communications. (Hereafter, the asynchronous serial port will simply be called the "serial port.") Data is transmitted through a serial port 1 bit at a time. This differs from the transmission of data through a parallel port, which sends 1 byte at a time. The transmission is called *asynchronous* because the length of time that passes between the transmission of each byte of data (1 bit at a time) does not matter. However, both the timing and sequence of the transmission of the bits that compose the byte and some other information are critical.

Each byte of data transmitted by the serial port uses this sequence of signals:

1. One start bit

2. Eight data bits (seven in some situations)

3. Optional parity bit

4. One or two stop bits

Between the transmission of each byte, any amount of time may pass.

The idle state of the transmission line is high. A bit set to 0 drives the line low; a bit set to 1 leaves the line high. The start bit signals the start of the transmission of a new byte by driving the line low for one cycle. The data bits are then transmitted, followed by an optional parity bit. Finally, 1 or 2 stop bits are sent, which also drive the line low. The stop bits determine the shortest time between bytes. Usually, it does not matter a great deal whether you use 1 or 2 stop bits, as long as both the transmitting port and the receiving port use the same number.

The parity bit, if supplied, checks for errors in transmission. Parity can be either even or odd. If even parity is selected, the parity bit is set in such a way that an even number of 1 bits will be transmitted. If odd parity is used, the parity bit will be set so that an odd number of 1 bits is transmitted.

The rate at which bits are transmitted is measured in *baud* (bits per second). The slowest baud rate in general use is 300, which is used mostly with older, slower modems. (Most modems today use either 1200 or 2400 baud.)

THE RS-232 STANDARD

Although it is not critical to understand the RS-232 asynchronous serial communications standard in any great detail for the purposes of this chapter, it is important to see how and why so many problems occur when serial ports are used.

The configuration of most serial ports is based, often loosely, upon the RS-232 standard, using a 25-pin connector on each end. (The IBM AT uses a 9-pin connector.) However, a great many serial ports do not support all the signals specified by the RS-232 standard. Some signals are not supported because they don't apply to the intended usage; others are not supported because the manufacturer sometimes elects not to provide full RS-232 support, offering instead a minimal subset. The most common RS-232 signals are

Signal	Abbreviation	Pin on Connector
Request to send	RTS	4
Clear to send	CTS	5
Data set ready	DSR	6
Data carrier detect	DCD	8
Data terminal ready	DTR	20
Transmit data	TxD	2
Receive data	RxD	3
Ground	GND	7

There are so many signals because the serial port was initially designed as a device to support a modem. Therefore, when it is used with other devices, several of these signals are not applicable. These signals are generally used to establish a hardware protocol between the modem and the computer so that the computer (1) does not send information to the modem before it is ready to transmit the information or (2) does not read data from the modem before it is ready.

A *framing error* is caused if the internal clocks that control the two ports are very different from each other. As you can guess, the serial port, upon seeing the start bit, samples the input register once every cycle to read the next bit. The length of that cycle is determined by the baud rate. However, the time each bit is actually in the register is determined by the clock that controls the system. If the receiving computer's clock rate is not close enough to the transmitter's clock, a bit gets overwritten, resulting in a framing error.

Hardware Handshaking

The proper way to transmit data over a serial port is to monitor the status of the clear-to-send signal of the receiving port. You must not send data until the clear-to-send signal indicates that it is safe to do so. Therefore, when hardware handshaking is used, the transmit routine, in pseudo-C code, looks like this:

```
do {
    while(not CTS) wait;
    send(byte);
} while(bytes to send);
```

If you have a properly wired cable and the hardware on both ends supports the RS-232 standard, you should definitely use hardware handshaking. However, in a less-than-perfect world, it is not always possible to do so.

COMMUNICATIONS PROBLEMS

To allow modem communications, several signals are used to determine when data is ready or when the next byte can be sent. However, when communication is occurring between computers, it is possible (although not necessarily advisable) to use only the GND, TxD, and RxD signals. The reasoning behind this is that running three wires is much less expensive than running five or six. If two computers of the same type are communicating with each other, when one is ready to send data, the other will, in theory, be ready to receive it. However, by bypassing the protocol signals built into the RS-232 standard, you open a Pandora's box of trouble.

When only three wires are used to connect two serial ports, it is necessary to "trick" the transmitting port into believing that the receiving port is always ready for data. This is usually accomplished by means of hooking pins 4 and 5 together and pins 6, 8, and 20 together on both connectors. This makes the serial port think that the device on the other end is always ready to receive data. Given this scenario, a data overrun error is very likely.

Assume that computer A is faster than computer B. If no hardware handshaking is being used, then it is possible for computer A to send a second byte to computer B before computer B has read the information from the input register of its serial port. This is called an *overrun error.* This error can occur even when computer B is faster than A, if its software is too slow. By tying pins 4 and 5 together, and pins 6, 8, and 20 together, the transmitting port will always think the receiving port is ready for data. Shortly, you will be shown a way around this difficulty.

ACCESSING THE PC SERIAL PORTS THROUGH BIOS

There are three ways to access the serial ports on a PC or compatible: through DOS, through the BIOS, or by bypassing DOS and BIOS and directly controlling the hardware. Accessing serial ports through DOS is not generally a good idea because it provides no feedback on the status of the port; it provides only blind reads or writes to the port. As such, the DOS interrupts will not be used. Although previous chapters have opted for direct hardware control of system resources, this method is not necessary for serial ports because adequate performance can be achieved through the BIOS interrupts.

Four BIOS services support access to the serial ports. These services are reached through interrupt 0x14. Let's look at each now.

Port Initialization

Before using the serial port, you will probably want to initialize it to a setting different from the default setting. (The default setting of the first

Table 6-1

The Encoding of the Baud in Bits 7, 6, and 5 of the Serial Port Initialization Byte

Baud	Bit Pattern
9600	1 1 1
4800	1 1 0
2400	1 0 1
1200	1 0 0
600	0 1 1
300	0 1 0
150	0 0 1
110	0 0 0

serial port is generally 1200 baud, even parity, 7 data bits, and 1 stop bit.) Interrupt 0x14, service 0, is used to initialize a serial port. As with other BIOS interrupts, the AH register holds the service number. The AL register holds the initialization parameters that are encoded into 1 byte, as shown here:

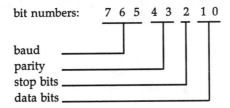

The baud is encoded as shown in Table 6-1. The parity bits are encoded as shown in Table 6-2.

Table 6-2

The Encoding of the Parity in Bits 4 and 3 of the Serial Port Initialization Byte

Parity	Bit Pattern
no parity	0 0 or 1 0
odd	0 1
even	1 1

The number of stop bits is determined by bit 2 of the serial port initialization byte. If bit 2 is 1, 2 stop bits are used; otherwise, 1 stop bit is used. Finally, the number of data bits is set by the code in bits 1 and 0 of the initialization byte. Of the four possible bit patterns, only two are valid. If bits 1 and 0 contain the pattern "1 0," 7 data bits are used. If they contain the pattern "1 1," 8 data bits are used.

For example, if you want to set the port to 9600 baud, even parity, 1 stop bit, and 8 data bits, you would use the bit pattern shown next. In decimal form, this value is 251.

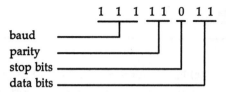

Up to seven serial ports are available on a standard PC (more on newer types of machines). You specify which serial port you want to use in the DX register. The first serial port is 0, the second is 1, and so on. The function shown here, called **init_port()**, initializes the value of any serial port in the system:

```c
/* Initialize the port. */
void port_init(int port, unsigned char code)
{
  union REGS r;

  r.x.dx = port; /* serial port */
  r.h.ah = 0;  /* initialize port function */
  r.h.al = code; /* initialization code - see text for details */
  int86(0x14, &r, &r);
}
```

This function relies upon the **int86()** function, which is found in many compilers, including Turbo C and Microsoft C, although the function may be called something else if you are using a different compiler. You might also be provided with a specific function that initializes the serial port. (For example, the **bioscom()** function in Turbo C allows port initialization.)

Transmitting Bytes

BIOS interrupt 0x14, service 1, transmits 1 byte through the serial port specified in DX. The byte you wish to send must be in AL. The status of the transmission is returned in the AH register. The function **sport()**, shown here, transmits 1 byte through the specified serial port:

```
/* Send a character out the serial port. */
void sport(int port, /* i/o port */
           char c) /* character to send */
{
  union REGS r;

  r.x.dx = port; /* serial port */
  r.h.al = c; /* char to send */
  r.h.ah = 1;  /* send character function */
  int86(0x14, &r, &r);
  if(r.h.ah & 128) {
    printf("Send error detected in serial port");
    exit(1);
  }
}
```

If bit 7 of AH is set upon return from the interrupt, a transmission error has occurred. To determine the cause of the error, you must read the status of the port; the method for doing this is discussed shortly. Although **sport()** simply exits upon an error, you could write an error handler routine that would attempt to recover from certain types of errors.

Checking a Port's Status

BIOS interrupt 0x14, service 3, is used to check a port's status. The port to be checked is specified in the DX register. Upon return from the interrupt, AH and AL will hold the port's status, encoded as shown in Table 6-3.

As you can see, most of the status conditions apply to modems and are less important when you are using the serial port to communicate with other devices. However, there is one status condition that is very important: data ready. By checking this condition, you can determine when a byte of data has been received by a port and is ready for reading. The function **rport()**, used to read data from a port, illustrates the use of the

---

Table 6-3

The Status Bytes of a Serial Port

Line Status (AH) Meaning When Set	Bit
Data ready	0
Overrun error	1
Parity error	2
Framing error	3
Break-detect error	4
Transfer holding register empty	5
Transfer shift register empty	6
Time-out error	7

Modem Status (AL) Meaning When Set	Bit
Change in clear-to-send	0
Change in data-set-ready	1
Trailing-edge ring detector	2
Change in line signal	3
Clear-to-send	4
Data-set-ready	5
Ring indicator	6
Line signal detected	7

---

data-ready status, as you'll see in the next section. The function **check_stat()**, shown here, returns a port's status information:

```
/* Check the status of the serial port. */
check_stat(int port) /* i/o port */
{
  union REGS r;

  r.x.dx = port; /* serial port */
  r.h.ah = 3; /* read status */
  int86(0x14, &r, &r);
  return r.x.ax;
}
```

Receiving a Byte

BIOS interrupt 0x14, service 2, reads a byte from a serial port. Again, the serial port to use is specified in the DX register. Upon return from the interrupt, the character read is in AL. As with transmitting a character, upon return, bit 7 of AH is used to indicate success or failure.

The function **rport()**, shown here, reads a byte from the specified port:

```
/* Read a character from a port. */
rport(int port) /* i/o port */
{
  union REGS r;

  /* wait for a character */
  while(!(check_stat(port)&256))
    if(kbhit()) { /* abort on keypress */
      getch();
      exit(1);
    }

  r.x.dx = port; /* serial port */
  r.h.ah = 2;  /* read character function */
  int86(0x14, &r, &r);
  if(r.h.ah & 128)
    printf("Read error detected in serial port");
  return r.h.al;
}
```

The read port interrupt waits until a byte has been received by the serial port before it returns. However, certain types of errors, such as an unplugged cable, can cause the computer to lock up because no byte is ever received. To avoid this, **rport()** reads the status of the specified port, checking the data-ready bit. At the same time, the function **kbhit()** checks to see if a keystroke has occurred. If a key has been pressed, the function exits. (In some cases, you may want it to call a custom error-handling function.) This gives you a way to abort if no data is received. As soon as data is received, interrupt 0x14, service 2, is called and the byte is read. Once again, bit 7 of AH is checked to see if the operation was a success. Finally, the byte is returned by the function.

TRANSFERRING FILES BETWEEN COMPUTERS

Today, many offices and individuals own more than one microcomputer, and these computers are frequently different brands or models with incompatible disk formats. For example, the 3 1/2-inch disks of the PS/2 systems are incompatible with the 5 1/4-inch disks of the older PC, XT, and AT line of IBM computers. When multiple computers are used, it is very helpful to have the computers communicate with each other via the serial ports in order to share information and/or programs. For various reasons, the creation of programs that allow the transfer of files through the serial port is problematic.

Although faster and more efficient file transfer programs exist, the one developed in this chapter has several significant advantages. It works for all types of files, with all types of computers—even those with different speeds—and requires no hardware handshaking. This last feature is important because it allows the use of three-wire cables. In addition, the program will work even when hardware handshaking is completely disabled and unavailable.

Although you should take advantage of hardware handshaking whenever possible because it lets you achieve the highest level of performance with the greatest reliability, it is not used here because often the proper signals are either not available or have been defeated through rewiring. This situation is slowly changing, but it is still quite common.

The file transfer routines developed here operate by performing software handshaking and work in virtually any environment. Sometimes it is better to sacrifice some performance to gain reliability.

Software Handshaking

When hardware handshaking is either unavailable or disabled, the only way to be sure that an overrun error will not occur during transmission is to implement handshaking in software. *Software handshaking* works like this: The transmitting computer sends the first byte and waits for the receiving computer to return an acknowledgment byte. Once the acknowledgment is received, the sender transmits the next byte and then waits again for acknowledgment. This process continues until the file has been transferred. In pseudo-C code, the sending and receiving routines look like this:

```
send()
{
  while (there are bytes to send) {
    send(a byte);
```

```
    wait();
  }
}

receive()
{
  do {
    receive_byte();
    send(acknowledgment):
  } while(there are still bytes to read);
}
```

In this way, the transmitter never overruns the receiver, no matter how much the two computers differ in speed of operation.

The only drawback to this type of handshaking is that it effectively halves the transmission rate because 2 bytes must be transmitted for each byte of information transferred. However, it will always work.

Seven Versus Eight Data Bits

If you only want to transfer text files, you need to use only 7 data bits because no letter or punctuation mark requires the 8th bit. By sending only 7 bits, you slightly increase the speed at which a file is sent, but a problem arises when you want to send a nontext file, such as a program file.

All program files and some data files contain information that uses all 8 bits of the byte. To transmit these files, you must send the full 8 bits. For this reason, the file transfer program will transmit all 8 bits. However, there is one slight problem when sending binary files: the EOF mark cannot be used to signal the end of the file. To solve this problem, a count of the number of bytes to be transferred must be sent to the receiver prior to sending the file.

Sending a File

The first routine needed is a function that transmits a file through the serial port. In general, it must open the file to be transmitted, count the number of bytes in the file, transmit the count, and finally send the file. The function **send_file()**, shown here, accomplishes these tasks:

```c
/* Send the specified file. */
void send_file(char *fname)
{
  FILE *fp;
  char ch;
  int i;
  union {
    char c[sizeof(long)];
    long count;
  } cnt;

  if(!(fp=fopen(fname, "rb"))) {
    printf("Cannot open input file\n");
    exit(1);
  }

  /* find out the size of the file */
  cnt.count = filesize(fp);

  printf("File size: %ld\n", cnt.count);

  send_file_name(fname); /* send the name of the file */

  /* send size */
  for(i=0; i<sizeof(long); i++) {
    sport(PORT, cnt.c[i]);
    wait(PORT);
  }

  i = 0;
  do {
    ch = getc(fp);
    if(ferror(fp)) {
      printf("Error reading input file.");
      break;
    }

    /* wait until receiver is ready */
    if(!feof(fp)) {
      sport(PORT, ch);
      wait(PORT);
```

```
  }

  i++;
  if(i==1024) {
    printf(".");
    i = 0;
  }
} while(!feof(fp));
fclose(fp);
}
```

The **filesize()** function returns the size of the file in bytes. The function **send_file_name()**, shown here, establishes a connection with the receiver and transmits the file name:

```
/* Send the file name */
void send_file_name(char *f)
{
  printf("Transmitter waiting...\n");
  do {
    sport(PORT, '?');
  } while(!kbhit() && !(check_stat(PORT)&256));
  if(kbhit()) {
    getch();
    exit(1);
  }
  wait(PORT);  /* wait for receiver to acknowledge */
  printf("Sending %s\n\n", f);

  /* actually send the name */
  while(*f) {
    sport(PORT, *f++);
    wait(PORT); /* wait for receiver to acknowledge */
  }
  sport(PORT, '\0'); /* null terminator */
  wait(PORT);
}
```

The **send_file_name()** function has two purposes. First, it establishes communication with the receiver by sending question marks until the receiver responds with a period. (The period is the acknowledgment symbol in the transfer program, but you can use any value you like.)

Once communication has been established, the file name is transmitted. Note that you can abort this function by pressing any key.

The function **wait()**, shown here, waits for an acknowledgment from the receiver, thus implementing the software handshaking:

```
/* Wait for a response. */
void wait(int port)
{
  if(rport(port) != '.') {
    printf("Communication error\n");
    exit(1);
  }
}
```

Although this function exits on error, you could substitute your own error handler if your application requires it.

Receiving a File

Receiving a file is just the opposite of sending one. First, the receiving function waits until it receives a question mark. It replies with a period (the acknowledgment symbol). Then the file name is read, followed by the number of bytes in the file. Finally, the file is read. Keep in mind that after each byte is received, an acknowledgment is sent. This creates the software handshaking. The **rec_file()** function is shown here:

```
/* Receive a file. */
void rec_file(void)
{
  FILE *fp;
  char ch;
  char fname[14];
  unsigned i;
  union {
    char c[sizeof(long)];
    long count;
  } cnt;

  get_file_name(fname); /* get the file name */

  printf("Receiving file %s\n", fname);
```

```
if(!(fp=fopen(fname, "wb"))) {
  printf("Cannot open output file\n");
  exit(1);
}

/* get file length */
for(i=0; i<sizeof(long); i++) {
  cnt.c[i] = rport(PORT);
  sport(PORT, '.'); /* acknowledge */
}

printf("File size: %ld\n", cnt.count);

for(i=0; cnt.count; cnt.count--) {
  ch = rport(PORT);
  putc(ch, fp);
  if(ferror(fp)) {
    printf("Error writing file");
    exit(1);
  }
  sport(PORT, '.'); /* acknowledge */

  i++;
  if(i==1024) {
    printf(".");
    i = 0;
  }
}
fclose(fp);
}
```

The function **get_file_name()** is shown next. It waits for the transmitting port to send it a question mark. Once it receives one, it sends its acknowledgment and then receives the file name.

```
/* Receive the file name. */
void get_file_name(char *f)
{
  printf("Receiver waiting...\n");
  while(rport(PORT) != '?') ;
  sport(PORT, '.'); /* acknowledge */
  while((*f=rport(PORT))) {
```

```
    if(*f != '?') {
      f++;
      sport(PORT, '.'); /* acknowledge */
    }
  }
  sport(PORT, '.'); /* acknowledge */
}
```

The Transfer Program

The entire file transfer program, including all necessary support functions,
is shown here. As it stands, port 0—the first serial port—is used; however,
you can change the definition of **PORT** near the top of the program if you
wish to use a different port.

```
/* File transfer program using software handshaking.

    Port initialized to
      9600 baud,
      no parity,
      eight data bits,
      two stop bits.

*/

#define PORT 0

#include "dos.h"
#include "stdio.h"
#include "conio.h"
#include "stdlib.h"
#include "ctype.h"

void send_file(char *fname), rec_file(void);
void send_file_name(char *f), get_file_name(char *f);
void wait(int port), sport(int port, char c);
void port_init(int port, unsigned char code);
int rport(int port), check_stat(int port);
long filesize(FILE *fp);

main(int argc, char *argv[])
{
  if(argc<2) {
    printf("Usage: trans s filename OR trans r\n");
```

```
    exit(1);
  }

  printf("File transfer program in operation.\n");
  printf("To abort, press any key.\n\n");

  port_init(PORT, 231); /* initialize the serial port */

  if(tolower(*argv[1]) == 's') send_file(argv[2]);
  else rec_file();

  return 0;
}

/* Send the specified file. */
void send_file(char *fname)
{
  FILE *fp;
  char ch;
  int i;
  union {
    char c[sizeof(long)];
    long count;
  } cnt;

  if(!(fp=fopen(fname, "rb"))) {
    printf("Cannot open input file\n");
    exit(1);
  }

  /* find out the size of the file */
  cnt.count = filesize(fp);

  printf("File size: %ld\n", cnt.count);

  send_file_name(fname); /* send the name of the file */

  /* send size */
  for(i=0; i<sizeof(long); i++) {
    sport(PORT, cnt.c[i]);
    wait(PORT);
  }

  i = 0;
  do {
```

```
    ch = getc(fp);
    if(ferror(fp)) {
      printf("Error reading input file.");
      break;
    }

    /* wait until receiver is ready */
    if(!feof(fp)) {
      sport(PORT, ch);
      wait(PORT);
    }

    i++;
    if(i==1024) {
      printf(".");
      i = 0;
    }
  } while(!feof(fp));
  fclose(fp);
}

/* Receive a file. */
void rec_file(void)
{
  FILE *fp;
  char ch;
  char fname[14];
  unsigned i;
  union {
    char c[sizeof(long)];
    long count;
  } cnt;

  get_file_name(fname); /* get the file name */

  printf("Receiving file %s\n", fname);

  if(!(fp=fopen(fname, "wb"))) {
    printf("Cannot open output file\n");
    exit(1);
  }

  /* get file length */
  for(i=0; i<sizeof(long); i++) {
    cnt.c[i] = rport(PORT);
```

```
      sport(PORT, '.'); /* acknowledge */
  }

  printf("File size: %ld\n", cnt.count);

  for(i=0; cnt.count; cnt.count--) {
    ch = rport(PORT);
    putc(ch, fp);
    if(ferror(fp)) {
      printf("Error writing file");
      exit(1);
    }
    sport(PORT, '.'); /* acknowledge */

    i++;
    if(i==1024) {
      printf(".");
      i = 0;
    }
  }
  fclose(fp);
}

/* Return the length, in bytes, of a file. */
long filesize(FILE *fp)
{
  unsigned i;

  fseek(fp, 0, SEEK_END);
  i = ftell(fp);
  rewind(fp);
  return i;
}

/* Send the file name. */
void send_file_name(char *f)
{
  printf("Transmitter waiting...\n");
  do {
    sport(PORT, '?');
  } while(!kbhit() && !(check_stat(PORT)&256));
  if(kbhit()) {
    getch();
    exit(1);
  }
```

```
    wait(PORT);  /* wait for receiver to acknowledge */
    printf("Sending %s\n\n", f);

    /* actually send the name */
    while(*f) {
      sport(PORT, *f++);
      wait(PORT); /* wait for receiver to acknowledge */
    }
    sport(PORT, '\0'); /* null terminator */
    wait(PORT);
}

/* Receive the file name */
void get_file_name(char *f)
{
  printf("Receiver waiting...\n");
  while(rport(PORT) != '?') ;
  sport(PORT, '.'); /* acknowledge */
  while((*f=rport(PORT))) {
    if(*f != '?') {
      f++;
      sport(PORT, '.'); /* acknowledge */
    }
  }
  sport(PORT, '.'); /* acknowledge */
}

/* Wait for a response. */
void wait(int port)
{
  if(rport(port) != '.') {
    printf("Communication error\n");
    exit(1);
  }
}

/* Send a character out the serial port. */
void sport(int port, /* i/o port */
           char c) /* character to send */
{
  union REGS r;

  r.x.dx = port; /* serial port */
  r.h.al = c; /* char to send */
  r.h.ah = 1;  /* send character function */
```

```
  int86(0x14, &r, &r);
  if(r.h.ah & 128) {
    printf("Send error detected in serial port");
    exit(1);
  }
}

/* Read a character from a port. */
rport(int port) /* i/o port */
{
  union REGS r;

  /* wait for a character */
  while(!(check_stat(port)&256))
    if(kbhit()) { /* abort on keypress */
      getch();
      exit(1);
    }

  r.x.dx = port; /* serial port */
  r.h.ah = 2;  /* read character function */
  int86(0x14, &r, &r);
  if(r.h.ah & 128)
    printf("Read error detected in serial port");
  return r.h.al;
}

/* Check the status of the serial port. */
check_stat(int port) /* i/o port */
{
  union REGS r;

  r.x.dx = port; /* serial port */
  r.h.ah = 3;  /* read status */
  int86(0x14, &r, &r);
  return r.x.ax;
}

/* Initialize the port. */
void port_init(int port, unsigned char code)
{
  union REGS r;

  r.x.dx = port; /* serial port */
  r.h.ah = 0;  /* initialize port function */
```

```
  r.h.al = code; /* initialization code - see text for details */
  int86(0x14, &r, &r);
}
```

Using the Transfer Program

The transfer program operates with command-line parameters. Assume that the transfer program is called TRANS. To send a file, use this general form:

TRANS S <*filename*>

where <*filename*> is the name of the file you wish to transfer.
    To receive a file, use this command line:

TRANS R

When receiving a file, the file name need not be specified because it is sent by the transmitting computer.

Enhancements

The transfer program just presented is fully functional and quite reliable. However, in highly critical situations that have no margin for error, you might want to add a few enhancements.

One way to ensure that the file has been correctly received is to echo each byte received back to the transmitter as acknowledgment instead of using the period. The transmitting routine has to be modified to check this byte against the one just transmitted. If a discrepancy is found, an error should be reported.

You might also want to add automatic retry on errors. Automatic retry greatly complicates both the sending and receiving functions but may be worth the effort when one or both of the systems is operating unattended.

Finally, you might want to print the specific nature of any error that occurs. This could be valuable when you are trying to diagnose problems.

A POOR MAN'S LAN

Local area networks, or *LANs* for short, have become increasingly popular in situations where multiple computers are in use. These networks allow the sharing of both data files and programs among several computers. The most common method of creating LANs uses a central computer solely for storing files and serving them to the other computers in the network. The central computer is often called the *file server.* The computers that access the file server are called *nodes, terminals,* or *workstations.* This is the simplest approach to a LAN and is very reliable. It is this approach that is examined more closely here.

Actually, the title to this section is something of an overstatement. In a true LAN, the file server is "transparent," that is, to a great extent each workstation appears to have direct access to the files on the file server. In the programs developed in this section, the user at a workstation must explicitly request a file. However, this approach has the advantage of being easy to develop and does not require any special hardware. You could also use it as a starting point for a full-featured LAN.

The File Server

At the center of the LAN is the file server, so it is appropriate to begin with it. The file server sequentially checks the status of each port in the system. A workstation makes a file request by sending either an "r" or an "s". An "s" is a request for the file server to send a file; an "r" is a request for the file server to receive a file (and store it). When a request is made, the file server fulfills the request and then returns to checking the status of the ports, waiting for the next request. The actual transmission or reception of a file is virtually the same as used in the file transfer program developed in the first part of this chapter.

The main loop of the file server is shown here. The code inserted as a comment shows how additional ports are added to the loop.

```
main(void)
{

  printf("File server in operation.\n");
  printf("To abort, press any key.\n\n");
```

```
    port_init(PORT, 231); /* initialize the serial port */

do {
   /* wait until a request is received */
   if(check_stat(PORT)&256) {
     switch(rport(PORT)) {
       case 's': send_file(PORT);
         printf("\nDone. File server waiting...\n\n");
         break;
       case 'r': rec_file(PORT);
         printf("\nDone. File server waiting...\n\n");
         break;
     }
   }
}


/*******************************
Add additional workstations by checking more ports
as shown here.
     if(check_stat(PORT1)&256) {
       switch(rport(PORT1)) {
         case 's': send_file(PORT1);
           printf("\nDone. File server waiting...\n\n");
           break;
         case 'r': rec_file(PORT1);
           printf("\nDone. File server waiting...\n\n");
           break;
       }
     }
   .
   .
   .

     if(check_stat(PORTn)&256) {
       switch(rport(PORTn)) {
         case 's': send_file(PORTn);
           printf("\nDone. File server waiting...\n\n");
           break;
         case 'r': rec_file(PORTn);
           printf("\nDone. File server waiting...\n\n");
           break;
       }
     }
*******************************/
```

```
  } while(!kbhit());

  return 0;
}
```

As shown, the file server works with only one workstation, but as the comments indicate, you can add as many as necessary. Notice that the file server program runs continuously until a key is pressed. This means that it is always ready to act upon a file request.

As you can see, the functions **send_file()** and **rec_file()** now accept the port with which they will communicate as an argument. This is necessary because the file server must be able to service several different ports. They must also send acknowledgment to the workstation that the request has been received. The reworked **send_file()** and **rec_file()** functions are shown here:

```
/* Send the specified file. */
void send_file(int port)
{
  FILE *fp;
  char ch, fname[128];
  int i;
  union {
    char c[sizeof(long)];
    long count;
  } cnt;

  sport(port, '.'); /* acknowledge */

  get_file_name(fname, port);

  if(!(fp=fopen(fname, "rb"))) {
    printf("Cannot open input file\n");
    exit(1);
  }

  /* find out the size of the file */
  cnt.count = filesize(fp);

  printf("Sending %s\n", fname);
  printf("File size: %ld\n", cnt.count);

  /* send size */
  for(i=0; i<sizeof(long); i++) {
```

```
      sport(port, cnt.c[i]);
      wait(port);
    }

    i = 0;
    do {
      ch = getc(fp);
      if(ferror(fp)) {
        printf("Error reading input file.");
        break;
      }

      /* wait until receiver is ready */
      if(!feof(fp)) {
        sport(port, ch);
        wait(port);
      }

      i++;
      if(i==1024) {
        printf(".");
        i = 0;
      }
    } while(!feof(fp));
    fclose(fp);
}

/* Receive a file. */
void rec_file(int port)
{
  FILE *fp;
  char ch;
  char fname[14];
  unsigned i;
  union {
    char c[sizeof(long)];
    long count;
  } cnt;

  sport(port, '.'); /* acknowledge */

  get_file_name(fname, port); /* get the file name */

  printf("Receiving file %s\n", fname);
```

```
if(!(fp=fopen(fname, "wb"))) {
  printf("Cannot open output file\n");
  exit(1);
}
/* get file length */
for(i=0; i<sizeof(long); i++) {
  cnt.c[i] = rport(port);
  sport(port, '.'); /* acknowledge */
}

printf("File size: %ld\n", cnt.count);

for(i=0; cnt.count; cnt.count--) {
  ch = rport(port);
  putc(ch, fp);
  if(ferror(fp)) {
    printf("Error writing file");
    exit(1);
  }
  sport(port, '.'); /* acknowledge */

  i++;
  if(i==1024) {
    printf(".");
    i = 0;
  }
}
fclose(fp);
}
```

The entire file server program, for use with port 0, is shown next. If you have more than one workstation, be sure to add the appropriate extra code.

```
/* Poor man's LAN file server. Port settings:

    9600 baud,
    no parity,
    eight data bits,
    two stop bits.
*/
```

```
#define PORT 0

#include "dos.h"
#include "stdio.h"

#include "conio.h"
#include "stdlib.h"
#include "ctype.h"

void send_file(int port);
void rec_file(int port);
void get_file_name(char *f, int port);
void wait(int port), sport(int port, char c);
void port_init(int port, unsigned char code);
int rport(int port), check_stat(int port);
long filesize(FILE *fp);

main(void)
{

  printf("File server in operation.\n");
  printf("To abort, press any key.\n\n");

  port_init(PORT, 231); /* initalize the serial port */

  do {
    /* wait until a request is received */
    if(check_stat(PORT)&256) {
      switch(rport(PORT)) {
        case 's': send_file(PORT);
          printf("\nDone. File server waiting...\n\n");
          break;
        case 'r': rec_file(PORT);
          printf("\nDone. File server waiting...\n\n");
          break;
      }
    }
  }

/*********************************
Add additional workstations by checking more ports
as shown here.
    if(check_stat(PORT1)&256) {
      switch(rport(PORT1)) {
        case 's': send_file(PORT1);
          printf("\nDone. File server waiting...\n\n");
```

```
        break;
      case 'r': rec_file(PORT1);
        printf("\nDone. File server waiting...\n\n");
        break;
    }
  }
    .
    .
    .

    if(check_stat(PORTn)&256) {
      switch(rport(PORTn)) {
        case 's': send_file(PORTn);
          printf("\nDone. File server waiting...\n\n");
          break;
        case 'r': rec_file(PORTn);
          printf("\nDone. File server waiting...\n\n");
          break;
      }
    }
*******************************/
  } while(!kbhit());

  return 0;
}

/* Send the specified file. */
void send_file(int port)
{
  FILE *fp;
  char ch, fname[128];
  int i;
  union {
    char c[sizeof(long)];
    long count;
  } cnt;

  sport(port, '.'); /* acknowledge */

  get_file_name(fname, port);

  if(!(fp=fopen(fname, "rb"))) {
    printf("Cannot open input file\n");
    exit(1);
  }
```

```
    /* find out the size of the file */
    cnt.count = filesize(fp);

    printf("Sending %s\n", fname);
    printf("File size: %ld\n", cnt.count);

    /* send size */
    for(i=0; i<sizeof(long); i++) {
      sport(port, cnt.c[i]);
      wait(port);
    }

    i = 0;
    do {
      ch = getc(fp);
      if(ferror(fp)) {
        printf("Error reading input file.");
        break;
      }

      /* wait until receiver is ready */
      if(!feof(fp)) {
        sport(port, ch);
        wait(port);
      }

      i++;
      if(i==1024) {
        printf(".");
        i = 0;
      }
    } while(!feof(fp));
    fclose(fp);
}

/* Receive a file. */
void rec_file(int port)
{
  FILE *fp;
  char ch;
  char fname[14];
  unsigned i;
  union {
    char c[sizeof(long)];
    long count;
```

```
  } cnt;

  sport(port, '.'); /* acknowledge */

  get_file_name(fname, port); /* get the file name */

  printf("Receiving file %s\n", fname);

  if(!(fp=fopen(fname, "wb"))) {
    printf("Cannot open output file\n");
    exit(1);
  }

  /* get file length */
  for(i=0; i<sizeof(long); i++) {
    cnt.c[i] = rport(port);
    sport(port, '.'); /* acknowledge */
  }

  printf("File size: %ld\n", cnt.count);

  for(i=0; cnt.count; cnt.count--) {
    ch = rport(port);
    putc(ch, fp);
    if(ferror(fp)) {
      printf("Error writing file");
      exit(1);
    }
    sport(port, '.'); /* acknowledge */

    i++;
    if(i==1024) {
      printf(".");
      i = 0;
    }
  }
  fclose(fp);
}

/* Return the length, in bytes, of a file. */
long filesize(FILE *fp)
{
  unsigned i;

  fseek(fp, 0, SEEK_END);
```

```
  i = ftell(fp);
  rewind(fp);
  return i;
}

/* Receive the file name */
void get_file_name(char *f, int port)
{
  while(rport(port) != '?') ;
  sport(port, '.'); /* acknowledge */
  while((*f=rport(port))) {
    if(*f != '?') {
      f++;
      sport(port, '.'); /* acknowledge */
    }
  }
  sport(port, '.'); /* acknowledge */
}

/* Wait for a response. */
void wait(int port)
{
  if(rport(port) != '.') {
    printf("Communication error\n");
    exit(1);
  }
}
/* Send a character out the serial port. */
void sport(int port, /* i/o port */
           char c) /* character to send */
{
  union REGS r;

  r.x.dx = port; /* serial port */
  r.h.al = c; /* char to send */
  r.h.ah = 1;  /* send character function */
  int86(0x14, &r, &r);
  if(r.h.ah & 128) {
    printf("Send error detected in serial port");
    exit(1);
  }
}

/* Read a character from a port. */
rport(int port) /* i/o port */
```

```
{
  union REGS r;

  /* wait for a character */
  while(!(check_stat(port)&256))
    if(kbhit()) { /* abort on keypress */
      getch();
      exit(1);
    }

  r.x.dx = port; /* serial port */
  r.h.ah = 2;  /* read character function */
  int86(0x14, &r, &r);
  if(r.h.ah & 128)
    printf("Read error detected in serial port");
  return r.h.al;
}

/* Check the status of the serial port. */
check_stat(int port) /* i/o port */
{
  union REGS r;

  r.x.dx = port; /* serial port */
  r.h.ah = 3;  /* read status */
  int86(0x14, &r, &r);
  return r.x.ax;
}

/* Initialize the port. */
void port_init(int port, unsigned char code)
{
  union REGS r;

  r.x.dx = port; /* serial port */
  r.h.ah = 0;  /* initialize port function */
  r.h.al = code; /* initialization code - see text for details */
  int86(0x14, &r, &r);
}
```

Loading Files

In order for a workstation to request and download a file from the file
server, a special program is required. This program is called GET and is

run by the workstation to request a file. It can be thought of as an extension to the DOS command set. The general form for using GET is

GET <*filename*>

where <*filename*> is the file to be downloaded.

There are two differences in the operation of the GET functions and those used in the file server. First, the **rec_file()** function sends the name of the file to the server. Second, the ports are hardcoded into the routines, not passed as in the file server.

The entire code to the GET program is shown here:

```c
/* Get a file from the file server. */

#define PORT 0

#include "dos.h"
#include "stdio.h"
#include "conio.h"
#include "stdlib.h"
#include "ctype.h"

void rec_file(char *fname);
void send_file_name(char *f), get_file_name(char *f);
void wait(int port), sport(int port, char c);
void port_init(int port, unsigned char code);
int rport(int port), check_stat(int port);
long filesize(FILE *fp);

main(int argc, char *argv[])
{
  if(argc!=2) {
    printf("Usage: get <filename>");
    exit(1);
  }

  port_init(PORT, 231); /* initialize the serial port */

  rec_file(argv[1]);
}

/* Receive a file. */
void rec_file(char *fname)
{
```

```
  FILE *fp;
  char ch;
  int i;
  union {
    char c[sizeof(long)];
    long count;
  } cnt;

  printf("Receiving file %s\n", fname);

  if(!(fp=fopen(fname, "wb"))) {
    printf("Cannot open output file\n");
    exit(1);
  }

  sport(PORT, 's'); /* tell server to send a file */
  wait(PORT); /* wait until server is ready */

  send_file_name(fname);

  /* get file length */
  for(i=0; i<sizeof(long); i++) {
    cnt.c[i] = rport(PORT);
    sport(PORT, '.'); /* acknowledge */
  }
  printf("File size: %ld\n", cnt.count);

  for(i=0; cnt.count; cnt.count--) {
    ch = rport(PORT);
    putc(ch, fp);
    if(ferror(fp)) {
      printf("Error writing file");
      exit(1);
    }
    sport(PORT, '.'); /* acknowledge */

    i++;
    if(i==1024) {
      printf(".");
      i = 0;
    }
  }
  fclose(fp);
}
```

```
/* Send the file name */
void send_file_name(char *f)
{
  do {
    sport(PORT, '?');
  } while(!kbhit() && !(check_stat(PORT)&256));
  if(kbhit()) {
    getch();
    exit(1);
  }
  wait(PORT);  /* wait for receiver to acknowledge */

  /* actually send the name */
  while(*f) {
    sport(PORT, *f++);
    wait(PORT); /* wait for receiver to acknowledge */
  }
  sport(PORT, '\0'); /* null terminator */
  wait(PORT);
}

/* Wait for a response. */
void wait(int port)
{
  if(rport(port) != '.') {
    printf("Communication error\n");
    exit(1);
  }
}

/* Send a character out the serial port. */
void sport(int port, /* i/o port */
           char c) /* character to send */
{
  union REGS r;

  r.x.dx = port; /* serial port */
  r.h.al = c; /* char to send */
  r.h.ah = 1;  /* send character function */
  int86(0x14, &r, &r);
  if(r.h.ah & 128) {
    printf("Send error detected in serial port");
    exit(1);
  }
```

```
}

/* Read a character from a port. */
rport(int port) /* i/o port */
{
  union REGS r;

  /* wait for a character */
  while(!(check_stat(port)&256))
    if(kbhit()) { /* abort on keypress */
      getch();
      exit(1);
    }

  r.x.dx = port; /* serial port */
  r.h.ah = 2;  /* read character function */
  int86(0x14, &r, &r);
  if(r.h.ah & 128)
    printf("Read error detected in serial port");
  return r.h.al;
}

/* Check the status of the serial port. */
check_stat(int port) /* i/o port */
{
  union REGS r;

  r.x.dx = port; /* serial port */
  r.h.ah = 3;  /* read status */
  int86(0x14, &r, &r);
  return r.x.ax;
}

/* Initialize the port. */
void port_init(int port, unsigned char code)
{
  union REGS r;

  r.x.dx = port; /* serial port */
  r.h.ah = 0;  /* initialize port function */
  r.h.al = code; /* initialization code - see text for details */
  int86(0x14, &r, &r);
}
```

Storing Files

In many networks, files may not only be downloaded but also uploaded onto the file server for storage. To support this, the program PUT is created. PUT is run by the workstation to transfer a file to a file server. Its usage is exactly like GET. The general form is

PUT <*filename*>

Its operation is virtually identical to the file transfer program.

The entire code for the PUT program is shown here:

```c
/* Send a file to the file server. */

#define PORT 0

#include "dos.h"
#include "stdio.h"

#include "conio.h"
#include "stdlib.h"
#include "ctype.h"

void send_file(char *fname);
void send_file_name(char *f);
void wait(int port), sport(int port, char c);
void port_init(int port, unsigned char code);
int rport(int port), check_stat(int port);
long filesize(FILE *fp);

main(int argc, char *argv[])
{
  if(argc!=2) {
    printf("Usage: get <filename>");
    exit(1);
  }

  port_init(PORT, 231); /* initialize the serial port */

  send_file(argv[1]);

  return 0;
}
```

```
/* Send the specified file. */
void send_file(char *fname)
{
  FILE *fp;
  char ch;
  int i;
  union {
    char c[sizeof(long)];
    long count;
  } cnt;

  if(!(fp=fopen(fname,"rb"))) {
    printf("Cannot open input file\n");
    exit(1);
  }
  printf("Sending file %s.\n", fname);

  /* request service */
  sport(PORT, 'r'); /* request server to receive a file */
  wait(PORT); /* wait until server is ready */

  send_file_name(fname); /* send the file name */

  /* find file size */
  cnt.count = filesize(fp);
  printf("File size: %ld\n", cnt.count);

  /* send size */
  for(i=0; i<sizeof(long); i++) {
    sport(PORT, cnt.c[i]);
    wait(PORT);
  }

  i = 0;
  do {
    ch = getc(fp);

    if(ferror(fp)) {
      printf("Error reading input file");
      break;
    }

    /* wait until receiver is ready */
    if(!feof(fp)) {
      sport(PORT, ch);
```

```
      wait(PORT);
    }

    i++;
    if(i==1024) {
      printf(".");
      i = 0;
    }
  } while(!feof(fp));
  fclose(fp);
}


/* Send the file name. */
void send_file_name(char *f)
{
  do {
    sport(PORT, '?');
  } while(!kbhit() && !(check_stat(PORT)&256));
  if(kbhit()) {
    getch();
    exit(1);
  }
  wait(PORT);  /* wait for receiver to acknowledge */

  /* actually send the name */
  while(*f) {
    sport(PORT, *f++);
    wait(PORT); /* wait for receiver to acknowledge */
  }
  sport(PORT, '\0'); /* null terminator */
  wait(PORT);
}


/* Return the length, in bytes, of a file. */
long filesize(FILE *fp)
{
  unsigned i;

  fseek(fp, 0, SEEK_END);
  i = ftell(fp);
  rewind(fp);
  return i;
}


/* Wait for a response. */
```

```
void wait(int port)
{
  if(rport(port) != '.') {
    printf("Communication error\n");
    exit(1);
  }
}

/* Send a character out the serial port. */
void sport(int port, /* i/o port */
           char c) /* character to send */
{
  union REGS r;

  r.x.dx = port; /* serial port */
  r.h.al = c; /* char to send */
  r.h.ah = 1;  /* send character function */
  int86(0x14, &r, &r);
  if(r.h.ah & 128) {
    printf("Send error detected in serial port");
    exit(1);
  }
}

/* Read a character from a port. */
rport(int port) /* i/o port */
{
  union REGS r;

  /* wait for a character */
  while(!(check_stat(port)&256))
    if(kbhit()) { /* abort on keypress */
      getch();
      exit(1);
    }

  r.x.dx = port; /* serial port */
  r.h.ah = 2;  /* read character function */
  int86(0x14, &r, &r);
  if(r.h.ah & 128)
    printf("Read error detected in serial port");
  return r.h.al;
}

/* Check the status of the serial port. */
```

```
check_stat(int port) /* i/o port */
{
  union REGS r;

  r.x.dx = port; /* serial port */
  r.h.ah = 3;  /* read status */
  int86(0x14, &r, &r);
  return r.x.ax;
}

/* Initialize the port. */
void port_init(int port, unsigned char code)
{
  union REGS r;

  r.x.dx = port; /* serial port */
  r.h.ah = 0;  /* initialize port function */
  r.h.al = code; /* initialization code - see text for details */
  int86(0x14, &r, &r);
}
```

Using the LAN

To use the LAN, run the file server on the central computer. Put the files GET.EXE and PUT.EXE on each workstation. When a file is needed, use the GET command. To store a file, use the PUT command.

Improving the LAN

One of the first improvements to make is to add the ability for a workstation to request a directory listing of the central computer. To do this, add the "d" (directory) command to the main loop and then transmit the directory listing as if it were a file when the command is received. At the workstation end, you would simply display the directory on the screen.

A very challenging enhancement would be to add a RUN command. This command would automatically download an executable file, place it in the workstation's memory, and begin execution.

An easier feature to add is electronic mail. You could allow users to leave messages to each other via the network.

Finally, you might want to not allow the system to upload certain files in order to protect their contents.

CHAPTER SEVEN

Language Interpreters

Have you ever wanted to create your own computer language? Most programmers find the idea of creating, controlling, enhancing, and modifying their own computer language very appealing. Few programmers, however, realize how easy and enjoyable the creation of a computer language can be. Developing a full-featured compiler is certainly a major undertaking, but creating a language interpreter is a much simpler task. Unfortunately, the methods used to create language interpreters are rarely taught in computer science classes, or they are taught only as abstractions. In this chapter, you learn the secrets of language interpretation and expression parsing by developing a working, practical example.

Language interpreters are important for three very different reasons. First, they can provide a truly interactive environment, as evidenced by the standard BASIC interpreter that comes with most microcomputers. Many novice users find an interactive environment easier to use than a compiler. Second, language interpreters can provide excellent interactive debugging facilities. Third, interpreters make excellent query languages for database management programs. In fact, most database query languages are designed as interpreters.

JOE DESANTIS

Joe DeSantis is the principal author of the Oakland Group's C-scape Interface Management System, a library of routines for creating portable user interfaces in C. He is currently the leader of a team that is developing a new generation of GUI-based programming tools.

I asked Joe what made him become a C programmer. "I chose C because it is elegant and offered the versatility of LISP and assembler, my favorite languages at the time. One thing that particularly impressed me about C is that it was obviously created by a few individuals with a vision and not by a committee. The language itself is very simple, but expressive enough to address almost any kind of problem," he explained.

I inquired what elements contribute to the creation of a great C program. He replied, "The most important part of a program is not that it is free from bugs, or that it is small and efficient. All programs should have these traits. The thing that sets apart a great program is how well it is organized." I asked him to elaborate. Joe continued, "A well-organized program is one that is consistent and based on a thorough plan. Its data structures and objects work together and are designed with future expansion in mind. When a program is consistent, looking at any one part of it helps you to understand the rest of it."

Joe offered some advice to other programmers. He said, "Strive to improve your development environment. Always be on the lookout for new programming tools and ideas. Never be satisfied with the way things are." Then Joe said something quite thought provoking. "Cultivate your nonprogramming interests. Take a close look at things you think are well made, such as books, songs, and films. Authors, composers, and film directors run into the same kinds of problems that programmers do and often come up with very interesting solutions. Other people's creativity can inspire you to improve your own work."

Joe DeSantis currently lives in Brookline, Massachusetts. He holds a degree in Electrical Engineering from MIT.

In this chapter, an interpreter for a subset of BASIC, hereafter referred to as "Small BASIC," is developed. BASIC is chosen over C because BASIC was designed to be an interpreter. As such, it is relatively easy to implement an interpreter for it. For example, standard BASIC does not support local variables, recursive functions, or block structures—all of which increase the complexity of an interpreter (this is why C is a much more difficult language to interpret than is BASIC.) However, the same principles used to interpret BASIC will also apply to any other language, and you can use the routines developed here as a starting point. For example, in my book *Born to Code in C* (Berkeley: Osborne/McGraw-Hill, 1989), a C interpreter is developed that builds from the routines discussed here. (Just as you must learn to crawl before you walk, it is necessary to learn the essentials of language interpretation before tackling the interpretation of something as complex as C.) If you don't know BASIC, don't worry. The commands used in Small BASIC are very easy to understand.

This discussion begins with the heart of any interpreter: the expression parser.

EXPRESSION PARSING

The most important part of a language interpreter is the *expression parser*, which transforms numeric expressions, such as (10−X)/23, into a form that the computer can understand and evaluate. In my book, *C: The Complete Reference, 2nd Ed* (Berkeley: Osborne/McGraw-Hill, 1990), an entire chapter is devoted to expression parsing, and the parser developed there will be used here, with slight modifications, as support for the Small BASIC interpreter. (This chapter presents only a brief explanation of expression parsing; for a detailed discussion, refer to *C: The Complete Reference*.)

Expression parsing is actually very straightforward and is a task like other programming tasks. (In some ways it is easier because it works with the very strict rules of algebra.) The expression parser developed in this chapter is commonly referred to as a *recursive descent parser*. Before developing the actual parser, you should first understand how to think about expressions.

Expressions

Although expressions can be composed of all types of information, this chapter deals only with *numeric expressions*. For our purposes, numeric expressions can be made up of the following items:

- Numbers

- The operators + − / * ^ = ( ) < >

- Variables

The ^ indicates exponentiation. The = is used as the assignment operator and for equality. These items can be combined in expressions according to the rules of algebra. Here are some examples:

```
7−8
(100−5) * 14/6
a+b−c
10^5
a = 7−b
```

Although the =, >, and < are operators, the way BASIC treats them, they do not fit easily into the expression parser and are instead handled explicitly by the specific functions that process the IF, PRINT, and assignment statements. As far as BASIC is concerned, the precedence of these operators is not defined (or you can think of them as having the highest precedence). For the operators that are actually processed by the parser, assume this precedence:

```
highest    ( )
                ^
.
.               * /
lowest     + −
```

Operators of equal precedence evaluate from left to right.

Small BASIC makes the following assumptions. All variables are single letters; this means that 26 variables (the letters A through Z) are available for use. Although most BASIC interpreters support more variables by allowing a number to follow a letter, such as X27, for simplicity the Small BASIC interpreter developed here does not. The variables are not case sensitive; "a" and "A" will be treated as the same variable. All numbers are integers, although you could easily write the routines to handle other types of numbers. Finally, no string variables are supported, although quoted string constants can be used for writing messages to the screen. These assumptions are built into the parser.

Tokens

Before you can develop a parser to evaluate expressions, you must have some way to decompose the string that contains the expression into its components. For example, the expression

A*B −(W + 10)

has the components A, *, B, −, (, W, +, 10, and). Each component represents an indivisible unit of the expression. Formally, each component or indivisible piece of an expression is called a *token*. In general, the function that breaks an expression into its component parts must do four tasks: (1) ignore spaces and tabs, (2) extract each token, (3) convert the token into an internal format, if necessary, and (4) determine the type of the token.

Each token has two formats: external and internal. The *external format* is the string form that you use when writing a program. For example, PRINT is the external form of the BASIC PRINT command. Although it is possible for an interpreter to be designed in such a way that each token is used in its external string format, this is seldom (if ever) done because it is horribly inefficient. Instead, the *internal format* of a token, which is simply an integer, is used. For example, the PRINT command might be represented by a 1, the INPUT command by a 2, and so on. The advantage of the internal representation is that much faster routines can be written by using integers rather than strings. It is the job of the function that returns the next token to convert the token from its external format into its internal format. Keep in mind that not all tokens have different formats. For example, there is no advantage to converting the operators because they are already single characters in their external form.

It is important to know what type of token is being returned. For example, the expression parser needs to know whether the next token is a number, an operator, or a variable. The importance of the token type will become evident as the interpreter is developed.

The function that returns the next token in the expression is called **get_token()**. In Small BASIC, the program is stored as one null-terminated string. The **get_token()** function progresses through the program one character at a time. A global character pointer points to the next character to be read. In the version of **get_token()** shown here, this pointer is called **prog**. The reason that **prog** is global is that it must maintain its value between calls to **get_token()** and allow other functions to use it. The parser developed in this chapter uses six types: **DELIMITER, VARIABLE, NUMBER, COMMAND, STRING,** and **QUOTE.**

DELIMITER is used for both operators and parentheses. VARIABLE is used when a variable is encountered. NUMBER is for numbers. COMMAND is assigned when a BASIC command is found. STRING is used temporarily inside get_token() until a determination is made about a token. QUOTE is for quoted strings. The global variable token_type holds the token type. The internal representation of the token is placed into the global variable tok.

Here is get_token(). Its necessary support functions are shown in the listing of the entire parser presented later in the chapter.

```c
/* Get a token. */
get_token(void)
{
  register char *temp;

  token_type = 0;
  tok = 0;
  temp = token;

  if(*prog=='\0') { /* end of file */
    *token = 0;
    tok = FINISHED;
    return(token_type=DELIMITER);
  }

  while(iswhite(*prog)) ++prog;  /* skip over white space */

  if(*prog=='\r') { /* crlf */
    ++prog; ++prog;
    tok = EOL; *token='\r';
    token[1]='\n'; token[2]=0;
    return (token_type = DELIMITER);
  }

  if(strchr("+-*^/=;(),><", *prog)){ /* delimiter */
    *temp = *prog;
    prog++; /* advance to next position */
    temp++;
    *temp = 0;
    return (token_type=DELIMITER);
  }

  if(*prog=='"') { /* quoted string */
```

```
    prog++;
    while(*prog!='"'&& *prog!='\r') *temp++ = *prog++;
    if(*prog=='\r') serror(MISS_QUOTE);
    prog++;*temp = 0;
    return(token_type=QUOTE);
  }

  if(isdigit(*prog)) { /* number */
    while(!isdelim(*prog)) *temp++ = *prog++;
    *temp = '\0';
    return(token_type = NUMBER);
  }

  if(isalpha(*prog)) { /* var or command */
    while(!isdelim(*prog)) *temp++ = *prog++;
    token_type = STRING;
  }

  *temp = '\0';

  /* see if a string is a command or a variable */
  if(token_type==STRING) {
    tok = look_up(token); /* convert to internal rep */
    if(!tok) token_type = VARIABLE;
    else token_type = COMMAND; /* is a command */
  }
  return token_type;
}
```

Look closely at **get_token()**. Because many programmers like to put spaces into expressions to add clarity, leading spaces are skipped over by using the function **iswhite()**, which returns "true" if its argument is a space or tab. Once the spaces have been skipped, **prog** points to a number, a variable, a command, a carriage return/linefeed, an operator, a quoted string, or a null if trailing spaces end the expression. If a carriage return is next, EOL is returned. If the next character is an operator or other type of delimiter, it is returned as a string in the global variable **token**, and **DELIMITER** is placed in **token_type**. Otherwise, a quoted string is checked for. If that is not the case, **get_token()** checks whether the next token is a number by seeing if the next character is a digit. If, instead, the next character is a letter, either a variable or a command (such as PRINT) is indicated. The function **look_up()** compares the token against commands in a table and, if it finds a match, returns the appropriate internal representation of the command. (The **look_up()** function is discussed later in this chapter.) If a match is not found, then the token is assumed to be a variable. Finally, if the character is none of the above, it is assumed that the end of the expression has been reached and **token** is null, signaling the end of the expression.

To better understand how **get_token()** works, study the type that the function returns for each token in the following expression:

PRINT A + 100 − (B*C)/2

Token	Token Type
PRINT	COMMAND
A	VARIABLE
+	DELIMITER
100	NUMBER
−	DELIMITER
(	DELIMITER
B	VARIABLE
*	DELIMITER
C	VARIABLE
)	DELIMITER
/	DELIMITER
2	NUMBER
null	FINISHED

Remember that **token** always holds a null-terminated string, even if it is just a single character.

Some of the functions in the interpreter need to look ahead one token to determine their next course of action. In some of these cases, the token must be returned to the input stream if it is not needed by the routine. The function **putback()** performs this task. It returns the previously read token by backing up **prog** appropriately:

```
/* Return a token to input stream. */
void putback(void)
{
  char *t;

  t = token;
  for(; *t; t++) prog--;
}
```

How Expressions Are Constructed

There are a number of ways to parse and evaluate an expression. For use with a recursive descent parser, you should think of expressions as *recursive data structures*, that is, expressions defined in terms of themselves. If, for the moment, expressions are restricted to using only +, −, *, /, and parentheses, then all expressions can be defined by using the following rules:

Expression = > Term [+ Term] [− Term]
Term = > Factor [* Factor] [/ Factor]
Factor = > Variable, Number or (Expression)

Any part of the above can be null. The square brackets mean "optional" and the = > means "produces." In fact, these rules are usually called the *production rules* of the expression. Therefore, you can say "Term produces Factor times Factor or Factor divided by Factor" for the definition of *term*. Notice that the precedence of the operators is implicit in the way an expression is defined.

The expression

10+5*B

has two terms: 10 and 5*B. It has two factors: 5 and B, consisting of one number and one variable.

On the other hand, the expression

14*(7−C)

has two factors, 14 and (7−C), consisting of one number and one parenthesized expression. The parenthesized expression evaluates to one number and one variable. You can transform the production rules for expressions into a set of mutually recursive chain-like functions that form a recursive descent parser. At each step, the parser performs the appropriate operations in the algebraically correct sequence. To see how this process works, let's parse the following expression and perform the arithmetic operations at the right time:

Input expression: 9/3−(100+56)

1. Get first term: 9/3.

2. Get each factor and divide integers. That value is 3.

3. Get second term: (100 + 56). At this point, start recursively analyzing the parenthesized expression.

4. Get each term and add. The value is 156.

5. Return from recursive call and subtract 156 from 3, yielding answer of −153.

If you are a little confused at this point, don't worry. This complex concept takes some getting used to. Remember two basic ideas about this recursive view of expressions: (1) the precedence of the operators is *implicit* in the way the production rules are defined, and (2) this method of parsing and evaluating expressions is very similar to the way human beings do the same operations.

The Expression Parser

Here is the entire simple recursive descent parser for integer expressions, along with some support functions. You should put this code into its own file. (The code to the parser and the interpreter when combined make a fairly large file, so two separately compiled files are recommended.) The meaning and use of the external variables are described shortly, in the discussion of the interpreter.

```
/* Recursive descent parser for integer expressions. */

#include "setjmp.h"
#include "math.h"
#include "ctype.h"
#include "stdlib.h"
#include "stdio.h"
#include "string.h"

enum tok_types {DELIMITER, VARIABLE, NUMBER, COMMAND,
                STRING, QUOTE};

enum tokens {PRINT=1, INPUT, IF, THEN, FOR, NEXT, TO,
             GOTO, GOSUB, RETURN, EOL, FINISHED, END};

extern char *prog;  /* points into the program */
extern char *p_buf; /* points to start of program */
```

```
extern jmp_buf e_buf; /* holds environment for longjmp() */
extern int variables[26]; /* variables */
extern struct commands {
  char command[20];
  char tok;
} table[];

extern char token[80]; /* holds string representation of token */
extern char token_type; /* contains type of token */
extern char tok; /* holds the internal representation of token */

void eval_exp1(int *answer), eval_exp2(int *answer);
void eval_exp3(int *answer), eval_exp4(int *answer);
void eval_exp5(int *answer), eval_exp6(int *answer);
void atom(int *answer), putback(void);
void serror(int error);
int get_token(void), look_up(char *s);
int isdelim(char c), iswhite(char c);
int find_var(char *s);

/* These are the constants used to call serror() when
   a syntax error occurs. Add more if you like.
   NOTE: SYNTAX is a generic error message used when
   nothing else seems appropriate.
*/
enum error_msg
     {SYNTAX, UNBAL_PARENS, NO_EXP, EQUALS_EXP,
      NOT_VAR, LAB_TAB_FULL, DUP_LAB, UNDEF_LAB,
      THEN_EXP, TO_EXP, TOO_MNY_FOR, NEXT_WO_FOR,
      TOO_MNY_GOSUB, RET_WO_GOSUB, MISS_QUOTE};

/* Entry point into parser. */
void eval_exp1(int *answer)
{
  get_token();
  if(!*token) {
    serror(NO_EXP);
    return;
  }
  eval_exp2(answer);
  putback(); /* return last token read to input stream */
}

/*  Add or subtract two terms. */
void eval_exp2(int *answer)
```

```
{
  register char  op;
  int temp;

  eval_exp3(answer);
  while((op = *token) == '+' || op == '-') {
    get_token();
    eval_exp3(&temp);
    switch(op) {
      case '-' :
        *answer = *answer - temp;
        break;
      case '+':
        *answer = *answer + temp;
        break;
    }
  }
}

/* Multiply or divide two factors. */
void eval_exp3(int *answer)
{
  register char  op;
  int temp;

  eval_exp4(answer);
  while((op = *token) == '*' || op == '/') {
    get_token();
    eval_exp4(&temp);
    switch(op) {
      case '*' :
        *answer = *answer * temp;
        break;
      case '/':
        *answer = *answer / temp;
        break;
    }
  }
}

/* Process integer exponent. */
void eval_exp4(int *answer)
{
  int temp, i, t;
```

```
    eval_exp5(answer);
   if(*token== '^') {
     get_token();
     eval_exp4(&temp);
     if(temp==0) {
       *answer = 1;
       return;
     }
     i = *answer;
     for(t=temp-1; t>0;   t--) *answer = (*answer) * i;
   }
}

/* Is a unary + or -. */
void eval_exp5(int *answer)
{
  register char  op;

  op = 0;
  if((token_type==DELIMITER) && *token=='+' ¦¦ *token=='-') {
    op = *token;
    get_token();
  }
  eval_exp6(answer);
  if(op=='-') *answer = -(*answer);
}

/* Process parenthesized expression. */
void eval_exp6(int *answer)
{
  if(*token == '(') {
    get_token();
    eval_exp2(answer);
    if(*token != ')')
      serror(UNBAL_PARENS);
    get_token();
  }
  else
    atom(answer);
}

/* Find value of number or variable. */
void atom(int *answer)
{
  switch(token_type) {
```

```
    case VARIABLE:
      *answer = find_var(token);
      get_token();
      return;
    case NUMBER:
      *answer = atoi(token);
      get_token();
      return;
    default:
      serror(SYNTAX);
    }
}

/* Find the value of a variable. */
int find_var(char *s)
{
  if(!isalpha(*s)){
    serror(NOT_VAR); /* not a variable */
    return 0;
  }
  return variables[toupper(*token)-'A'];
}

/* Display an error message. */
void serror(int error)
{
  char *p, *temp;
  int linecount = 0;
  register int i;

  static char *e[]= {
    "syntax error",
    "unbalanced parentheses",
    "no expression present",
    "equal sign expected",
    "not a variable",
    "Label table full",
    "duplicate label",
    "undefined label",
    "THEN expected",
    "TO expected",
    "too many nested FOR loops",
    "NEXT without FOR",
    "too many nested GOSUBs",
    "RETURN without GOSUB",
```

```
     "double qoutes needed"
   };
   printf("%s", e[error]);

   p = p_buf;
   while(p != prog) {  /* find line number of error */
     p++;
     if(*p == '\r') {
       linecount++;
     }
   }
   printf(" in line %d\n", linecount);

   temp = p;  /* display line with error */
   for(i=0; i<20 && p>p_buf && *p!='\n'; i++, p--);
   for(; p<=temp; p++) printf("%c", *p);

   longjmp(e_buf, 1); /* return to save point */
}

/* Get a token. */
get_token(void)
{
  register char *temp;

  token_type = 0;
  tok = 0;
  temp = token;

  if(*prog=='\0') { /* end of file */
    *token = 0;
    tok = FINISHED;
    return(token_type=DELIMITER);
  }

  while(iswhite(*prog)) ++prog;  /* skip over white space */

  if(*prog=='\r') { /* crlf */
    ++prog; ++prog;
    tok = EOL; *token='\r';
    token[1]='\n'; token[2]=0;
    return (token_type = DELIMITER);
  }

  if(strchr("+-*^/=;(),><", *prog)){ /* delimiter */
```

```
    *temp = *prog;
    prog++; /* advance to next position */
    temp++;
    *temp = 0;
    return (token_type=DELIMITER);
  }

  if(*prog=='"') { /* quoted string */
    prog++;
    while(*prog!='"'&& *prog!='\r') *temp++ = *prog++;
    if(*prog=='\r') serror(MISS_QUOTE);
    prog++;*temp = 0;
    return(token_type=QUOTE);
  }

  if(isdigit(*prog)) { /* number */
    while(!isdelim(*prog)) *temp++ = *prog++;
    *temp = '\0';
    return(token_type = NUMBER);
  }

  if(isalpha(*prog)) { /* var or command */
    while(!isdelim(*prog)) *temp++ = *prog++;
    token_type = STRING;
  }

  *temp = '\0';

  /* see if a string is a command or a variable */
  if(token_type==STRING) {
    tok = look_up(token); /* convert to internal rep */
    if(!tok) token_type = VARIABLE;
    else token_type = COMMAND; /* is a command */
  }
  return token_type;
}

/* Return a token to input stream. */
void putback(void)
{

  char *t;

  t = token;
```

```
    for(; *t; t++) prog--;
}

/* Look up a token's internal representation in the
   token table.
*/
look_up(char *s)
{
  register int i;
  char *p;

  /* convert to lowercase */
  p = s;
  while(*p){
    *p = tolower(*p);
    p++;
  }

  /* see if token is in table */
  for(i=0; *table[i].command; i++)
      if(!strcmp(table[i].command, s)) return table[i].tok;
  return 0; /* unknown command */
}

/* Return true if c is a delimiter. */
isdelim(char c)
{
  if(strchr(" ;,+-<>/*%^=()", c) || c==9 || c=='\r' || c==0)
    return 1;
  return 0;
}

/* Return 1 if c is space or tab. */
iswhite(char c)
{
  if(c==' ' || c=='\t') return 1;
  else return 0;
}
```

The parser as shown can handle the following operators: +, −, *, /, integer exponentiation (^), and the unary minus. It also deals with parentheses correctly. Notice that it has six levels as well as the **atom()** function, which returns the value of a number. Also included are various support routines, as well as the **get_token()** code.

To evaluate an expression, set **prog** to point to the beginning of the string that holds the expression and call **eval_exp1()** with the address of the variable you want to hold the result.

Pay special attention to the **serror()** function, which is used to report errors. When a syntax error is detected, **serror()** is called with the number of the error. It then displays the appropriate error message, the line number in which the error occurred, and part of the line that contains the error. It is easiest to call **serror()** by using the enumerated values defined by **error_msg** near the start of the parser code instead of trying to remember the actual number of each error message. As the comments preceding the **error_msg** enumeration indicate, the "syntax error" message is used when nothing else applies. Otherwise, a specific error is reported. Notice that **serror()** ends with a call to **longjmp()**. The **longjmp()** function performs a nonlocal GOTO, returning to the point defined by its companion function **setjmp()**—presumably a safe place. (The **setjmp()** function is found in the interpreter code, not the parser code.) The first argument in **longjmp()** is an environment buffer that is initialized by **setjmp()** that resets the state of the computer to what it was at the time of the **setjmp()** call. The second argument is a value that will appear to be "returned" by **setjmp()**. The use of **longjmp()** simplifies error handling because the parser routines do not have to abort explicitly when errors occur. If your compiler does not support **setjmp()** and **longjmp()**, each function will have to return manually when an error occurs.

How the Parser Handles Variables

As stated earlier, the Small BASIC interpreter recognizes only the variables A through Z. Each variable uses one array location in a 26-element array of integers called **variables**. This array is defined in the interpreter code with each variable initialized to 0, as shown here:

```
int variables[26]= {    /* 26 user variables, A-Z */
  0, 0, 0, 0, 0, 0, 0, 0, 0, 0,
  0, 0, 0, 0, 0, 0, 0, 0, 0, 0,
  0, 0, 0, 0, 0, 0
};
```

Because the variable names are the letters A through Z, they can easily be used to index the array **variables** by subtracting the ASCII value for A from the variable name. The function **find_var()**, which finds a variable's value, is shown here:

```
/* Find the value of a variable. */
int find_var(char *s)
{
  if(!isalpha(*s)){
    serror(NOT_VAR); /* not a variable */
    return 0;
  }
  return variables[toupper(*token)-'A'];
}
```

As this function is written, it actually accepts long variable names, but only the first letter is significant. You can modify it to enforce single-letter variable names if you like.

THE SMALL BASIC INTERPRETER

Now that expressions can be parsed and evaluated, it is time to develop the Small BASIC interpreter. The interpreter will recognize the following BASIC keywords:

PRINT
INPUT
IF
THEN
FOR
NEXT
TO
GOTO
GOSUB
RETURN
END

The internal representations of these commands (plus EOL for end-of-line and FINISHED for signaling the end of the program) are enumerated as shown here. The **tokens** enumeration begins with 1 because the value 0 is used by the **look_up()** function (discussed shortly) to indicate an unknown command.

```
enum tokens {PRINT=1, INPUT, IF, THEN, FOR, NEXT, TO,
             GOTO, GOSUB, RETURN, EOL, FINISHED, END};
```

In order for the external representation of a token to be converted into the internal representation, both the external and internal formats are held in a table of structures called **table**, shown here:

```
/* keyword lookup table */
struct commands {
  char command[20]; /* string form */
  char tok; /* internal representation */
} table[] = { /* Commands must be entered lowercase */
  "print", PRINT, /* in this table. */
  "input", INPUT,
  "if", IF,
  "then", THEN,
  "goto", GOTO,
  "for", FOR,
  "next", NEXT,
  "to", TO,
  "gosub", GOSUB,
  "return", RETURN,
  "end", END,
  "", END  /* mark end of table */
};
```

Notice that a null string marks the end of the table. The function **look_up**(), shown here, uses **table** to return either a token's internal representation or a null if no match is found. (This function is in the parser file. It is shown here for your convenience.)

```
/* Look up a token's internal representation in the
   token table.
*/
look_up(char *s)
{
  register int i;
  char *p;

  /* convert to lowercase */
  p = s;
  while(*p){
    *p = tolower(*p);
    p++;
  }
```

```
/* see if token is in table */
for(i=0; *table[i].command; i++)
    if(!strcmp(table[i].command, s)) return table[i].tok;
return 0; /* unknown command */
}
```

The Small BASIC interpreter does not support an integral editor. Instead, you must create a BASIC program by using a standard text editor. The program is then read in and executed by the interpreter. The function that loads the program is called **load_program()** and is shown here:

```
/* Load a program. */
load_program(char *p, char *fname)
{
  FILE *fp;
  int i=0;

  if(!(fp=fopen(fname, "rb"))) return 0;

  i = 0;
  do {
    *p = getc(fp);
    p++; i++;
  } while(!feof(fp) && i<PROG_SIZE);
  *(p-2) = '\0'; /* null terminate the program */
  fclose(fp);
  return 1;
}
```

The Main Loop

Almost all interpreters are driven by a top-level loop that operates by reading the next token from the program and selecting the right function to process it. The Small BASIC interpreter is no exception. The main loop for the Small BASIC interpreter looks like this:

```
do {
  token_type = get_token();
  /* check for assignment statement */
```

```
    if(token_type==VARIABLE) {
      putback(); /* return the var to the input stream */
      assignment(); /* must be assignment statement */
    }
    else /* is command */
      switch(tok) {
        case PRINT:
      print();
      break;
        case GOTO:
      exec_goto();
      break;
    case IF:
      exec_if();
      break;
    case FOR:
      exec_for();
      break;
    case NEXT:
      next();
      break;
    case INPUT:
      input();
      break;
        case GOSUB:
      gosub();
      break;
    case RETURN:
      greturn();
      break;
        case END:
      return 0;
      }
  } while (tok != FINISHED);
```

First, a token is read from the program. In BASIC, the first token on
each line determines what kind of statement occurs on that line. (No
look-ahead is required for this step.) Assuming no syntax errors have been
made, if the token is a variable, an assignment statement is occurring.
(The Small BASIC interpreter does not support the antiquated LET com-

mand.) Otherwise, the token must be a command, and the appropriate **case** statement is selected based on the value of **tok**. Let's see how each of these commands works.

The Assignment Function

In BASIC, the general form of an assignment statement is

<var-name> = <expression>

The **assignment()** function shown here supports this type of assignment:

```
/* Assign a variable a value. */
void assignment(void)
{
  int var, value;

  /* get the variable name */
  get_token();
  if(!isalpha(*token)) {
    serror(NOT_VAR);
    return;
  }

  /* convert to index into variable table */
  var = toupper(*token)-'A';

  /* get the equal sign */
  get_token();
  if(*token != '=') {
    serror(EQUALS_EXP);
    return;
  }

  /* get the value to assign */
  eval_exp1(&value);

  /* assign the value */
  variables[var] = value;
}
```

First, **assignment()** reads a token from the program. This token is the variable that has its value assigned. If it is not a valid variable, an error is reported. Next, the equal sign is read. Next, **eval_exp1()** is called so that the value to assign the variable can be computed. Finally, the value is assigned to the variable. The function is surprisingly simple and uncluttered because the expression parser and the **get_token()** function do much of the "messy" work.

The PRINT Command

The standard BASIC PRINT command is actually quite powerful and flexible, especially when PRINT USING is employed. Although it is beyond the scope of this chapter to create a function that supports all the functionality of the PRINT command, the one developed here embodies its most important functions. The general form of the Small BASIC PRINT command is

PRINT <*arg-list*>

where *arg-list* is a list of expressions or quoted strings that are separated by commas or semicolons. The function **print()**, shown here, executes a BASIC PRINT command:

```
/* Execute a simple version of the BASIC PRINT statement. */
void print(void)
{
  int answer;
  int len=0, spaces;
  char last_delim;

  do {
    get_token(); /* get next list item */
    if(tok==EOL || tok==FINISHED) break;
    if(token_type==QUOTE) { /* is string */
      printf(token);
      len += strlen(token);
      get_token();
    }
    else { /* is expression */
      putback();
```

```
      eval_exp1(&answer);
      get_token();
      len += printf("%d", answer);
    }
    last_delim = *token;

    /* if comma, move to next tab stop */
    if(*token==',') {
      /* compute number of spaces to move to next tab */
      spaces = 8 - (len % 8);
      len += spaces; /* add in the tabbing position */
      while(spaces) {
    printf(" ");
        spaces--;
      }
    }
    else if(*token==';') printf(" ");
    else if(tok!=EOL && tok!=FINISHED) serror(SYNTAX);
  } while (*token==';' ¦¦ *token==',');

  if(tok==EOL ¦¦ tok==FINISHED) {
    if(last_delim != ';' && last_delim!=',') printf("\n");
  }
  else serror(SYNTAX); /* error is not , or ; */
}
```

The PRINT command can print a list of variables and quoted strings
on the screen. If two items are separated by a semicolon, then one space is
printed between them. If two items are separated by a comma, the second
item is displayed beginning with the next tab position. If the list ends in a
comma or semicolon, then no newline is issued. Here are some examples
of valid PRINT statements. The last example simply prints a newline.

```
PRINT X; Y; "THIS IS A STRING"

PRINT 10 / 4

PRINT
```

Notice that **print()** makes use of the **putback()** function to return a
token to the input stream. This is because **print()** must look ahead to see
whether the next item to be printed is a quoted string or a numeric

expression. If it is an expression, the first term in the expression must be placed back in the input stream so the expression parser can correctly compute the value of the expression.

The INPUT Command

In BASIC, the INPUT command reads information from the keyboard into a variable. It has two general forms. The first is

INPUT < *var-name* >

which displays a question mark and waits for input. The second is

INPUT " < *prompt-string* >", < *var-name* >

which displays a prompting message and waits for input. The function **input()**, shown here, implements the BASIC INPUT command:

```
/* Execute a simple form of the BASIC INPUT command. */
void input(void)
{
  char var;
  int i;

  get_token(); /* see if prompt string is present */
  if(token_type==QUOTE) {
    printf(token); /* if so, print it and check for comma */
    get_token();
    if(*token!=',') serror(SYNTAX);
    get_token();
  }
  else printf("? "); /* otherwise, prompt with ? */
  var = toupper(*token)-'A'; /* get the input var */

  scanf("%d", &i); /* read input */

  variables[var] = i; /* store it */
}
```

The operation of this function is straightforward and should be clear after you read the comments.

The GOTO Command

Now that you have seen the way a few simple commands work, it is time to develop a somewhat more difficult command. In standard BASIC, the most important form of program control is the lowly GOTO. In standard BASIC, the object of a GOTO must be a line number, and in Small BASIC, this traditional approach is preserved. However, Small BASIC does not require a line number for each line; a number is needed only if that line is the target of a GOTO. The general form of the GOTO is

GOTO *<line-number>*

The main complexity associated with GOTO is that both forward and backward jumps must be allowed. To satisfy this constraint in an efficient manner requires the entire program to be scanned prior to execution and the location of each label to be placed in a table that holds both the label name and a pointer to its location in the program. Then, each time a GOTO is executed, the location of the target line can be looked up and program control transferred to that point. The table that holds the labels is declared as shown here:

```
/* label lookup table */
struct label {
  char name[LAB_LEN]; /* label */
  char *p; /* points to label's location in source file */
} label_table[NUM_LAB];
```

The routine that scans the program and puts each label's location in the table is called **scan_labels()** and is shown here, along with several of its support functions:

```
/* Find all labels. */
void scan_labels(void)
{
  int addr;
  char *temp;
```

```
     label_init();  /* zero all labels */
     temp = prog;    /* save pointer to top of program */

     /* if the first token in the file is a label */
     get_token();
     if(token_type==NUMBER) {
       strcpy(label_table[0].name, token);
       label_table[0].p = prog;
     }

     find_eol();
     do {
       get_token();
       if(token_type==NUMBER) {
         addr = get_next_label(token);
         if(addr==-1 || addr==-2) {
           (addr==-1) ? serror(LAB_TAB_FULL):serror(DUP_LAB);
         }
         strcpy(label_table[addr].name, token);

         /* save current location in program */
         label_table[addr].p = prog;
       }
       /* if not on a blank line, find next line */
       if(tok!=EOL) find_eol();
     } while(tok!=FINISHED);
     prog = temp;  /* restore original location */
}

/* Find the start of the next line. */
void find_eol(void)
{
   while(*prog!='\n'  && *prog!='\0') ++prog;
   if(*prog) prog++;
}

/* Return index of next free position in label array.
   -1 is returned if the array is full.
   -2 is returned when duplicate label is found.
*/
get_next_label(char *s)
{
   register int t;
```

```
  for(t=0;t<NUM_LAB;++t) {
    if(label_table[t].name[0]==0) return t;
    if(!strcmp(label_table[t].name,s)) return -2; /* dup */
  }

  return -1;
}
```

Two types of errors are reported by **scan_labels()**. The first is duplicate labels. In BASIC (and most other languages), no two labels can be the same. Second, a full label table is reported. The table's size is defined by **NUM_LAB**, which you can set to any size you desire.

Once the label table has been built, it is quite easy to execute a GOTO instruction with **exec_goto()**, as shown here:

```
/* Execute a GOTO statement. */
void exec_goto(void)
{
  char *loc;

  get_token(); /* get label to go to */
  /* find the location of the label */
  loc = find_label(token);
  if(loc=='\0')
    serror(UNDEF_LAB); /* label not defined */

  else prog = loc;  /* start program running at that loc */
}

/* Find location of given label. A null is returned if
   label is not found; otherwise a pointer to the position
   of the label is returned.
*/
char *find_label(char *s)
{
  register int t;

  for(t=0; t<NUM_LAB; ++t)
    if(!strcmp(label_table[t].name,s)) return label_table[t].p;
  return '\0'; /* error condition */
}
```

The support function **find_label()** looks up a label in the label table and returns a pointer to it. If the label is not found, a null—which can never be a valid pointer—is returned. If the address is not null, it is assigned to the global **prog**, causing execution to resume at the location of the label. (Remember, **prog** is the pointer that keeps track of where the program is currently being executed.) If the label is not found, an undefined label message is issued.

The IF Statement

The Small BASIC interpreter executes a subset of the standard BASIC's IF statement. In Small BASIC, no ELSE is allowed and only the conditions "greater than," "less than," and "equal to" are supported. (However, you will find it easy to enhance the IF, once you understand its operation.) The IF statement takes this general form:

IF *<expression>* *<operator>* *<expression>* THEN *<statement>*

The statement that follows the THEN is executed only if the relational expression is true. The function **exec_if()**, shown here, executes this form of the IF statement:

```
/* Execute an IF statement. */
void exec_if(void)
{
  int x, y, cond;
  char op;

  eval_exp1(&x); /* get left expression */

  get_token(); /* get the operator */
  if(!strchr("=<>", *token)) {
    serror(SYNTAX); /* not a legal operator */
    return;
  }
  op = *token;

  eval_exp1(&y); /* get right expression */

  /* determine the outcome */
  cond = 0;
  switch(op) {
```

```
    case '<':
      if(x<y) cond = 1;
      break;
    case '>':
      if(x>y) cond = 1;
      break;
    case '=':
      if(x==y) cond = 1;
      break;
  }
  if(cond) { /* is true so process target of IF */
    get_token();
    if(tok!=THEN) {
      serror(THEN_EXP);
      return;
    }/* else, target statement will be executed */
  }
  else find_eol(); /* find start of next line */
}
```

The **exec_if()** function operates as follows:

1. The value of the left expression is computed.

2. The operator is read.

3. The value of the right expression is computed.

4. The relational operation is evaluated.

5. If the condition is true, the target of the THEN is executed; otherwise, **find_eol()** finds the start of the next line.

Notice that if the condition is true, the **exec_if()** function simply returns. This causes the main loop to iterate and the next token is read. Since the target of an IF is a statement, returning to the main loop simply causes the target statement to be executed as if it were on its own line.

The FOR Loop

The implementation of the BASIC FOR loop presents a challenging problem that lends itself to a rather elegant solution. The general form of the FOR loop is

FOR *<control var-name>* = *<initial value>* TO *<target value>*

.

.

.

statement sequence

.

.

.

NEXT

The Small BASIC version of the FOR allows only positively running loops that increment the control variable by one for each iteration. The STEP command is not supported.

In BASIC, as in C, FOR loops may be nested to several levels. The main challenge this presents is keeping track of the information associated with each loop. (That is, each NEXT must be associated with the proper FOR.) The solution to this problem is to implement the FOR loop using a stack-based mechanism. At the top of the loop, information about the status of the control variable, the target value, and the location of the top of the loop in the program is pushed onto a stack. Each time the NEXT is encountered, this information is popped, the control variable updated, and its value checked against the target value. If the control value exceeds the target, the loop stops and execution continues with the next line following the NEXT statement. Otherwise, the updated information is placed on the stack, and execution resumes at the top of the loop. Implementing a FOR loop in this way works not only for a single loop but also for loops nested to any level because the innermost NEXT will always be associated with the innermost FOR. (The last information pushed on the stack will be the first information popped.) Once an inner loop terminates, its information is popped from the stack and, if it exists, an outer loop's information comes to the top of the stack. Thus, each NEXT is automatically associated with its corresponding FOR.

To support the FOR loop, a stack that holds the loop information must be created, as shown here:

```
/* support for FOR loops */
struct for_stack {
  int var; /* counter variable */
  int target;  /* target value */
  char *loc; /* place in source code to loop to */
} fstack[FOR_NEST]; /* stack for FOR/NEXT loop */
int ftos;  /* index to top of FOR stack */
```

The value of **FOR_NEST** defines how deeply nested the FOR loops may be. (Twenty-five is generally more than adequate.) The **ftos** variable holds the index to the top of the stack.

You will need two stack routines, called **fpush()** and **fpop()**, both of which are shown here:

```
/* Push the FOR stack. */
void fpush(struct for_stack i)
{
   if(ftos>FOR_NEST)
    serror(TOO_MNY_FOR);

  fstack[ftos] = i;
  ftos++;
}

/* Pop the FOR stack. */
struct for_stack fpop(void)
{
  ftos--;
  if(ftos<0) serror(NEXT_WO_FOR);
  return(fstack[ftos]);
}
```

Now that the necessary support is in place, the functions that execute the FOR and NEXT statements can be developed as shown here:

```
/* Execute a FOR loop. */
void exec_for(void)
{
  struct for_stack i;
  int value;

  get_token(); /* read the control variable */
  if(!isalpha(*token)) {
    serror(NOT_VAR);
    return;
  }

  i.var = toupper(*token)-'A'; /* save its index */

  get_token(); /* read the equals sign */
  if(*token!='=') {
```

```
      serror(EQUALS_EXP);
      return;
   }

   eval_exp1(&value); /* get initial value */

   variables[i.var] = value;

   get_token();
   if(tok!=TO) serror(TO_EXP); /* read and discard the TO */

   eval_exp1(&i.target); /* get target value */

   /* if loop can execute at least once, push info on stack */
   if(value >= variables[i.var]) {
      i.loc = prog;
      fpush(i);
   }
   else  /* otherwise, skip loop code altogether */
      while(tok!=NEXT) get_token();
}

/* Execute a NEXT statement. */
void next(void)
{
   struct for_stack i;

   i = fpop(); /* read the loop info */

   variables[i.var]++; /* increment control variable */
   if(variables[i.var]>i.target) return;  /* all done */
   fpush(i);  /* otherwise, restore the info */
   prog = i.loc;  /* loop */
}
```

You should be able to follow the operation of these routines by reading the comments. As the code is written, it does not prevent a GOTO out of a FOR loop. However, jumping out of a FOR loop will corrupt the FOR stack and should be avoided.

The stack-based solution to the FOR loop problem can be generalized to all loops. Although Small BASIC does not implement any other types of loops, you can apply the same sort of procedure to WHILE and DO-WHILE loops. As you will see in the next section, the stack-based solution can also be applied to any language element that may be nested, including calling subroutines.

The GOSUB

Although standard BASIC does not support true stand-alone subroutines, it does allow portions of a program to be called and returned from by using the GOSUB and RETURN statements. The general form of a GOSUB-RETURN is

GOSUB *< line-num >*

.

.

.

< line-num >

. *subroutine code*

.

RETURN

Calling a subroutine, even as simply as subroutines are implemented in BASIC, requires the use of a stack. The reason for this is similar to that given for the FOR statement. Because it is possible to have one subroutine call another, a stack is required to ensure that a RETURN statement is associated with its proper GOSUB. The definition of a GOSUB stack is shown here:

```
char *gstack[SUB_NEST]; /* stack for gosub */

int gtos;  /* index to top of GOSUB stack */
```

As you can see, the **gstack** is simply an array of character pointers. It holds the location in the program to return to once a subroutine has finished.

The function **gosub()** and its support routines are shown here:

```
/* Execute a GOSUB command. */
void gosub(void)
{
  char *loc;

  get_token();
  /* find the label to call */
  loc = find_label(token);
  if(loc=='\0')
```

```
      serror(UNDEF_LAB); /* label not defined */
    else {
      gpush(prog); /* save place to return to */
      prog = loc;  /* start program running at that loc */
    }
}


/* Return from GOSUB. */
void greturn(void)
{
    prog = gpop();
}


/* Push GOSUB stack. */
void gpush(char *s)
{
  gtos++;

  if(gtos==SUB_NEST) {
    serror(TOO_MNY_GOSUB);
    return;
  }

  gstack[gtos]=s;
}

/* Pop GOSUB stack. */
char *gpop(void)
{
  if(gtos==0) {
    serror(RET_WO_GOSUB);
    return 0;
  }

  return(gstack[gtos--]);
}
```

The GOSUB command works as follows. When a GOSUB is encoun-
terd, the current value of **prog** is pushed on the GOSUB stack. (This is the
point in the program that the subroutine will return to once it is finished.)
The target line number that begins the subroutine is looked up, and its
address is assigned to **prog**. This causes program execution to resume at
the start of the subroutine. When a RETURN is encountered, the GOSUB
stack is popped, and this value is assigned to **prog**, causing execution to

continue on the next line after the GOSUB statement. Because the return address is pushed on the GOSUB stack, subroutines may be nested. In each case, the most recently called subroutine will be the one returned from when its RETURN statement is encountered. (That is, the return address of the most recently called subroutine will be on the top of the **gstack** stack.) This process allows GOSUBs to be nested to any depth.

The Entire Interpreter File

All the code for the Small BASIC interpreter, except those routines found in the expression parser file, is shown here. Once you have entered it into your computer, you should compile both the interpreter and the parser files and link them together.

```
/* A Small BASIC interpreter */

#include "stdio.h"
#include "setjmp.h"
#include "math.h"
#include "ctype.h"
#include "stdlib.h"
#include "string.h"

#define NUM_LAB 100
#define LAB_LEN 10
#define FOR_NEST 25
#define SUB_NEST 25
#define PROG_SIZE 10000

enum tok_types {DELIMITER, VARIABLE, NUMBER, COMMAND,
                STRING, QUOTE};

enum tokens {PRINT=1, INPUT, IF, THEN, FOR, NEXT, TO,
             GOTO, GOSUB, RETURN, EOL, FINISHED, END};

char *prog; /* points into the program */
char *p_buf; /* points to start of program */
jmp_buf e_buf; /* holds environment for longjmp() */

int variables[26]= {    /* 26 user variables,  A-Z */
  0, 0, 0, 0, 0, 0, 0, 0, 0, 0,
```

```
  0, 0, 0, 0, 0, 0, 0, 0, 0, 0,
  0, 0, 0, 0, 0, 0
};

/* keyword lookup table */
struct commands {
  char command[20]; /* string form */
  char tok; /* internal representation */
} table[] = { /* Commands must be entered lowercase */
  "print", PRINT, /* in this table. */
  "input", INPUT,
  "if", IF,
  "then", THEN,
  "goto", GOTO,
  "for", FOR,
  "next", NEXT,
  "to", TO,
  "gosub", GOSUB,
  "return", RETURN,
  "end", END,
  "", END  /* mark end of table */
};

char token[80];
char token_type, tok;

/* label lookup table */
struct label {
  char name[LAB_LEN]; /* label */
  char *p; /* points to label's location in source file */
} label_table[NUM_LAB];

/* support for FOR loops */
struct for_stack {
  int var; /* counter variable */
  int target;  /* target value */
  char *loc; /* place in source code to loop to */
} fstack[FOR_NEST]; /* stack for FOR/NEXT loop */

char *gstack[SUB_NEST]; /* stack for gosub */

int ftos;  /* index to top of FOR stack */
int gtos;  /* index to top of GOSUB stack */
```

```
void print(void), scan_labels(void), find_eol(void);
void exec_goto(void), exec_if(void), exec_for(void);
void next(void), fpush(struct for_stack i);
void input(void), gosub(void), greturn(void);
void gpush(char *s), label_init(void);
void assignment(void);
char *find_label(char *s), *gpop(void);
struct for_stack fpop(void);
int load_program(char *p, char *fname);
int get_next_label(char *s);

/* prototypes for functions in the parser file */
int eval_exp1(int *answer), get_token(void);
void serror(int error), putback(void);

/* These are the constants used to call serror() when
   a syntax error occurs. Add more if you like.
   NOTE: SYNTAX is a generic error message used when
   nothing else seems appropriate.
*/
enum error_msg
    {SYNTAX, UNBAL_PARENS, NO_EXP, EQUALS_EXP,
     NOT_VAR, LAB_TAB_FULL, DUP_LAB, UNDEF_LAB,
     THEN_EXP, TO_EXP, TOO_MNY_FOR, NEXT_WO_FOR,
     TOO_MNY_GOSUB, RET_WO_GOSUB, MISS_QUOTE};

main(int argc, char *argv[])
{
  if(argc!=2) {
    printf("usage: run <filename>\n");
    exit(1);
  }

  /* allocate memory for the program */
  if(!(prog=(char *) malloc(PROG_SIZE))) {
    printf("allocation failure");
    exit(1);
  }
  p_buf = prog;

  /* load the program to execute */
  if(!load_program(prog, argv[1])) exit(1);

  if(setjmp(e_buf)) exit(1); /* initialize the long jump buffer */
```

```
scan_labels(); /* find the labels in the program */
ftos = 0; /* initialize the FOR stack index */
gtos = 0; /* initialize the GOSUB stack index */
do {
  token_type = get_token();
  /* check for assignment statement */
  if(token_type==VARIABLE) {
    putback(); /* return the var to the input stream */
    assignment(); /* must be assignment statement */
  }
  else /* is command */
    switch(tok) {
      case PRINT:
    print();
    break;
      case GOTO:
    exec_goto();
    break;
  case IF:
    exec_if();
    break;
  case FOR:
    exec_for();
    break;
  case NEXT:
    next();
    break;
  case INPUT:
    input();
    break;
      case GOSUB:
    gosub();
    break;
  case RETURN:
    greturn();
    break;
      case END:
    return 0;
    }
} while (tok != FINISHED);
return 0;
}
```

```
/* Load a program. */
load_program(char *p, char *fname)
{
  FILE *fp;
  int i=0;

  if(!(fp=fopen(fname, "rb"))) return 0;

  i = 0;
  do {
    *p = getc(fp);
    p++; i++;
  } while(!feof(fp) && i<PROG_SIZE);
  *(p-2) = '\0'; /* null terminate the program */
  fclose(fp);
  return 1;
}

/* Find all labels. */
void scan_labels(void)
{
  int addr;
  char *temp;

  label_init();  /* zero all labels */
  temp = prog;   /* save pointer to top of program */

  /* if the first token in the file is a label */
  get_token();
  if(token_type==NUMBER) {
    strcpy(label_table[0].name, token);
    label_table[0].p = prog;
  }

  find_eol();
  do {
    get_token();
    if(token_type==NUMBER) {
      addr = get_next_label(token);
      if(addr==-1 || addr==-2) {
        (addr==-1) ? serror(LAB_TAB_FULL):serror(DUP_LAB);
      }
      strcpy(label_table[addr].name, token);
```

```
      /* save current location in program */
      label_table[addr].p = prog;
    }
    /* if not on a blank line, find next line */
    if(tok!=EOL) find_eol();
  } while(tok!=FINISHED);
  prog = temp;  /* restore original location */
}


/* Find the start of the next line. */
void find_eol(void)
{
  while(*prog!='\n'  && *prog!='\0') ++prog;
  if(*prog) prog++;
}


/* Return index of next free position in label array.
   -1 is returned if the array is full.
   -2 is returned when duplicate label is found.
*/
get_next_label(char *s)
{
  register int t;

  for(t=0;t<NUM_LAB;++t) {
    if(label_table[t].name[0]==0) return t;
    if(!strcmp(label_table[t].name,s)) return -2; /* dup */
  }

  return -1;
}


/* Find location of given label. A null is returned if
   label is not found; otherwise a pointer to the position
   of the label is returned.
*/
char *find_label(char *s)
{
  register int t;

  for(t=0; t<NUM_LAB; ++t)
    if(!strcmp(label_table[t].name,s)) return label_table[t].p;
  return '\0'; /* error condition */
}
```

```
/* Initialize the array that holds the labels.
   By convention, a null label name indicates that
   array position is unused.
*/
void label_init(void)
{
  register int t;

  for(t=0; t<NUM_LAB; ++t) label_table[t].name[0]='\0';
}

/* Assign a variable a value. */
void assignment(void)
{
  int var, value;

  /* get the variable name */
  get_token();
  if(!isalpha(*token)) {
    serror(NOT_VAR);
    return;
  }

  /* convert to index into variable table */
  var = toupper(*token)-'A';

  /* get the equal sign */
  get_token();
  if(*token != '=') {
    serror(EQUALS_EXP);
    return;
  }

  /* get the value to assign */
  eval_exp1(&value);

  /* assign the value */
  variables[var] = value;
}

/* Execute a simple version of the BASIC PRINT statement. */
void print(void)
{
  int answer;
```

```
  int len=0, spaces;
  char last_delim;

  do {
    get_token(); /* get next list item */
    if(tok==EOL ¦¦ tok==FINISHED) break;
    if(token_type==QUOTE) { /* is string */
      printf(token);
      len += strlen(token);
      get_token();
    }
    else { /* is expression */
      putback();
      eval_exp1(&answer);
      get_token();
      len += printf("%d", answer);
    }
    last_delim = *token;

    /* if comma, move to next tab stop  */
    if(*token==',') {
      /* compute number of spaces to move to next tab */
      spaces = 8 - (len % 8);
      len += spaces; /* add in the tabbing position */
      while(spaces) {
    printf(" ");
        spaces--;
      }
    }
    else if(*token==';') printf(" ");
    else if(tok!=EOL && tok!=FINISHED) serror(SYNTAX);
  } while (*token==';' ¦¦ *token==',');

  if(tok==EOL ¦¦ tok==FINISHED) {
    if(last_delim != ';' && last_delim!=',') printf("\n");
  }
  else serror(SYNTAX); /* error is not , or ; */

}


/* Execute a GOTO statement. */
void exec_goto(void)
{
  char *loc;
```

```
get_token(); /* get label to go to */
/* find the location of the label */
loc = find_label(token);
if(loc=='\0')
  serror(UNDEF_LAB); /* label not defined */

else prog = loc;  /* start program running at that loc */
}

/* Execute an IF statement. */
void exec_if(void)
{
  int x, y, cond;
  char op;

  eval_exp1(&x); /* get left expression */

  get_token(); /* get the operator */
  if(!strchr("=<>", *token)) {
    serror(SYNTAX); /* not a legal operator */
    return;
  }
  op = *token;

  eval_exp1(&y); /* get right expression */

  /* determine the outcome */
  cond = 0;
  switch(op) {
    case '<':
      if(x<y) cond = 1;
      break;
    case '>':
      if(x>y) cond = 1;
      break;
    case '=':
      if(x==y) cond = 1;
      break;
  }
  if(cond) { /* is true so process target of IF */
    get_token();
    if(tok!=THEN) {
      serror(THEN_EXP);
      return;
    }/* else, target statement will be executed */
```

```
  }
  else find_eol(); /* find start of next line */
}

/* Execute a FOR loop. */
void exec_for(void)
{
  struct for_stack i;
  int value;

  get_token(); /* read the control variable */
  if(!isalpha(*token)) {
    serror(NOT_VAR);
    return;
  }

  i.var = toupper(*token)-'A'; /* save its index */

  get_token(); /* read the equal sign */
  if(*token!='=') {
    serror(EQUALS_EXP);
    return;
  }

  eval_exp1(&value); /* get initial value */

  variables[i.var] = value;

  get_token();
  if(tok!=TO) serror(TO_EXP); /* read and discard the TO */

  eval_exp1(&i.target); /* get target value */

  /* if loop can execute at least once, push info on stack */
  if(value >= variables[i.var]) {
    i.loc = prog;
    fpush(i);
  }
  else  /* otherwise, skip loop code altogether */
    while(tok!=NEXT) get_token();
}

/* Execute a NEXT statement. */
void next(void)
{
```

```
   struct for_stack i;

   i = fpop(); /* read the loop info */

   variables[i.var]++; /* increment control variable */
   if(variables[i.var]>i.target) return;  /* all done */
   fpush(i);  /* otherwise, restore the info */
   prog = i.loc;  /* loop */
}

/* Push the FOR stack. */
void fpush(struct for_stack i)
{
   if(ftos>FOR_NEST)
     serror(TOO_MNY_FOR);

   fstack[ftos] = i;
   ftos++;
}

/* Pop the FOR stack. */
struct for_stack fpop(void)
{
  ftos--;
  if(ftos<0) serror(NEXT_WO_FOR);
  return(fstack[ftos]);
}

/* Execute a simple form of the BASIC INPUT command. */
void input(void)
{
  char var;
  int i;

  get_token(); /* see if prompt string is present */
  if(token_type==QUOTE) {
    printf(token); /* if so, print it and check for comma */
    get_token();
    if(*token!=',') serror(SYNTAX);
    get_token();
  }
  else printf("? "); /* otherwise, prompt with ? */
  var = toupper(*token)-'A'; /* get the input var */

  scanf("%d", &i); /* read input */
```

```
  variables[var] = i; /* store it */
}

/* Execute a GOSUB command. */
void gosub(void)
{
  char *loc;

  get_token();
  /* find the label to call */
  loc = find_label(token);
  if(loc=='\0')
    serror(UNDEF_LAB); /* label not defined */
  else {
    gpush(prog); /* save place to return to */
    prog = loc;  /* start program running at that loc */
  }
}

/* Return from GOSUB. */
void greturn(void)
{
   prog = gpop();
}

/* Push GOSUB stack. */
void gpush(char *s)
{
  gtos++;

  if(gtos==SUB_NEST) {
    serror(TOO_MNY_GOSUB);
    return;
  }

  gstack[gtos]=s;
}

/* Pop GOSUB stack. */
char *gpop(void)
{
  if(gtos==0) {
    serror(RET_WO_GOSUB);
```

```
    return 0;
  }

  return(gstack[gtos--]);
}
```

Using Small BASIC

Here are some sample programs that Small BASIC will execute. Notice that both upper- and lowercase characters are supported.

```
PRINT "This program demostrates all commands."
FOR X = 1 TO 100
PRINT X; X/2, X; X*X
NEXT
GOSUB 300
PRINT "hello"
INPUT H
IF H<11 THEN GOTO 200
PRINT 12-4/2
PRINT 100
200 A = 100/2
IF A>10 THEN PRINT "this is ok"
PRINT A
PRINT A+34
INPUT H
PRINT H
INPUT "this is as test ",y
PRINT H+Y
END
300 PRINT "this is a subroutine"
    RETURN


PRINT "This program demonstrates nested GOSUBs."
INPUT "enter a number: ", I
GOSUB 100

END

100 FOR T = 1 TO I
  X = X + I
```

```
   GOSUB 150
NEXT
RETURN

150 PRINT X;
    RETURN
```

```
print "This program computes the volume of a cube."
input "Enter length of first side ", l
input "Enter length of second side ", w
input "Enter length of third side ", d
t = l * w * d
print "Volume is ",t
```

```
PRINT "This program demostrates nested FOR loops."
FOR X = 1 TO 100
  FOR Y = 1 TO 10
    PRINT X; Y; X*Y
  NEXT
NEXT
```

ENHANCING AND EXPANDING THE INTERPRETER

The most important thing to understand about expanding or enhancing the interpreter is that you are not limited to the BASIC language. The techniques described in this chapter will work on any procedural language. You can even invent your own language to reflect your own programming style and personality.

To add commands, follow the general format taken by the ones presented in the chapter. To add different variable types, you must use an array of structures to hold the variables; one field in the structure should indicate the type of the variable and the other field should hold the value. To add strings, you need to establish a string table. The easiest approach is to require fixed-length strings where each string is allocated 255 bytes of storage.

One final thought: the types of statements that you can interpret are bounded only by your imagination.

CHAPTER EIGHT

Of Screens and Speakers

Throughout this book, you have been exploring those aspects of C programming that add professional appeal to the programs you develop. Because the user's opinion of your brilliance is determined by the user interface, it is only fitting that we look closely at screen manipulation one last time, with special emphasis on displaying text in different colors. In addition, some other screen-related topics are covered: how to change the size of the cursor, how to scroll part of the screen, and how to save what is on the screen to a disk file. Since the tasteful use of sound can dramatically enhance your work, the chapter concludes with a section on using the speaker to generate tones and special effects.

The routines in this chapter are hardware dependent. They will work with IBM PCs, XTs, ATs, PS/2s, and compatibles. Some of the functions require that the computer support a color display. If you have a different computer, you will have to modify the functions.

FRED CRIGGER

Fred Crigger, Vice President of Research and Development at Watcom, is the leader of the team that developed the award-winning WATCOM C and C/386 optimizing compilers. He originally wrote most of the C runtime libraries that accompany these compilers. He is a member of the ANSI standards committee and frequently lectures on topics regarding C compiler technology and optimization techniques.

Given Fred's impressive accomplishments, the first question I asked him was what magic he employed to create a compiler as technically excellent as WAT-COM C. He said, "I know and understand the assembly language! In the early days, it was easy to outperform a C program with assembly code. That is changing. The C compilers available today are far better and are constantly improving. Microprocessors are becoming more sophisticated with features such as caching, instruction pipelining, and parallelism. The only way to harness the speed and power of these advanced microprocessors effectively is to use an optimizing compiler that is capable of choosing the right instruction sequence to take advantage of these capabilities. In essence, the key to exploiting the new microprocessors is to make the compiler smarter and teach it about the new aspects of the processor architecture."

I asked Fred what misconceptions non-C programmers have about C. He remarked, "Non-C programmers often look at C the way most people look at APL, that is, it looks like Greek to them. For example, to the non-C programmer, this is a very cryptic statement:

```
while (*p++ = *s++) ;
```

Of course, as all C programmers know, once you master the basics of C, this statement makes perfect sense."

On the future of C, Fred related this thought: "C will be around for a long time. For many people, C provides the lowest level access to the machine. As many others have said, C is used as a universal assembly language." I asked Fred specifically about C++. He said, "There is now a strong movement towards C++. Many people will migrate to it, but C will still be an important part of the landscape for quite some time." I am certain that sentiment is shared by many C programmers.

When Fred is not coding or lecturing, he can often be found practicing his ballroom dancing technique at the local dance studio.

Fred Crigger is an honors graduate of the University of Waterloo with a Bachelor of Mathematics in Computer Science. He currently lives in Waterloo, Ontario, Canada.

USING COLOR IN TEXT MODE

It is rare to see a professionally written program today that does not take full advantage of color. As you learned in Chapter 1, the PC family of computers supports a variety of video modes. If you have a color adapter, the default mode is 3, which specifies 80x25 color text. By default, the color of the text that appears on the screen is white, but it is possible to display text in other colors.

The Attribute Byte in Text Mode

Each character displayed on the screen is associated with an attribute byte that defines the way the character is displayed (see Chapter 1). When the computer is in video mode 3, the attribute byte that is associated with each character determines the foreground color, the background color, the intensity of the character, and whether it is blinking or nonblinking. The attribute byte is organized as shown in Table 8-1.

Bits 0, 1, and 2 of the attribute byte determine the foreground color component of the character associated with the attribute. For example, setting bit 0 causes the character to appear blue. If all bits are off, the character is not displayed. Keep in mind that the colors are additive. When all three bits are on, the character is displayed as white. If you set two of the bits, then either magenta or cyan is produced. The same conditions apply to the background colors. When bits 4 through 6 are off, the background is black; otherwise the background appears in the color specified.

Table 8-1

The Attribute Byte Organization in Video Mode 3

Bit	Meaning When Set
0	Foreground blue
1	Foreground green
2	Foreground red
3	High intensity
4	Background blue
5	Background green
6	Background red
7	Blinking character

In the early days of microcomputers, the default operation of the video system displayed characters in full intensity and gave you the option of displaying in low intensity. When the IBM PC was released, it worked the opposite way: the default video operation of the PC line is in "normal" intensity, but you can display characters in high intensity by setting the high-intensity bit. In addition, you can cause the character to blink by setting the blinking bit.

Previous chapters developed functions that wrote characters to the screen by using both BIOS calls and direct video RAM access. Direct video RAM accessing was necessary in the context of pop-up or pull-down menus or windows for speed of execution. However, direct accessing of the video RAM reduces the portability of the code and can interfere with multitasking operating systems like OS/2. The functions developed in this chapter use BIOS calls because the code is more portable and because extremely fast execution is not usually required for normal display output. However, feel free to use the direct video RAM routines if you prefer.

Writing a String in Color

Writing a string in color is not quite as simple as you might think because of the way the BIOS write-character function operates. The BIOS interrupt 0x10, function 9, writes one character and its attribute to the current cursor location. The problem is that it does not advance the cursor location; this must be done by your routine. To accomplish this, it is first necessary to determine the current cursor position. The function **read_cursor_xy()**, shown here, uses BIOS interrupt 0x10, function 3, to read the cursor's current X,Y position. This position is returned in the variables pointed to by the arguments to the function.

```
/* Read the current cursor position. */
void read_cursor_xy(char *x, char *y)
{
  union REGS r;

  r.h.ah = 3; /* read cursor postion */
  r.h.bh = 0; /* video page */
  int86(0x10, &r, &r);
  *x = r.h.dl;
  *y = r.h.dh;
}
```

Once the position of the cursor is known, the function that prints a string must manually advance the cursor with each character written by using the **goto_xy()** routine developed earlier and repeated here for your convenience.

```c
/* Send the cursor to the specified X,Y position. */
void goto_xy(int x, int y)
{
  union REGS r;

  r.h.ah = 2; /* cursor addressing function */
  r.h.dl = x; /* column coordinate */
  r.h.dh = y; /* row coordinate */
  r.h.bh = 0; /* video page */
  int86(0x10, &r, &r);
}
```

The function **color_puts()**, shown here, displays the specified string in the specified color:

```c
/* Print a string in color. */
void color_puts(char *s, char color)
{
  union REGS r;
  char x, y;

  read_cursor_xy(&x, &y); /* get current cursor position */
  while(*s) {
    if(*s=='\n') { /* process a newline */
      printf("\n");
      s++;
      x = 0; y++; /* advance to next line */
      continue;
    }

    r.h.ah = 9; /* write character and attribute */
    r.h.al = *s++; /* character to write */
    r.h.bl = color; /* color attribute */
    r.h.bh = 0; /* video page 0 */
    r.x.cx = 1; /* write it one time */
    int86(0x10, &r, &r);
```

```
    x++;
    goto_xy(x, y); /* advance the cursor */
  }
}
```

As you can see, the character is placed in AL, the color attribute in BL, the video page in BH, and the number of times to write the character is placed in CX. Since each character will be written only once, CX will always be given the value 1. Notice that the function properly processes a newline character. You might also want it to process tabs and other special characters.

To use the **color_puts()** function, define the macros shown here at the top of your program:

```
#define BLUE        1
#define GREEN       2
#define RED         4
#define INTENSE     8
#define BLUE_BACK   16
#define GREEN_BACK  32
#define RED_BACK    64
#define BLINK       128
```

By using these macros, you can print a string with any foreground or background color that you desire. You can also control whether the string blinks or is in high intensity. To combine colors, blinking, and high intensity, simply OR together the characteristics that you want to appear. For example, the following code prints the string "this is a test" in high-intensity cyan:

```
color_puts("this is a test", GREEN | RED | INTENSE);
```

Using Color

The effective use of multicolored text is more art than science, but a few general suggestions can be offered.

- Do not overuse color. It is generally best to use the standard white characters on a black background for most of the screen, relying upon different-colored text to highlight a relatively few bits of important information.

- A colored border around a screen or window can be a very effective use of color.

- In some situations it is helpful to display negative dollar amounts in red.

- Displaying the active line (or part of a line) in a different color can be an excellent way to prompt the user.

CHANGING THE SIZE OF THE CURSOR

An often overlooked feature of the IBM PC and derivatives is that it is possible to change the size of the cursor. In its default size, the cursor appears as one short blinking line, but you can vary the size of the cursor from 1 scan line to the full height of a character. In color text modes, the cursor can be from 0 to 8 scan lines tall. In monochrome, the cursor can be from 0 to 14 scan lines, but this discussion is concerned only with color modes. The top scan line is number 0.

To set the size of the cursor, you need to use the BIOS interrupt 0x10, function 1, which sets the cursor size. Place the starting (upper) scan line of the cursor in CH and the ending (lower) scan line in CL. The function **size_cursor()**, shown here, sets the size of the cursor.

```
/* Set the size of the cursor. */
void size_cursor(char start, char end)
{
  union REGS r;

  r.h.ah = 1; /* cursor sizing function */
  r.h.ch = start;
  r.h.cl = end;
  int86(0x10, &r, &r);
}
```

To use **size_cursor()**, call the function with the beginning and ending scan lines of the cursor size you want. For example, the following constructs a block cursor that is the full height of a character.

```
size_cursor(0, 7);
```

The following constructs the default cursor:

```
size_cursor(6, 7);
```

The cursor remains the specified size until it is reset either by another call to **size_cursor()** or by a change in the video mode.

The use of different cursors can give any program a custom look. Be careful, though; large blinking cursors can be very annoying.

SCROLLING PART OF THE SCREEN

Two seldom-used BIOS interrupt functions allow you to scroll up or down a portion of the screen. As you know, when the cursor is positioned on the twenty-fifth line of the display and you press ENTER, the entire display scrolls up one line and a new, blank line appears on the bottom of the screen. It is possible to make this same type of scroll occur on only part of the screen using BIOS interrupt 0x10, functions 6 and 7. Function 6 scrolls a window up, 7 scrolls it down.

Both functions are called by using the register assignments that follow. Put the number of lines to scroll in the AL register. To define the size of the region to be scrolled, put the upper-left row number in CH, the upper-left column number in CL, the lower-right row number into DH, and the lower-right column number into DL. Finally, put the display attribute, which determines how the scrolled-in blank lines appear, into BH. The **scroll_window()** function is shown here:

```
/* Scroll a window up or down. */
void scroll_window(
  char startx, char starty, /* upper-left corner */
  char endx, char endy, /* lower-right corner */
  char lines, /* number of lines to scroll */
  char direct /* up or down */
)
{
  union REGS r;

  if(direct==UP) r.h.ah = 6; /* scroll up */
  else r.h.ah = 7; /* scroll down */
```

```
   r.h.al = lines;
   r.h.ch = starty;
   r.h.cl = startx;
   r.h.dh = endy;
   r.h.dl = endx;
   r.h.bh = 0; /* display attribute */
   int86(0x10, &r, &r);
}
```

You can define the macro **UP** as having any value. You should also define another macro called **DOWN** that has a different value than **UP** and use it to call **scroll_window()** when you want to scroll a window down. The **scroll_window()** function assigns the attribute 0 to BH to ensure a blank line, but you can change this if you wish.

A SIMPLE DEMONSTRATION PROGRAM

This program demonstrates the functions developed so far in this chapter: changing the size of the cursor, outputting a message in color, and scrolling a portion of the screen. Its output is shown in Figure 8-1.

```
/* Demonstration program for printing text in color,
   sizing the cursor, and scrolling a window.
*/
#include "stdio. h"
#include "dos. h"

#define BLUE       1
#define GREEN      2
#define RED        4
#define INTENSE    8
#define BLUE_BACK  16
#define GREEN_BACK 32
#define RED_BACK   64
#define BLINK      128

#define UP   0
#define DOWN 1
```

```
void color_puts(char *s, char color);
void read_cursor_xy(char *x, char *y);
void mode(int mode_code), goto_xy(int x, int y);
void size_cursor(char start, char end);
void scroll_window(char startx, char starty,
                   char endx, char endy, char lines,
                   char direct);

main(void)
{
  int i, j;

  /* set video mode to 80 column color */
  mode(3); /* color text */

  /* make the cursor a small block */
  size_cursor(4, 7);

  /* write in color */
  goto_xy(0, 0);
  color_puts("this is a test\n", BLUE | RED | INTENSE);

  for(i=0; i<22; i++ ) {
    for(j=0; j<79; j++)
      printf("%c", i+'a');
    printf("\n");
  }
  getchar();
  /* scroll part of the screen down 3 lines */
  scroll_window(10, 10, 50, 15, 3, DOWN);
  getchar();
  /* reset the cursor */
  size_cursor(6, 7);

  return 0;
}

/* Print a string in color. */
void color_puts(char *s, char color)
{
  union REGS r;
```

```
  char x, y;

  read_cursor_xy(&x, &y); /* get current cursor position */
  while(*s) {
    if(*s=='\n') { /* process a newline */
      printf("\n");
      s++;
      x = 0; y++; /* advance to next line */
      continue;
    }

    r.h.ah = 9; /* write character and attribute */
    r.h.al = *s++; /* character to write */
    r.h.bl = color; /* color attribute */
    r.h.bh = 0; /* video page 0 */
    r.x.cx = 1; /* write it one time */
    int86(0x10, &r, &r);
    x++;
    goto_xy(x, y); /* advance the cursor */
  }
}

/* Read the current cursor position. */
void read_cursor_xy(char *x, char *y)
{
  union REGS r;

  r.h.ah = 3; /* read cursor postion */
  r.h.bh = 0; /* video page */
  int86(0x10, &r, &r);
  *x = r.h.dl;
  *y = r.h.dh;
}

/* Set the video mode. */
void mode(int mode_code)
{
  union REGS r;

  r.h.al = mode_code;
  r.h.ah = 0;
  int86(0x10, &r, &r);
}
```

```c
/* Send the cursor to the specified X,Y position. */
void goto_xy(int x, int y)
{
  union REGS r;

  r.h.ah = 2; /* cursor addressing function */
  r.h.dl = x; /* column coordinate */
  r.h.dh = y; /* row coordinate */
  r.h.bh = 0; /* video page */
  int86(0x10, &r, &r);
}
/* Set the size of the cursor. */
void size_cursor(char start, char end)
{
  union REGS r;

  r.h.ah = 1; /* cursor sizing function */
  r.h.ch = start;
  r.h.cl = end;
  int86(0x10, &r, &r);
}

/* Scroll a window up or down. */
void scroll_window(
  char startx, char starty, /* upper-left corner */
  char endx, char endy, /* lower-right corner */
  char lines, /* number of lines to scroll */
  char direct /* up or down */
)
{
  union REGS r;

  if(direct==UP) r.h.ah = 6; /* scroll up */
  else r.h.ah = 7; /* scroll down */

  r.h.al = lines;
  r.h.ch = starty;
  r.h.cl = startx;
  r.h.dh = endy;
  r.h.dl = endx;
  r.h.bh = 0; /* display attribute */
  int86(0x10, &r, &r);
}
```

Figure 8-1

Output from the screen demonstration program

(a)
```
this is a test
aaaaaaaaaaaaaaaaaaaaaaaaaaaaaaaaaaaaaaaaaaaaaaaaaaaaaaaaaaaaaaaaaaaaaaaaaaa
bbbbbbbbbbbbbbbbbbbbbbbbbbbbbbbbbbbbbbbbbbbbbbbbbbbbbbbbbbbbbbbbbbbbbbbbbbb
ccccccccccccccccccccccccccccccccccccccccccccccccccccccccccccccccccccccccccc
ddddddddddddddddddddddddddddddddddddddddddddddddddddddddddddddddddddddddddd
eeeeeeeeeeeeeeeeeeeeeeeeeeeeeeeeeeeeeeeeeeeeeeeeeeeeeeeeeeeeeeeeeeeeeeeeeee
fffffffffffffffffffffffffffffffffffffffffffffffffffffffffffffffffffffffffff
ggggggggggggggggggggggggggggggggggggggggggggggggggggggggggggggggggggggggggg
hhhhhhhhhhhhhhhhhhhhhhhhhhhhhhhhhhhhhhhhhhhhhhhhhhhhhhhhhhhhhhhhhhhhhhhhhhh
iiiiiiiiiiiiiiiiiiiiiiiiiiiiiiiiiiiiiiiiiiiiiiiiiiiiiiiiiiiiiiiiiiiiiiiiiii
jjjjjjjjjjjjjjjjjjjjjjjjjjjjjjjjjjjjjjjjjjjjjjjjjjjjjjjjjjjjjjjjjjjjjjjjjjj
kkkkkkkkkkkkkkkkkkkkkkkkkkkkkkkkkkkkkkkkkkkkkkkkkkkkkkkkkkkkkkkkkkkkkkkkkkk
lllllllllllllllllllllllllllllllllllllllllllllllllllllllllllllllllllllllll
mmmmmmmmmmmmmmmmmmmmmmmmmmmmmmmmmmmmmmmmmmmmmmmmmmmmmmmmmmmmmmmmmmmmmmmmmmm
nnnnnnnnnnnnnnnnnnnnnnnnnnnnnnnnnnnnnnnnnnnnnnnnnnnnnnnnnnnnnnnnnnnnnnnnnnn
ooooooooooooooooooooooooooooooooooooooooooooooooooooooooooooooooooooooooooo
ppppppppppppppppppppppppppppppppppppppppppppppppppppppppppppppppppppppppppp
qqqqqqqqqqqqqqqqqqqqqqqqqqqqqqqqqqqqqqqqqqqqqqqqqqqqqqqqqqqqqqqqqqqqqqqqqqq
rrrrrrrrrrrrrrrrrrrrrrrrrrrrrrrrrrrrrrrrrrrrrrrrrrrrrrrrrrrrrrrrrrrrrrrrrrr
sssssssssssssssssssssssssssssssssssssssssssssssssssssssssssssssssssssssssss
ttttttttttttttttttttttttttttttttttttttttttttttttttttttttttttttttttttttttttt
uuuuuuuuuuuuuuuuuuuuuuuuuuuuuuuuuuuuuuuuuuuuuuuuuuuuuuuuuuuuuuuuuuuuuuuuuuu
vvvvvvvvvvvvvvvvvvvvvvvvvvvvvvvvvvvvvvvvvvvvvvvvvvvvvvvvvvvvvvvvvvvvvvvvvvv
```

(b)
```
this is a test
aaaaaaaaaaaaaaaaaaaaaaaaaaaaaaaaaaaaaaaaaaaaaaaaaaaaaaaaaaaaaaaaaaaaaaaaaaa
bbbbbbbbbbbbbbbbbbbbbbbbbbbbbbbbbbbbbbbbbbbbbbbbbbbbbbbbbbbbbbbbbbbbbbbbbbb
ccccccccccccccccccccccccccccccccccccccccccccccccccccccccccccccccccccccccccc
ddddddddddddddddddddddddddddddddddddddddddddddddddddddddddddddddddddddddddd
eeeeeeeeeeeeeeeeeeeeeeeeeeeeeeeeeeeeeeeeeeeeeeeeeeeeeeeeeeeeeeeeeeeeeeeeeee
fffffffffffffffffffffffffffffffffffffffffffffffffffffffffffffffffffffffffff
ggggggggggggggggggggggggggggggggggggggggggggggggggggggggggggggggggggggggggg
hhhhhhhhhhhhhhhhhhhhhhhhhhhhhhhhhhhhhhhhhhhhhhhhhhhhhhhhhhhhhhhhhhhhhhhhhhh
iiiiiiiiiiiiiiiiiiiiiiiiiiiiiiiiiiiiiiiiiiiiiiiiiiiiiiiiiiiiiiiiiiiiiiiiiii
jjjjjjjjjj                              jjjjjjjjjjjjjjjjjjjjjjjjjjjjjjjjjjj
kkkkkkkkkk                              kkkkkkkkkkkkkkkkkkkkkkkkkkkkkkkkkkk
llllllllll                              lllllllllllllllllllllllllllllllll
mmmmmmmmmjjjjjjjjjjjjjjjjjjjjjjjjjjjjjjjjjjjjjjjjjjjjjjjjmmmmmmmmmmmmmmmmmmmmmmmmmmmmmmmmmm
nnnnnnnnnnkkkkkkkkkkkkkkkkkkkkkkkkkkkkkkkkkkkkkkkkkkkkkkknnnnnnnnnnnnnnnnnnnnnnnnnnnnnnnnnn
oooooooooollllllllllllllllllllllllllllllllllllllllllllllooooooooooooooooooooooooooooooooo
ppppppppppppppppppppppppppppppppppppppppppppppppppppppppppppppppppppppppppp
qqqqqqqqqqqqqqqqqqqqqqqqqqqqqqqqqqqqqqqqqqqqqqqqqqqqqqqqqqqqqqqqqqqqqqqqqqq
rrrrrrrrrrrrrrrrrrrrrrrrrrrrrrrrrrrrrrrrrrrrrrrrrrrrrrrrrrrrrrrrrrrrrrrrrrr
sssssssssssssssssssssssssssssssssssssssssssssssssssssssssssssssssssssssssss
ttttttttttttttttttttttttttttttttttttttttttttttttttttttttttttttttttttttttttt
uuuuuuuuuuuuuuuuuuuuuuuuuuuuuuuuuuuuuuuuuuuuuuuuuuuuuuuuuuuuuuuuuuuuuuuuuuu
vvvvvvvvvvvvvvvvvvvvvvvvvvvvvvvvvvvvvvvvvvvvvvvvvvvvvvvvvvvvvvvvvvvvvvvvvvv
```

SAVING THE SCREEN TO A DISK FILE

One utility not provided by DOS, OS/2, or most other operating systems
is the ability to save the current contents of the screen to a disk file in a
fashion similar to the print screen command. However, all is not lost
because, as you will see in this section, it is quite easy to create a program
that saves the screen to a disk file.

The program works by using BIOS interrupt 0x10, function 8, to read the character at the current cursor position. This character is then written to the file. Once again, the function **goto_xy()** is used to move the cursor around on the screen, beginning with the upper-left corner and stopping at the lower-right corner.

Here, the file name is specified as an argument to the program. Assuming that the program is called **screen**, this line evokes the program and saves the screen in a file called **scr.sav**:

```
C>screen scr.sav
```

The **screen** program is shown here:

```c
/* This program saves what is currently on the screen
   in the disk file specified on the command line.

   It assumes that the computer is using an 80-column
   text video mode.
*/

#include "dos.h"
#include "stdio.h"
#include "stdlib.h"

void save_screen(char *fname), goto_xy(int x, int y);

main(int argc, char *argv[])
{
  if(argc!=2) {
    printf("usage: screen <filename>");
    exit(1);
  }
  save_screen(argv[1]);

  return 0;
}

/* Save the contents of the screen to a disk file. */
void save_screen(char *fname)
{
  FILE *fp;
  union REGS r;
  register char x, y;
```

```
  if(!(fp=fopen(fname, "w"))) {
    printf("cannot open file");
    exit(1);
  }

  for(y=0; y<25; y++)
    for(x=0; x<80; x++) {
      goto_xy(x, y);
      r.h.ah = 8; /* read a character */
      r.h.bh = 0; /* video page */
      int86(0x10, &r, &r);
      putc(r.h.al, fp); /* write the character */
    }
  fclose(fp);
}

/* Send the cursor to the specified X,Y position. */
void goto_xy(int x, int y)
{
  union REGS r;

  r.h.ah = 2; /* cursor addressing function */
  r.h.dl = x; /* column coordinate */
  r.h.dh = y; /* row coordinate */
  r.h.bh = 0; /* video page */
  int86(0x10, &r, &r);
}
```

As it stands, only the characters on the screen are saved, not the attribute associated with each character. However, this addition is easy to make, and you might want to try it on your own.

ADDING SOUND

Tastefully applied, sound greatly enhances a program's appeal. Sound can range from a subtle "beep" to music or sound effects. In this section, you learn how to control the pitch and duration of a note produced by your computer's speaker. Although most compilers available today provide their own sound-producing function, the one developed here gives you full control over how sound is produced. (Also, it is interesting to see how sound is generated on a PC.) You will also see demonstrations of some of the interesting effects available to you.

Using the Programmable Timer

Without going into too many hardware details, it is sufficient to say that sound is generated on a PC by using one of its programmable timers. This timer is used to pulse the speaker on and off at a frequency determined by the contents of various internal registers. These registers are set by writing to certain ports. Port 66 is used to specify a count that the timer uses as an interval between speaker pulses. The timer operates by counting system clock pulses up to the specified count, pulsing the speaker, resetting, and counting up again. The value of the count is determined by the formula

count = 1,193,180 / desired frequency

where 1,193,180 is the speed at which the system clock oscillates.

The timer register is set using the following sequence:

1. Output to port 67 the value 182. This tells the timer that a count will follow.

2. Output to port 66 the low-order byte of the integer that contains the count.

3. Output to port 66 the high-order byte of the integer that contains the count.

The speaker in most PCs is not designed to reproduce the full range of human hearing (20-18,000 Hz). Instead, it plays some notes better than others and "tops out" at around 12,000 to 14,000 Hz. Its most practical range is 100-5000 Hz.

Once the timer is set, the speaker does not sound because it has not been turned on. The timer counts continuously, but the speaker responds only when it is turned on.

Turning on the speaker requires setting bits 0 and 1 of a register in a programmable peripheral interface circuit accessed through port 97. When these two bits are on, the speaker sounds at the current timer frequency.

When the bits are 0, no sound is heard. The other bits in the byte are used by other devices and must be left unaltered. Therefore, to set the speaker bits, the following sequence must be followed:

1. Input the current value at port 97.

2. OR that value with 3.

3. Output the result to port 97.

To turn off the speaker, AND the current value with 253.

The easiest way to read and write a port in C is to use functions that read and write a byte to or from a port. In Turbo C, these functions are called **inportb()** and **outportb()**. In Microsoft C, they are called **inp()** and **outp()**. They take the following prototypes:

int inportb(int *port*);
void outportb(int *port*, char *value*);
int inp(unsigned *port*);
int outp(unsigned *port*, int *value*);

These functions may not have the same name in every C compiler, but almost without fail, you will have functions similar to these in your library. The examples that follow use either the Microsoft or the Turbo C functions.

A Simple Hearing Tester

You can construct a crude but effective hearing tester that may disclose certain types of hearing loss. As stated earlier, the speaker in the average PC barely works past about 12,000 Hz. However, a person with acute hearing loss often cannot hear frequencies anywhere near that high. In fact, when you try the tester, you might be surprised at how high-pitched 12,000 Hz is. (*Caution:* This hearing tester is provided only for fun. It is by no means an accurate hearing test. If you suspect that you suffer from hearing loss, see your doctor.)

The heart of the hearing tester is the function **tone()**, which sounds a specified note of short duration. As presented here, this function also shows all the code necessary to produce sound on the speaker.

```
/* Beep the speaker using the specified frequency. */
void tone(int freq)
{
  unsigned long i;
  union {
    long divisor;
    unsigned char c[2];
  } count;

  unsigned char p;

  count.divisor = 1193280 / freq;  /* compute the proper count */
  outportb(67, 182); /* tell 8253 that a count is coming */
  outportb(66, count.c[0]); /* send low-order byte */
  outportb(66, count.c[1]); /* send high-order byte */
  p = inportb(97); /* get existing bit pattern */
  outportb(97, p | 3); /* turn on bits 0 and 1 */

  for(i=0; i<DELAY; ++i) ; /* delay loop */

  outportb(97, p); /* restore original bits to turn off speaker */
}
```

Notice that the frequency of the note to be reproduced is specified as an argument. The delay loop determines how long the specified tone is sounded. Without the delay, you would, at most, hear only a click. You can change the delay to suit the clock rate of the processor in your computer. You could even specify it as a parameter. The **tone()** function can also be used to supply a custom beep.

The **main()** function to the hearing tester program is shown here. Notice the commented **#define** statement. As shown, it uses Turbo C's **inportb()** and **outportb()** functions. If you uncomment the **#define**, it will substitute the equivalent Microsoft functions.

```
/* A simple hearing tester. */

#include "stdio.h"
#include "dos.h"

#define DELAY 100000

/*
If you use Microsoft C, include these #defines:
```

```
#define inportb inp
#define outportb outp
*/

void tone(int freq);

main(void)
{
  int freq;

  do {
    printf("enter frequency (0 to exit): ");
    scanf("%d", &freq);
    if(freq) tone(freq);
  } while(freq);

  return 0;
}
```

To use the tester, simply specify increasingly higher pitches until you cannot hear them anymore. To exit, enter a value of 0.

Creating a Siren and a "Laser Blast"

You can use the speaker to create sound effects such as those that might be applied to a video game. The key to most sound effects is to vary the frequency of the sound—often in some unusual way.

For example, to create a siren effect, you vary the frequency of the sound between two end points. The pitch should ascend from the low to the high and then descend back to the low pitch. The function **siren()**, shown here, uses this method to produce a siren-like effect:

```
#include "stdio.h"
#include "stdlib.h"
#include "dos.h"

#define DELAY 10000
#define RATE 10

/*
```

```
If you use Microsoft C, include these #defines:

#define inportb inp
#define outportb outp
*/

void siren(void);

main(void)
{
  siren();

  return 0;
}

/* Create a siren effect. */
void siren(void)
{
  unsigned freq;
  unsigned long i;
  union {
    long divisor;
    unsigned char c[2];
  } count;

  unsigned char p;

  p = inportb(97); /* get existing bit pattern */
  outportb(97, p | 3); /* turn on bits 0 and 1 */
  /* ascending siren */
  for(freq=1000; freq<3000; freq+=RATE) {
    count.divisor = 1193280 / freq;  /* compute the proper count */
    outportb(67, 182); /* tell 8253 that a count is coming */
    outportb(66, count.c[0]); /* send low-order byte */
    outportb(66, count.c[1]); /* send high-order byte */

    for(i=0; i<DELAY; ++i) ;
  }

  /* descending siren */
  for( ; freq>1000; freq-=RATE) {
    count.divisor = 1193280 / freq;  /* compute the proper count */
    outportb(67, 182); /* tell 8253 that a count is coming */
    outportb(66, count.c[0]); /* send low-order byte */
```

```
    outportb(66, count.c[1]); /* send high-order byte */

    for(i=0; i<DELAY; ++i) ;
  }
  outportb(97, p); /* restore original bits to turn off speaker */
}
```

You should define the macro **DELAY** to match the speed of your system and personal preferences. The value of **RATE** determines how quickly the pitch changes. As shown, **siren()** produces one full cycle and then returns. To create a continuous cycle, simply place the call to **siren()** in a loop.

To produce the laser blast sound effect used by many video games, modify **siren()** so that only a descending sound is heard. Also, you will need to experiment with the values of **DELAY** and **RATE** to produce the desired effect. The function **laser()** is shown here:

```
#include "stdio.h"
#include "stdlib.h"
#include "dos.h"

#define DELAY 5000
#define RATE 50

/*
If you use Microsoft C, include these #defines:

#define inportb inp
#define outportb outp
*/

void laser(void);

main(void)
{
  laser();
  laser();
  laser();
  laser();
  laser();

  return 0;
```

```
}

/* Create a laser blast effect. */
void laser(void)
{
  unsigned freq;
  unsigned long i;

  union {
    long divisor;
    unsigned char c[2];
  } count;

  unsigned char p;

  p = inportb(97); /* get existing bit pattern */
  outportb(97, p | 3); /* turn on bits 0 and 1 */
  /* laser blast */
  for(freq = 3000; freq>1000; freq-=RATE) {
    count.divisor = 1193280 / freq;  /* compute the proper count */
    outportb(67, 182); /* tell 8253 that count is coming */
    outportb(66, count.c[0]); /* send low-order byte */
    outportb(66, count.c[1]); /* send high-order byte */

    for(i=0; i<DELAY; ++i) ;
  }
  outportb(97, p); /* restore original bits to turn off speaker */
}
```

With a little ingenuity and experimentation, you can produce just about any type of effect you want. One thing to try is varying the rate of change as the effect is produced.

Making Celestial Music

By connecting the standard C random-number function **rand()** to the **tone()** function, you can create "celestial music." The sounds produced by the program shown here are reminiscent of the "space music" used in old science fiction movies. Although all the tones are generated at random, bits and pieces of melodies emerge from time to time in a most haunting fashion.

```
/* Celestial Music of the Cosmic Spheres. */

#include "dos.h"
#include "stdio.h"
#include "conio.h"
#include "stdlib.h"

#define DELAY 64000

/*
If you use Microsoft C, include these #defines:

#define inportb inp
#define outportb outp
*/

void tone(int freq);

main(void)
{
  int freq;

  do {
    do {
      freq = rand();
    } while(freq>5000); /* alter to your personal taste */
    tone(freq);
  } while(!kbhit());

  return 9;
}

/* Beep the speaker using the specified frequency. */
void tone(int freq)
{
  unsigned long i;
  union {
    long divisor;
    unsigned char c[2];
  } count;

  unsigned char p;

  count.divisor = 1193280 / freq;  /* compute the proper count */
  outportb(67, 182); /* tell 8253 that count is coming */
```

```
outportb(66, count.c[0]); /* send low-order byte */
outportb(66, count.c[1]); /* send high-order byte */
p = inportb(97); /* get existing bit pattern */
outportb(97, p ¦ 3); /* turn on bits 0 and 1 */

for(i=0; i<DELAY; ++i) ;

outportb(97, p); /* restore original bits to turn off speaker */
}
```

The program uses frequencies less than 5000 because higher frequencies are either very soft or are outside the average hearing range.

You should experiment with this program because it's really quite fascinating. There are three things especially you'll want to try: allow a random length of time between notes; filter the values actually sent to **tone()** in different ways; and adjust the value of **DELAY** to suit your personal preference.

CHAPTER NINE

Interfacing to the Mouse

After the keyboard, the most popular input device for microcomputers is the mouse. Although the mouse and similar technologies, such as the roller ball, have been available for some time, the mouse became popular with the advent of the Apple Lisa, which came with a mouse and an icon interface to its operating system. The Lisa eventually evolved into the Macintosh, which kept the mouse and icon interface. Prior to the advent of the IBM PS/2 line of computers, the mouse had been a third-party add-on to the PC. However, with the introduction of the IBM PS/2 system, which offers a mouse port and mouse, and the release of Windows and DOS 5, both of which include mouse support, the mouse has found an important place in the PC environment.

Several types and brands of mice are available, and some function differently from others. The routines in this chapter use the Microsoft two-button mouse, which is functionally identical to the IBM PS/2 mouse.

DAVE BURNS

Dave Burns is the project manager for Solution Systems' BRIEF for Windows. As you may know, BRIEF is one of the most popular programming editors in the world. It was initially created by Dave Nanian and Mike Strickman. It is Dave's task to guide BRIEF's transition to the Windows environment. Dave is a veteran programmer and manager who has also worked on software tools at Phoenix Technologies and on both Lotus Express and Agenda at Lotus Development Corporation.

Dave told me why he liked the C language. "What is great about C is how much was left out. Useless distractions like nested procedures and language-defined I/O don't clutter the compiler or your code. C helps programmers write great programs because it's not in their way," he said.

I asked Dave how he manages his team of programmers. He responded, "The best software is designed by one or two people at most. But that doesn't mean that managers like myself should hoard all the design decisions to ourselves. I try to control the design through intelligence and persuasion, because any design imposed by force will be bad. My job as manager is to help my team create the best functional design we can and then keep myself and the rest of the company out of the way while they implement it in code." Since C programmers are a notoriously independent lot, Dave's approach makes sense.

I asked Dave to name one of his favorite C programs. He said, "Well, right now I'm really excited about BRIEF. This code was written back in 1984 and was optimized to run on a 192K machine. Yet, Dave Nanian and Mike Strickman's architecture is incredibly forward-looking. The display code, for instance, is completely isolated from the editing code. This is the kind of architecture that is more easily supported by an object-oriented language, but here it was implemented by the intelligence and discipline of the initial design."

Dave Burns currently lives in Cambridge, Massachusetts.

SOME MOUSE BASICS

Before the mouse can be used, its device driver must be installed. For the Microsoft mouse, the line of code that is shown here must be put in the CONFIG.SYS file.

```
device = mouse.sys
```

Alternatively, the program MOUSE.COM can be executed instead. For this mouse, place the line shown here in the AUTOEXEC.BAT file:

```
mouse
```

Either way, the device driver is installed.

Once the mouse driver is in place, whenever you move the mouse or press a button an interrupt, 0x33, is generated. The mouse driver processes the interrupt, setting the appropriate internal variables and returns. Because an interrupt is generated only when the mouse changes state, an idle mouse has no effect on the performance of the computer.

Just as a cursor is associated with the keyboard, a cursor (sometimes called a *pointer*) is associated with the mouse. The mouse pointer is an arrow in the graphics modes and a solid block in the text modes. The cursor shows the current mouse position on the screen. Like the keyboard cursor, the mouse cursor can be turned on or off.

Although physically separate, the mouse can be thought of as being linked to the screen because the mouse driver automatically maintains counters that indicate where the mouse cursor is currently located. As you move the mouse, the cursor automatically moves across the screen in the same direction as the mouse.

The distance traveled by the mouse is measured in *mickeys*. One mickey equals 1/200th of an inch. For the most part, however, you will not need to know the actual distance moved by the mouse.

THE VIRTUAL VERSUS THE ACTUAL SCREEN

The mouse device driver operates on a *virtual screen* with pixel dimensions that may be different from the actual physical screen. As the mouse is moved, the cursor location counters are updated. When the cursor is displayed on the screen, the virtual cursor coordinates are mapped onto the actual screen coordinates. In video modes 6, 14, 15, 16, 17, and 18, this is a one-to-one mapping. In modes 4 and 5, only every other point of the virtual horizontal position is mapped to the actual screen. This means that the size of the virtual screen in mode 4 graphics is 640x200. To translate the X virtual coordinate into a screen coordinate, you divide the virtual coordinate by 2. You must keep this fact in mind because the paint program to which the mouse interface will be added uses mode 4 graphics.

ACCESSING THE MOUSE DEVICE DRIVER

The mouse device driver is accessed by using interrupt 0x33. It contains 35 functions that are selected by the value of the AX register. (This is somewhat similar to the way you access DOS or BIOS functions.) While some mouse functions require no extra parameters, several take up to three. The extra parameters are specified in the BX, CX, and DX registers, respectively. When the mouse interrupt returns, any information that a specific mouse function generates is returned in the AX, BX, CX, and DX registers. The mouse interrupt will be executed by using the **int86()** function.

Of the 35 mouse functions defined by Microsoft, only a few are needed by the paint program. A brief discussion of these follows.

Reset and Status

Function 0 resets the mouse. It places the mouse in the center of the screen with the cursor turned off. It returns the number of buttons the mouse has in BX. Upon return, AX will be 0 if the mouse and software are not installed and −1 if they are.

Display Cursor

Function 1 displays the mouse cursor. There are no return values.

Remove Cursor

Function 2 removes the cursor from the screen. There are no return values.

Read Button Status and Cursor Position

Function 3 returns the status of the buttons in BX. The virtual horizontal cursor position is in CX and the virtual vertical cursor position is in DX.

The status of the buttons is encoded in BX in bits 0 and 1. When bit 0 is set, the left button is being pressed; when bit 1 is set, the right button is being pressed. When a bit is off, its associated button is not being pressed.

Set Cursor Location

Function 4 sets the mouse cursor location. The value of CX determines the horizontal position, and the value of DX sets the vertical position. You must make sure that only valid values within the range of the virtual screen are used.

Motion Indication

Function 11 returns the vertical and horizontal mickey count since the last call to function 11. It also resets its internal counting registers to 0. The horizontal count is returned in CX and the vertical count in DX. This means that if the mouse has not been moved since the last call, both the horizontal and vertical counts will be 0. If either count (or both counts) is any value other than 0, the mouse has moved.

A positive vertical mickey count means that the mouse has moved downward. A negative count indicates that the mouse has moved upward. A positive horizontal count means that the mouse moved to the right. A negative count indicates that the mouse moved to the left.

THE HIGH-LEVEL MOUSE FUNCTIONS

Using the mouse interrupts just described, you can construct a set of high-level C routines that make programming for the mouse much easier. Let's look at these now.

Resetting the Mouse

The function shown here, **mouse_reset()**, resets the mouse. Notice that it confirms that the proper hardware and software are present and that a two-button mouse is installed.

```
/* Reset the mouse. */
void mouse_reset(void)
{
  union REGS r;

  r.x.ax = 0; /* reset the mouse */
  int86(0x33, &r, &r);
  if((int) r.x.ax != -1) {
    printf("mouse hardware or software not installed");
    exit(1);
  }
  if(r.x.bx != 2) {
   printf("two-button mouse required");
    exit(1);
  }
}
```

Displaying and Removing the Mouse Cursor

The companion functions **cursor_on()** and **cursor_off()**, shown here, activate and deactivate the visual mouse cursor:

```
/* Turn off the mouse cursor. */
void cursor_off(void)
{
  union REGS r;

  r.x.ax = 2; /* remove the cursor */
  int86(0x33, &r, &r);
}

/* Turn on the mouse cursor. */
void cursor_on(void)
{
  union REGS r;
```

```
   r.x.ax = 1; /* show the cursor */
   int86(0x33, &r, &r);
}
```

Determining if a Button Is Pressed

Another pair of companion functions, **rightb_pressed()** and **leftb_pressed()**, shown here, return true if the right button or left button is pressed.

```
/* Return true if right button is pressed,
   false otherwise. */
rightb_pressed(void)
{
  union REGS r;

  r.x.ax = 3; /* get position and button status */
  int86(0x33, &r, &r);
  return r.x.bx & 2;
}

/* Return true if left button is pressed,
   false otherwise. */
leftb_pressed(void)
{
  union REGS r;

  r.x.ax = 3; /* get position and button status */
  int86(0x33, &r, &r);
  return r.x.bx & 1;
}
```

Detecting Motion

Function 11, which returns the change in the mickey count since the last call, detects mouse motion. The function **mouse_motion()**, shown here, returns the change in the horizontal and vertical directions in variables pointed to by its arguments. If both **deltax** and **deltay** are 0, no motion has occurred.

```
/* Return the direction of travel. */
void mouse_motion(char *deltax, char *deltay)
{
  union REGS r;

  r.x.ax = 11; /* get direction of motion */
  int86(0x33, &r, &r);

  if(r.x.cx>0) *deltax = RIGHT;
  else if(r.x.cx<0) *deltax = LEFT;
  else *deltax = NOT_MOVED;

  if(r.x.dx>0) *deltay = DOWN;
  else if(r.x.dx<0) *deltay = UP;
  else *deltay = NOT_MOVED;
}
```

The macros **RIGHT, LEFT, UP, DOWN,** and **NOT_MOVED** are defined as shown here:

```
#define NOT_MOVED 0
#define RIGHT     1
#define LEFT      2
#define UP        3
#define DOWN      4
```

Reading and Setting the Cursor Position

The functions **set_mouse_position()** and **mouse_position()**, shown here, set and read the current position of the mouse:

```
/* Set mouse cursor coordinates. */
void set_mouse_position(int x, int y)
{
  union REGS r;

  r.x.ax = 4; /* set position */
  r.x.cx = x;
  r.x.dx = y;
  int86(0x33, &r, &r);
}
```

```
/* Return mouse cursor coordinates. */
void mouse_position(int *x, int *y)
{
  union REGS r;

  r.x.ax = 3; /* get position and button status */
  int86(0x33, &r, &r);
  *x = r.x.cx;
  *y = r.x.dx;
}
```

A Simple Demonstration Program

The program shown here demonstrates the use of the high-level mouse functions. You should enter it into your computer now.

```
/* Interfacing to the Microsoft/IBM mouse. */

#include "dos.h"
#include "stdio.h"
#include "stdlib.h"

#define NOT_MOVED 0
#define RIGHT     1
#define LEFT      2
#define UP        3
#define DOWN      4

void mouse(int *ax, int *bx, int *cx, int *dx);
void set_mouse_position(int x, int y);
void cursor_off(void), cursor_on(void);
void mouse_position(int *x, int *y);
void mouse_motion(char *deltax, char *deltay);
void mouse_reset(void), read_mouse(void);
int leftb_pressed(void), rightb_pressed(void);

void goto_xy(int x, int y);
void mode(int mode_code);

main(int argc, char *argv[])
{
```

```
char deltax, deltay;
int x, y;

if(argc!=2) {
  printf("usage:mouser <video mode>");
  exit(1);
}
mode(atoi(argv[1]));

mouse_reset(); /* initialize the mouse */
cursor_on(); /* turn on the cursor */

do {
  goto_xy(0, 0);
  if(leftb_pressed()) printf("left button ");
  if(rightb_pressed()) printf("right button");

  /* show mouse location */
  mouse_position(&x, &y);
  goto_xy(0, 2);
  printf(" %d %d - ", x, y);
  goto_xy(0, 0);

  /* see if change in position */
  mouse_motion(&deltax, &deltay);
  if(deltax || deltay) {
    printf("X Direction: ");
    switch(deltax) {
      case NOT_MOVED: printf("      ");
        break;
      case RIGHT: printf("right ");
        break;
      case LEFT: printf("left  ");
        break;
    }
    printf("Y Direction: ");
    switch(deltay) {
      case NOT_MOVED: printf("      ");
        break;
      case UP: printf("up    ");
        break;
      case DOWN: printf("down  ");
        break;
    }
  }
```

```
  /* loop until both buttons are pressed at the same time */
  } while(!(leftb_pressed() && rightb_pressed()));
  mode(3);

  return 0;
}

/* Set the video mode. */
void mode(int mode_code)
{
  union REGS r;

  r.h.al = mode_code;
  r.h.ah = 0;
  int86(0x10, &r, &r);
}

/* Send the cursor to the specified X,Y position. */
void goto_xy(int x, int y)
{
  union REGS r;

  r.h.ah = 2; /* cursor addressing function */
  r.h.dl = x; /* column coordinate */
  r.h.dh = y; /* row coordinate */
  r.h.bh = 0; /* video page */
  int86(0x10, &r, &r);
}


/*********************************************/
/* Mouse interface functions.               */
/*********************************************/

/* Turn off the mouse cursor. */
void cursor_off(void)
{
  union REGS r;

  r.x.ax = 2; /* remove the cursor */
  int86(0x33, &r, &r);
}

/* Turn on the mouse cursor. */
void cursor_on(void)
{
  union REGS r;
```

```
  r.x.ax = 1; /* show the cursor */
  int86(0x33, &r, &r);
}

/* Return true if right button is pressed,
   false otherwise. */
rightb_pressed(void)
{
  union REGS r;

  r.x.ax = 3; /* get position and button status */
  int86(0x33, &r, &r);
  return r.x.bx & 2;
}

/* Return true if left button is pressed,
   false otherwise. */
leftb_pressed(void)
{
  union REGS r;

  r.x.ax = 3; /* get position and button status */
  int86(0x33, &r, &r);
  return r.x.bx & 1;
}

/* Set mouse cursor coordinates. */
void set_mouse_position(int x, int y)
{
  union REGS r;

  r.x.ax = 4; /* set position */
  r.x.cx = x;
  r.x.dx = y;
  int86(0x33, &r, &r);
}

/* Return mouse cursor coordinates. */
void mouse_position(int *x, int *y)
{
  union REGS r;

  r.x.ax = 3; /* get position and button status */
```

```
    int86(0x33, &r, &r);
    *x = r.x.cx;
    *y = r.x.dx;
}

/* Return the direction of travel. */
void mouse_motion(char *deltax, char *deltay)
{
    union REGS r;

    r.x.ax = 11; /* get direction of motion */
    int86(0x33, &r, &r);

    if(r.x.cx>0) *deltax = RIGHT;
    else if(r.x.cx<0) *deltax = LEFT;
    else *deltax = NOT_MOVED;

    if(r.x.dx>0) *deltay = DOWN;
    else if(r.x.dx<0) *deltay = UP;
    else *deltay = NOT_MOVED;
}

/* Reset the mouse. */
void mouse_reset(void)
{
    union REGS r;

    r.x.ax = 0; /* reset the mouse */
    int86(0x33, &r, &r);
    if((int) r.x.ax != -1) {
        printf("mouse hardware or software not installed");
        exit(1);
    }
    if(r.x.bx != 2) {
        printf("two-button mouse required");
        exit(1);
    }
}
```

To use the program, specify on the command line the number of the video mode that you wish to use. The program reports the direction that the mouse travels and also reports when a button is pressed. In addition, the program shows the current X,Y position. Pressing both buttons terminates the program. You should try this program using different video modes to see the effect.

INTEGRATING MOUSE INPUT INTO THE PAINT PROGRAM

This section develops the routines that allow the mouse to control the paint program developed in Chapter 4. The mouse interface will be added to the existing control routines rather than substituted for them. This means that the arrow keys will still be 100 percent functional, and the user will be able to choose the best input device for the situation.

Before the mouse can be integrated into the paint program, it is necessary to develop two additional mouse-related routines. The first, **wait_on()**, waits until the specified button is released. This function is needed because pressing a button causes interrupts to be continuously generated until the button is released. (It is impossible to press the button quickly enough to generate only one interrupt.) In many routines, it is important to avoid this situation and make each button press generate (or rather, appear to generate) only one interrupt until it is released. To accomplish this, your routines must call **wait_on()**, shown here, before continuing after a button press:

```
/* Return 1 when specified button released. */
void wait_on(int button)
{
  if(button==LEFTB)
    while(leftb_pressed()) ;
  else
    while(rightb_pressed()) ;
}
```

The macros **LEFTB** and **RIGHTB**, shown here, should be used when calling **wait_on()**:

```
#define LEFTB    1
#define RIGHTB   2
```

The second required routine is called **mouse_menu()**. This routine displays a one-line menu and allows the user to make a selection by moving the mouse to the appropriate item and pressing either button. The function is passed a two-dimensional character array that holds the menu selections, the number of selections, and the X,Y position to display the menu. The character array allows each item in the list a maximum length of 19 characters. It returns the number of the selection beginning with 0, or −1 if no selection is made. When the function begins, it computes the length, in pixels, of each menu item and stores the pixel location of the beginning and ending horizontal pixel position of each in the array **len**. (In mode 4 graphics, each character is 16 pixels wide and 8 pixels high.) After this computation, the function waits until a button is pressed and then checks to see if the mouse is pointing to a menu selection. If it is, the number of that selection is returned to the calling routine. The **mouse_menu()** function is shown here:

```
/* Display a one-line mouse menu and return selection. */
mouse_menu(int count, /* number of menu items */
          char item[][20], /* menu items */
          int x, int y) /* display position */
{
  int i, len[MENU_MAX][2], t;
  int mousex, mousey;

  goto_xy(x, y);
  t = 0;
  for(i=0; i<count; i++) {
   printf("%s  ", item[i]);
   len[i][0] = t;
   len[i][1] = t + strlen(item[i])*16;
   t = len[i][1] + 32;
  }

  do {
    if(rightb_pressed() ¦¦ leftb_pressed()) break;
  } while(!kbhit());
  /* wait until button not pressed */
  while(rightb_pressed() ¦¦ leftb_pressed()) ;

  mouse_position(&mousex, &mousey);

  /* see if mouse cursor is on a menu selection */
  if(mousey >= 0 && mousey < 8)
    for(i=0; i<count; i++) {
      if(mousex > len[i][0] && mousex < len[i][1])
        return i;
    }
  return -1; /* no selection made */
}
```

The Main Loop

Although most of the original code to the paint program remains un-changed, the **main()** function, shown here, is significantly altered to ac-commodate the mouse routines:

```
main(void)
{
  char done = 0;

  mode(4);  /* switch to mode 4 graphics */
  palette(0); /* palette 0 */

  mouse_reset(); /* initialize the mouse */

  xhairs(x, y); /* show the cross hairs */
  set_mouse_position(x*2, y); /* set initial mouse position */
  do {
    /* see if mouse has been moved */
    mouse_motion(&deltax, &deltay);
    if(deltax || deltay) read_mouse();
    /* check for button press */
    if(leftb_pressed() || rightb_pressed())
      read_mouse();
    if(kbhit()) {
      done = read_kb();
      /* reposition mouse to match new cross hairs location */
      set_mouse_position(x*2, y);
    }
  } while (!done);
  mode(3);

  return 0;
}
```

As you can see, except for **done, main()** has no local variables. Instead, all the control and counter variables necessary to the operation of the program have been made global so that both the keyboard and mouse routines can access them without having to be passed a large number of arguments. As you can see, the status of the mouse and the keyboard are monitored inside the loop. Whenever the state of either device changes, the appropriate function is called. Note that the mouse cursor is not turned on. Instead, during the drawing part of the program, the cross hairs are used to show the current screen position. The mouse cursor is activated only when a menu selection is made.

The **read_kb()** function, which processes keyboard input, is shown here. It is basically the same as in the original program.

```
/* Read and process a keyboard command. */
read_kb(void)
{
  union k{
    char c[2];
    int i;
  } key;

  key.i = readkey();
  xhairs(x, y);   /* erase the cross hairs */
  if(!key.c[0]) switch(key.c[1]) {
    case 75: /* left */
      if(on_flag) line(x, y, x-inc, y, cc);
      x -= inc;
      break;
    case 77: /* right */
      if(on_flag) line(x, y, x+inc, y, cc);
      x += inc;
      break;
    case 72: /* up */
      if(on_flag) line(x, y, x, y-inc, cc);
      y -= inc;
      break;
    case 80: /* down */
      if(on_flag) line(x, y, x, y+inc, cc);
      y += inc;
      break;
    case 71: /* up left */
      if(on_flag) line(x, y, x-inc, y-inc, cc);
      x -= inc; y -= inc;
      break;
    case 73: /* up right */
      if(on_flag) line(x, y, x+inc, y-inc, cc);
      x += inc; y -= inc;
      break;
    case 79: /* down left*/
      if(on_flag) line(x, y, x-inc, y+inc, cc);
      x -= inc; y += inc;
      break;
```

```
      case 81: /* down right */
        if(on_flag) line(x, y, x+inc, y+inc, cc);
        x += inc; y += inc;
        break;
      case 59: inc = 1;  /* F1 - slow speed */
        break;
      case 60: inc = 5;  /* F2 - fast speed */
        break;
    }
    else switch(tolower(key.c[0])) {
      case 'o': on_flag = !on_flag; /* toggle brush */
        break;
      case '1': cc = 1; /* color 1 */
        break;
      case '2': cc = 2; /* color 2 */
        break;
      case '3': cc = 3; /* color 3 */
        break;
      case '0': cc = 0; /* color 0 */
        break;
      case 'b': box(startx, starty, endx, endy, cc);
        break;
      case 'f': fill_box(startx, starty, endx, endy, cc);
        break;
      case 'l': line(startx, starty, endx, endy, cc);
        break;
      case 'c':
        if(starty < endy)
          circle(startx, starty, endy-starty, cc);
        else
          circle(startx, starty, starty-endy, cc);
        break;
      case 'h':
        if(starty < endy)
          fill_circle(startx, starty, endy-starty, cc);
        else
          fill_circle(startx, starty, starty-endy, cc);
        break;
      case 's': save_pic();
        break;
      case 'r': load_pic();
        break;
      case 'm': /* move a region */
        move(startx, starty, endx, endy, x, y);
```

```
        break;
    case 'x': /* copy a region */
        copy(startx, starty, endx, endy, x, y);
        break;
    case 'd':  /* define an object to rotate */
        sides = define_object(object, x, y);
        break;
    case 'a': /* rotate the object */
        rotate_object(object, 0.05, x, y, sides);
        break;
    case '\r': /* set end points for line, circle, or box */
        if(first_point) {
            startx = x; starty = y;
        }
        else {
            endx = x; endy = y;
        }
        first_point = !first_point;
        break;
    case 'p': pal_num = pal_num==1 ? 2:1;
        palette(pal_num);
    }
    xhairs(x, y); /* redisplay the cross hairs */

    if(tolower(key.c[0])=='q') return 1;
    return 0;
}
```

The **read_mouse()** function, which processes mouse input, is shown
here:

```
/* Read and process mouse input. */
void read_mouse(void)
{
    int oldx, oldy;
    int choice;

    oldx = x; oldy = y;
    xhairs(x, y); /* erase from current position */

    /* press both buttons to activate mouse menu */
    if(rightb_pressed() && leftb_pressed()) {
        choice = menu(); /* get mouse menu selection */
        switch(choice) {
```

```
        case 0: box(startx, starty, endx, endy, cc);
          break;
        case 1:
          if(starty < endy)
            circle(startx, starty, endy-starty, cc);
          else
            circle(startx, starty, starty-endy, cc);
          break;
        case 2: line(startx, starty, endx, endy, cc);
          break;
        case 3: fill_box(startx, starty, endx, endy, cc);
          break;
        case 4:
          if(starty < endy)
            fill_circle(startx, starty, endy-starty, cc);
          else
            fill_circle(startx, starty, starty-endy, cc);
          break;
      }
    }
    /* right button defines end points for shapes */
    else if(rightb_pressed()) {
      if(first_point) {
        startx = x; starty = y;
      }
      else {
        endx = x; endy = y;
      }
      first_point = !first_point;
      wait_on(RIGHTB); /* wait until button released */
    }

    if(deltax || deltay) {
      mouse_position(&x, &y);
      x = x / 2; /* normalize virtual screen coordinates */

      /* press left button to draw */
      if(leftb_pressed()) mouse_on_flag = 1;
      else mouse_on_flag = 0;
      if(mouse_on_flag) line(oldx, oldy, x, y, cc);
    }
    xhairs(x, y); /* redisplay cross hairs */
}
```

The **read_mouse()** function works as follows. First it checks to see if both buttons are pressed. If they are, the mouse menu is activated by calling **menu()**, which sets up the call to **mouse_menu()**. If a menu selection is made, the appropriate action is taken. As currently implemented, the mouse menu allows only boxes, circles, lines, and fills to be selected by the mouse. (You might also want to allow the mouse to select color and palette.)

The right button is used to define the end points of lines, boxes, and circles exactly the same as the ENTER key, which is used for the same purpose. Simply position the mouse at the first end point of the object and press the button. Next, move the mouse to the location of the second end point and press the button again.

When the left button is not pressed, the mouse can be moved around the screen without leaving a trail; that is, the default state of the mouse is pen up. To cause the mouse to write to the screen, you must press the left button. While the button is pressed, the pen is down.

Finally, if the mouse has moved, the X,Y counters are updated.

The **menu()** function, shown here, sets up a call to **mouse_menu()**:

```c
/* Display a menu. */
menu(void)
{
  register int i, j;

  /* pointer to mode 4 graphics RAM */
  char far *ptr = (char far *) 0xB8000000;

  char far *temp;
  unsigned char buf[14][80]; /* hold the contents of screen */
  int choice;
  char items[][20] = {
    "BOX",
    "CIRCLE",
    "LINE",
    "FILL BOX",
    "FILL CIRCLE"
  };

  temp = ptr;
  /* save the top of the current screen */
  for(i=0; i<14; i++)
    for(j=0; j<80; j+=2) {
      buf[i][j] = *temp; /* even byte */
      buf[i][j+1] = *(temp+8152); /* odd byte */
      *temp = 0; *(temp+8152) = 0;  /* clear top of screen */
      temp++;
```

```
    }

  goto_xy(0, 0);
  /* wait until last button press has cleared */
  while(rightb_pressed() || leftb_pressed()) ;
  cursor_on();

  choice = mouse_menu(5, items, 0, 0);

  cursor_off();
  temp = ptr;
  /* restore the top of the current screen */
  for(i=0; i<14; i++)
    for(j=0; j<80; j+=2) {
      *temp = buf[i][j];
      *(temp+8152) = buf[i][j+1];
      temp++;
    }
  return choice;
}
```

The function operates by first saving the top of the screen and then making sure that neither button is pressed. It then turns on the mouse cursor and calls **mouse_menu()**. Upon return from **mouse_menu()**, the cursor is turned off, the top of the screen is restored, and the function returns the value of the selection.

Defining Objects with the Mouse

The original paint program allowed an object to be defined, using the **define_object()** function, by specifying the end points of each line segment. Once the object is defined, it can then be rotated. The version of **define_object()** shown here allows the mouse to select the end points of the object as well:

```
/* Define an object by specifying its end points using
   either the mouse or the keyboard. */
define_object(double ob[][5], int x, int y)
{

  union k{
    char c[2];
```

```
   int i;
} key;
register int i, j;

/* pointer to mode 4 graphics RAM */
char far *ptr = (char far *) 0xB8000000;

char far *temp;
unsigned char buf[14][80]; /* hold the contents of screen */
int sides = 0;
char deltax, deltay;
int oldx, oldy;

temp = ptr;
/* save the top of the current screen */
for(i=0; i<14; i++)
  for(j=0; j<80; j+=2) {
    buf[i][j] = *temp;
    buf[i][j+1] = *(temp+8152);
    *temp = 0; *(temp+8152) = 0; /* clear the top of the screen */
    temp++;
  }

i = 0;
key.i = 0;
xhairs(x, y);
do {
  goto_xy(0, 0);
  printf("Define side %d,", sides+1);
  if(i==0) printf(" enter first end point");
  else printf(" enter second end point");

  do {
    /* mouse additions ****************************/
    /* see if mouse has moved */
    mouse_motion(&deltax, &deltay);
    /* use left button to define a point */
    if(leftb_pressed()) {
      xhairs(x, y);    /* erase the cross hairs */
      /* store coordinates of the point */
      ob[sides][i++] = (double) x;
      ob[sides][i++] = (double) y;
      if(i==4) {
        ob[sides][4] = read_point(x, y); /* get color */
        i = 0;
```

```
      sides++;
    }
    break;
  }
} while(!kbhit() && !deltax && !deltay);
if(leftb_pressed()) wait_on(LEFTB);

if(deltax || deltay) {
  /* if mouse moved, update position */
  oldx = x; oldy = y;
  mouse_position(&x, &y);
  x = x / 2; /* normalize virtual screen coordinates */
  xhairs(oldx, oldy);   /* erase the cross hairs */
}
/* end of mouse code ******************************/
else if(kbhit()) {
  key.i = readkey();
  xhairs(x, y);   /* plot the cross hairs */
  if(key.c[0]=='\r') {
    /* use RETURN to define a point */
    ob[sides][i++] = (double) x;
    ob[sides][i++] = (double) y;
    if(i==4) {
      ob[sides][4] = read_point(x, y); /* get color */
      i = 0;
      sides++;
    }
  }
  /* if arrow key, move the cross hairs */
  if(!key.c[0]) switch(key.c[1]) {
    case 75: /* left */
      x -= 1;
      break;
    case 77: /* right */
      x += 1;
      break;
    case 72: /* up */
      y -= 1;
      break;
    case 80: /* down */
      y += 1;
      break;
    case 71: /* up left */
      x -= 1; y -= 1;
```

```
          break;
        case 73: /* up right */
          y -= 1; x += 1;
          break;
        case 79: /* down left*/
          y += 1; x -= 1;
          break;
        case 81: /* down right */
          y += 1; x += 1;
          break;
      }
    }
  if(key.c[1]!=59) xhairs(x, y);
} while(key.c[1] != 59); /* F1 to stop */

  temp = ptr;
  /* restore the top of the current screen */
  for(i=0; i<14; i++)
    for(j=0; j<80; j+=2) {
      *temp = buf[i][j];
      *(temp+8152) = buf[i][j+1];
      temp++;
    }
  return sides;
}
```

As you can see, the left button is used to select the end points. The mouse
motion code is the same as in the **read_mouse()** function. Aside from the
addition of the mouse input code, the function is unchanged. To define a
point, move the mouse to the proper location and press the button.

The Entire Revised Paint Program

The code to the entire paint program is shown here:

```
/* This version of the paint program allows
   the use of a Microsoft/IBM mouse as an
   alternate input device.
 */

#include "dos.h"
```

```
#include "stdio.h"
#include "math.h"
#include "conio.h"
#include "stdlib.h"
#include "ctype.h"
#include "string.h"

#define NUM_SIDES 20 /* Number of sides an object may
                        have. Enlarge as needed */
#define NOT_MOVED 0
#define RIGHT     1
#define LEFT      2
#define UP        3
#define DOWN      4


#define LEFTB    1
#define RIGHTB   2


#define MENU_MAX 20 /* number of mouse menu items */

#define XMAX 319
#define YMAX 199


void line(int startx, int starty, int endx, int endy,
        int color);
void box(int startx, int starty, int endx, int endy,
        int color);
void fill_box(int startx, int starty, int endx, int endy,
        int color);
void circle(int x_center, int y_center, int radius, int color);
void fill_circle(int x_center, int y_center, int radius,
                int color);
void plot_circle(int x, int y, int x_center, int y_center,
                int color);
void mempoint(int x, int y, int color);
void palette(int pnum);
void mode(int mode_code);
void rotate_point(double theta, double *x, double *y,
                int x_org, int y_org);
void display_object(double ob[][5], int lines);
void rotate_object(double ob[][5], double theta,
                int x, int y, int lines);
void move(int startx, int starty, int endx, int endy,
        int x, int y);
void copy(int startx, int starty, int endx, int endy,
```

```
             int x, int y);
void xhairs(int x, int y), goto_xy(int x, int y);
void save_pic(void), load_pic(void);
int define_object(double ob[][5], int x, int y);
int readkey(void);

void set_mouse_position(int x, int y);
void cursor_off(void), cursor_on(void);
void mouse_position(int *x, int *y);
void mouse_motion(char *deltax, char *deltay);
void mouse_reset(void),  wait_on(int button);
int mouse_menu(int count, char item[][20], int x, int y);
int menu(void), leftb_pressed(void), rightb_pressed(void);
void read_mouse(void);
int read_kb(void);

unsigned char read_point();

/* This array will hold the coordinates of an object
   defined dynamically.
*/
double object[NUM_SIDES][5];

double asp_ratio; /* holds aspect ratio for cirlces */

int x = 10, y = 10; /* current screen position */
int cc = 2; /* current color */
int on_flag = 1, mouse_on_flag = 0; /* pen on or off */
int pal_num = 1; /* palette number */
/* the end points of a defined line, circle, or box */
int startx=0, starty=0, endx=0, endy=0, first_point=1;
int inc = 1; /* movement increment */
int sides = 0; /* number of sides of a defined object */
char deltax, deltay; /* mouse change in position indicators */

main(void)
{
  char done = 0;

  mode(4);  /* switch to mode 4 graphics */
  palette(0); /* palette 0 */

  mouse_ reset(); /* initialize the mouse */

  xhairs(x, y); /* show the cross hairs */
  set_mouse_position(x*2, y); /* set initial mouse position */
```

```
  do {
    /* see if mouse has been moved */
    mouse_motion(&deltax, &deltay);
    if(deltax || deltay) read_mouse();
    /* check for button press */
    if(leftb_pressed() || rightb_pressed())
      read_mouse();
    if(kbhit()) {
      done = read_kb();
      /* reposition mouse to match new cross hairs location */
      set_mouse_position(x*2, y);
    }
  } while (!done);
  mode(3);

  return 0;
}

/* Read and process mouse input. */
void read_mouse(void)
{
  int oldx, oldy;
  int choice;

  oldx = x; oldy = y;
  xhairs(x, y); /* erase from current position */

  /* press both buttons to activate mouse menu */
  if(rightb_pressed() && leftb_pressed()) {
    choice = menu(); /* get mouse menu selection */
    switch(choice) {
      case 0: box(startx, starty, endx, endy, cc);
        break;
      case 1:
        if(starty < endy)
          circle(startx, starty, endy-starty, cc);
        else
          circle(startx, starty, starty-endy, cc);
        break;
      case 2: line(startx, starty, endx, endy, cc);
        break;
      case 3: fill_box(startx, starty, endx, endy, cc);
        break;
      case 4:
        if(starty < endy)
```

```
          fill_circle(startx, starty, endy-starty, cc);
        else
          fill_circle(startx, starty, starty-endy, cc);
        break;
    }
  }
  /* right button defines end points for shapes */
  else if(rightb_pressed()) {
    if(first_point) {
      startx = x; starty = y;
    }
    else {
      endx = x; endy = y;
    }
    first_point = !first_point;
    wait_on(RIGHTB); /* wait until button released */
  }

  if(deltax ¦¦ deltay) {
    mouse_position(&x, &y);
    x = x / 2; /* normalize virtual screen coordinates */
    /* press left button to draw */
    if(leftb_pressed()) mouse_on_flag = 1;
    else mouse_on_flag = 0;
    if(mouse_on_flag) line(oldx, oldy, x, y, cc);
  }
  xhairs(x, y); /* redisplay cross hairs */
}

/* Read and process a keyboard command. */
read_kb(void)
{
  union k{
    char c[2];
    int i;
  } key;

  key.i = readkey();
  xhairs(x, y);    /* erase the cross hairs */
  if(!key.c[0]) switch(key.c[1]) {
    case 75: /* left */
      if(on_flag) line(x, y, x-inc, y, cc);
      x -= inc;
      break;
    case 77: /* right */
```

```
      if(on_flag) line(x, y, x+inc, y, cc);
      x += inc;
      break;
    case 72: /* up */
      if(on_flag) line(x, y, x, y-inc, cc);
      y -= inc;
      break;
    case 80: /* down */
      if(on_flag) line(x, y, x, y+inc, cc);
      y += inc;
      break;
    case 71: /* up left */
      if(on_flag) line(x, y, x-inc, y-inc, cc);
      x -= inc; y -= inc;
      break;
    case 73: /* up right */
      if(on_flag) line(x, y, x+inc, y-inc, cc);
      x += inc; y -= inc;
      break;
    case 79: /* down left*/
      if(on_flag) line(x, y, x-inc, y+inc, cc);
      x -= inc; y += inc;
      break;
    case 81: /* down right */
      if(on_flag) line(x, y, x+inc, y+inc, cc);
      x += inc; y += inc;
      break;
    case 59: inc = 1;   /* F1 - slow speed */
      break;
    case 60: inc = 5;   /* F2 - fast speed */
      break;
  }
  else switch(tolower(key.c[0])) {
    case 'o': on_flag = !on_flag; /* toggle brush */
      break;
    case '1': cc = 1; /* color 1 */
      break;
    case '2': cc = 2; /* color 2 */
      break;
    case '3': cc = 3; /* color 3 */
      break;
    case '0': cc = 0; /* color 0 */
      break;
    case 'b': box(startx, starty, endx, endy, cc);
      break;
```

```
    case 'f': fill_box(startx, starty, endx, endy, cc);
      break;
    case 'l': line(startx, starty, endx, endy, cc);
      break;
    case 'c':
      if(starty < endy)
        circle(startx, starty, endy-starty, cc);
      else
        circle(startx, starty, starty-endy, cc);
      break;
    case 'h':
      if(starty < endy)
        fill_circle(startx, starty, endy-starty, cc);
      else
        fill_circle(startx, starty, starty-endy, cc);
      break;
    case 's': save_pic();
      break;
    case 'r': load_pic();
      break;
    case 'm': /* move a region */
      move(startx, starty, endx, endy, x, y);
      break;
    case 'x': /* copy a region */
      copy(startx, starty, endx, endy, x, y);
      break;
    case 'd':  /* define an object to rotate */
      sides = define_object(object, x, y);
      break;
    case 'a': /* rotate the object */
      rotate_object(object, 0.05, x, y, sides);
      break;
    case '\r': /* set end points for line, circle, or box */
      if(first_point) {
        startx = x; starty = y;
      }
      else {
        endx = x; endy = y;
      }
      first_point = !first_point;
      break;
    case 'p': pal_num = pal_num==1 ? 2:1;
      palette(pal_num);
  }
  xhairs(x, y); /* redisplay the cross hairs */
```

```
  if(tolower(key.c[0])=='q') return 1;
  return 0;
}

/* Set the palette. */
void palette(int pnum)
{
  union REGS r;

  r.h.bh = 1;   /* code for palette select */
  r.h.bl = pnum;
  r.h.ah = 11;  /* set palette function */
  int86(0x10, &r, &r);
}

/* Set the video mode. */
void mode(int mode_code)
{
  union REGS r;

  r.h.al = mode_code;
  r.h.ah = 0;
  int86(0x10, &r, &r);
}

/* Draw a box. */
void box(int startx, int starty, /* upper-left corner */
         int endx, int endy, /* lower-right corner */
         int color) /* color */
{
  line(startx, starty, endx, starty, color);
  line(startx, starty, startx, endy, color);
  line(startx, endy, endx, endy, color);
  line(endx, starty, endx, endy, color);
}


/* Draw a line in specified color
   using Bresenham's integer-based algorithm.
*/
void line(int startx, int starty, /* upper-left corner */
          int endx, int endy, /* lower-right corner */
          int color) /* color */
{
  register int t, distance;
```

```
  int x=0, y=0, delta_x, delta_y;
  int incx, incy;

  /* Compute the distances in both directions. */
  delta_x = endx-startx;
  delta_y = endy-starty;

  /* Compute the direction of the increment.
     An increment of 0 means either a vertical
     or horizontal line.
  */
  if(delta_x>0) incx = 1;
  else if(delta_x==0) incx = 0;
  else incx = -1;

  if(delta_y>0) incy = 1;
  else if(delta_y==0) incy = 0;
  else incy = -1;

  /* determine which distance is greater */
  delta_x = abs(delta_x);
  delta_y = abs(delta_y);
  if(delta_x>delta_y) distance = delta_x;
  else distance = delta_y;

  /* draw the line */
  for(t=0; t<=distance+1; t++) {
    mempoint(startx, starty, color);
    x += delta_x;
    y += delta_y;
    if(x>distance) {
      x -= distance;
      startx += incx;
    }
    if(y>distance) {
      y -= distance;
      starty += incy;
    }
  }
}

/* Fill box with specified color. */
void fill_box(int startx, int starty, /* upper-left corner */
        int endx, int endy, /* lower-right corner */
        int color) /* color */
{
```

```
  register int i, begin, end;

  begin = startx<endx ? startx : endx;
  end = startx>endx ? startx : endx;

  for(i=begin; i<=end;i++)
    line(i, starty, i, endy, color);
}

/* Draw a circle using Bresenham's integer-based algorithm. */
void circle(int x_center, int y_center, /* center */
            int radius, /* radius */
            int color) /* color */
{
  register int x, y, delta;

  asp_ratio = 1.0;  /* for different aspect ratios, alter
                       this number */

  y = radius;
  delta = 3 - 2 * radius;

  for(x=0; x<y; ) {
    plot_circle(x, y, x_center, y_center, color);

    if (delta < 0)
      delta += 4*x+6;
    else {
      delta += 4*(x-y)+10;
      y--;
    }
    x++;
  }
  x = y;
  if(y) plot_circle(x, y, x_center, y_center, color);
}

/* Plot_circle actually prints the points that
   define the circle.
*/
void plot_circle(int x, int y,
                 int x_center, int y_center,
                 int color)
{
  int startx, endx, x1, starty, endy, y1;
```

```
  starty = y*asp_ratio;
  endy = (y+1)*asp_ratio;
  startx = x*asp_ratio;
  endx = (x+1)*asp_ratio;

  for (x1=startx; x1<endx; ++x1)  {
    mempoint(x1+x_center, y+y_center, color);
    mempoint(x1+x_center, y_center-y, color);
    mempoint(x_center-x1, y_center-y, color);
    mempoint(x_center-x1, y+y_center, color);
  }

  for (y1=starty; y1<endy; ++y1) {
    mempoint(y1+x_center, x+y_center, color);
    mempoint(y1+x_center, y_center-x, color);
    mempoint(x_center-y1, y_center-x, color);
    mempoint(x_center-y1, x+y_center, color);
  }
}

/* Fill a circle by repeatedly calling circle()
   with smaller radius.
*/
void fill_circle(int x_center, int y_center,
                 int radius, int color)
{
  while(radius) {
    circle(x_center, y_center, radius, color);
    radius--;
  }
}

/* Write a point directly to mode 4 graphics RAM. */
void mempoint(int x, int y, /* coordinate of point */
              int color) /* color */
{
  union mask {
    char c[2];
    int i;
  } bit_mask;
  int index, bit_position;
  unsigned char t;
  char xor; /* xor color in or overwrite */

  /* pointer to mode 4 graphics RAM */
```

```
   char far *ptr = (char far *) 0xB8000000;

   bit_mask.i = 0xFF3F;   /* 11111111 00111111 in binary */

   /* check range */
   if(x<0 || x>XMAX || y<0 || y>YMAX) return;

   xor = color & 128; /* see if xor mode is set */
   color = color & 127; /* mask off high bit */

   /* set bit_mask and color bits to the right location */
   bit_position = x%4;
   color <<= 2*(3-bit_position);
   bit_mask.i >>= 2*bit_position;

   /* find the correct byte in screen memory */
   index = y*40 + (x >> 2);
   if(y % 2) index += 8152; /* if odd use 2nd bank */

   /* write the color */
   if(!xor) { /* overwrite mode */
     t = *(ptr+index) & bit_mask.c[0];
     *(ptr+index) = t | color;
   }
   else { /* xor mode */
     t = *(ptr+index) | (char) 0;
     *(ptr+index) = t ^ color;
   }
}

/* Display cross hairs locator. */
void xhairs(int x, int y)
{
  line(x-4, y, x+3, y, 1 | 128);
  line(x, y+4, x, y-3, 1 | 128);
}

/* Return the 16-bit scan code from the keyboard. */
readkey(void)
{
  union REGS r;

  r.h.ah = 0;
  return int86(0x16, &r, &r);
}
```

```
/* Read byte directly from the video RAM in mode 4. */
unsigned char read_point(int x, int y)
{
  union mask {
    char c[2];
    int i;
  } bit_mask;
  int index, bit_position;
  unsigned char t;

  /* pointer to mode 4 graphics RAM */
  char far *ptr = (char far *) 0xB8000000;

  bit_mask.i = 3;        /* 11111111 00111111 in binary */

  /* check range for mode 4 */
  if(x<0 || x>XMAX || y<0 || y>YMAX) return 0;

  /* set bit_mask and color_code bits to the right location */
  bit_position = x%4;
  bit_mask.i <<= 2*(3-bit_position);
  /* find the correct byte in screen memory */
  index = y*40 +(x >> 2);
  if(y % 2) index += 8152; /* if odd use 2nd bank */

  /* read the color */
  t = *(ptr+index) & bit_mask.c[0];
  t >>= 2*(3-bit_position);
  return t;
}

/* Save the video graphics display. */
void save_pic(void)
{
  char fname[80];
  FILE *fp;
  register int i, j;
  int e=0;

  /* pointer to mode 4 graphics RAM */
  char far *ptr = (char far *) 0xB8000000;

  char far *temp;
  unsigned char buf[14][80]; /* hold the contents of screen */
```

```
    temp = ptr;
    /* save the top of the current screen */
    for(i=0; i<14; i++)
      for(j=0; j<80; j+=2) {
        buf[i][j] = *temp; /* even byte */
        buf[i][j+1] = *(temp+8152); /* odd byte */
        *temp = 0; *(temp+8152) = 0;  /* clear top of screen */
        temp++;
      }

  goto_xy(0, 0);
  printf("Filename: ");
  gets(fname);
  if(!(fp=fopen(fname, "wb"))) {
    goto_xy(0, 0);
    printf("cannot open file - press a key ");
    getch();
    e = 1;  /* flag error */
  }

    temp = ptr;
    /* restore the top of the current screen */
    for(i=0; i<14; i++)
      for(j=0; j<80; j+=2) {
        *temp = buf[i][j];
        *(temp+8152) = buf[i][j+1];
        temp++;
      }

  if(e) return; /* if file could not be opened, exit */

  /* save image to file */
  for(i=0; i<8152; i++) {
    putc(*ptr, fp); /* even byte */
    putc(*(ptr+8152), fp); /* odd byte */
    ptr++;
  }

  fclose(fp);
}

/* Load the video graphics display. */
void load_pic(void)
{
  char fname[80];
  FILE *fp;
```

```
register int i, j;

/* pointer to mode 4 graphics RAM */
char far *ptr = (char far *) 0xB8000000;

char far *temp;
unsigned char buf[14][80]; /* hold the contents of screen */

temp = ptr;
/* save the top of the current screen */
for(i=0; i<14; i++)
  for(j=0; j<80; j+=2) {
    buf[i][j] = *temp;
    buf[i][j+1] = *(temp+8152);
    *temp = 0; *(temp+8152) = 0; /* clear the top of the screen */
    temp++;
  }

goto_xy(0, 0);
printf("Filename: ");
gets(fname);
if(!(fp=fopen(fname, "rb"))) {
  goto_xy(0, 0);
  printf("cannot open file\n");
  temp = ptr;
  /* restore the top of the current screen */
  for(i=0; i<14; i++)
    for(j=0; j<80; j+=2) {
      *temp = buf[i][j];
      *(temp+8152) = buf[i][j+1];
      temp++;
    }
  return;
}

/* load image from file */
for(i=0; i<8152; i++) {
  *ptr = getc(fp); /* even byte */
  *(ptr+8152) = getc(fp); /* odd byte */
  ptr++;
}

fclose(fp);
}
```

```
/* Send the cursor to the specified X,Y position. */
void goto_xy(int x, int y)
{
  union REGS r;

  r.h.ah = 2; /* cursor addressing function */
  r.h.dl = x; /* column coordinate */
  r.h.dh = y; /* row coordinate */
  r.h.bh = 0; /* video page */
  int86(0x10, &r, &r);
}

/* Move one region to another location. */
void move(int startx, int starty, /* upper-left coordinate */
  int endx, int endy, /* lower-right coordinate */
  int x, int y) /* upper left of region receiving the image */
{
  int i, j;
  unsigned char c;

  for(; startx<=endx; startx++, x++)
    for(i=starty, j=y; i<=endy; i++, j++) {
      c = read_point(startx, i); /* read point */
      mempoint(startx, i, 0); /* erase old image */
      mempoint(x, j, c); /* write it to new location */
    }
}

/* Copy one region to another location. */
void copy(int startx, int starty, /* upper-left coordinate */
  int endx, int endy, /* lower-right coordinate */
  int x, int y) /* upper left of region receiving the image */
{
  int i, j;
  unsigned char c;

  for(; startx<=endx; startx++, x++)
    for(i=starty, j=y; i<=endy; i++, j++) {
      c = read_point(startx, i); /* read point */
      mempoint(x, j, c); /* write it to new location */
    }
}

/* Rotate a point around the origin, specified by
   x_org and y_org, by angle theta.
*/
```

```
void rotate_point(double theta, /* angle of rotation */
                  double *x, double *y, /* point to rotate */
                  int x_org, int y_org) /* origin */
{
  double tx, ty;

  /* normalize x and y */
  tx = *x - x_org;
  ty = *y - y_org;

  /* rotate */
  *x = tx * cos(theta) - ty * sin(theta);
  *y = tx * sin(theta) + ty * cos(theta);

  /* return to PC coordinate values */
  *x += x_org;
  *y += y_org;

}

/* Rotate the specified object. */
void rotate_object(double ob[][5], /* object definition */
           double theta, /* angle of rotation in radians */
           int x, int y, /* location of origin */
           int lines) /* number of lines in image */
{
  register int j;
  char ch;

  for(;;) {
    ch = getch(); /* see which direction to rotate */
    switch(tolower(ch)) {
      case 'l': /* counterclockwise */
        theta = theta < 0 ? -theta : theta;
        break;
      case 'r': /* clockwise */
        theta = theta > 0 ? -theta : theta;
        break;
      default: return;
    }

    for(j=0; j<lines; j++) {
      /* erase old line */
      line((int) ob[j][0], (int) ob[j][1],
        (int) ob[j][2], (int) ob[j][3], 0);
```

```
      rotate_point(theta, &ob[j][0],
        &ob[j][1], x, y);

      rotate_point(theta, &ob[j][2],
        &ob[j][3], x, y);

      line((int) ob[j][0], (int) ob[j][1],
        (int) ob[j][2], (int) ob[j][3], (int) ob[j][4]);
    }
  }
}

/* Display an object. */
void display_object(double ob[][5], int lines)
{
  register int i;

  for(i=0; i<lines; i++)
    line((int) ob[i][0], (int) ob[i][1],
      (int) ob[i][2], (int) ob[i][3], (int) ob[i][4]);
}

/* Define an object by specifying its end points using
   either the mouse or the keyboard. */
define_object(double ob[][5], int x, int y)
{

  union k{
    char c[2];
    int i;
  } key;
  register int i, j;

  /* pointer to mode 4 graphics RAM */
  char far *ptr = (char far *) 0xB8000000;

  char far *temp;
  unsigned char buf[14][80]; /* hold the contents of screen */
  int sides = 0;
  char deltax, deltay;
  int oldx, oldy;

  temp = ptr;
  /* save the top of the current screen */
  for(i=0; i<14; i++)
```

```
    for(j=0; j<80; j+=2) {
      buf[i][j] = *temp;
      buf[i][j+1] = *(temp+8152);
      *temp = 0; *(temp+8152) = 0; /* clear the top of the screen */
      temp++;
    }
  i = 0;
  key.i = 0;
  xhairs(x, y);
  do {
    goto_xy(0, 0);
    printf("Define side %d,", sides+1);
    if(i==0) printf(" enter first end point");
    else printf(" enter second end point");

    do {
      /* mouse additions *****************************/
      /* see if mouse has moved */
      mouse_motion(&deltax, &deltay);
      /* use left button to define a point */
      if(leftb_pressed()) {
        xhairs(x, y);    /* erase the cross hairs */
        /* store coordinates of the point */
        ob[sides][i++] = (double) x;
        ob[sides][i++] = (double) y;
        if(i==4) {
          ob[sides][4] = read_point(x, y); /* get color */
          i = 0;
          sides++;
        }
        break;
      }
    } while(!kbhit() && !deltax && !deltay);
    if(leftb_pressed()) wait_on(LEFTB);

    if(deltax || deltay) {
      /* if mouse moved, update position */
      oldx = x; oldy = y;
      mouse_position(&x, &y);
      x = x / 2; /* normalize virtual screen coordinates */
      xhairs(oldx, oldy);    /* erase the cross hairs */
    }
    /* end of mouse code *****************************/
    else if(kbhit()) {
      key.i = readkey();
```

```
        xhairs(x, y);   /* plot the cross hairs */
        if(key.c[0]=='\r') {
          /* use RETURN to define a point */
          ob[sides][i++] = (double) x;
          ob[sides][i++] = (double) y;
          if(i==4) {
            ob[sides][4] = read_point(x, y); /* get color */
            i = 0;
            sides++;
          }
        }

        /* if arrow key, move the cross hairs */
        if(!key.c[0]) switch(key.c[1]) {
          case 75: /* left */
            x -= 1;
            break;
          case 77: /* right */
            x += 1;
            break;
          case 72: /* up */
            y -= 1;
            break;
          case 80: /* down */
            y += 1;
            break;
          case 71: /* up left */
            x -= 1; y -= 1;
            break;
          case 73: /* up right */
            y -= 1; x += 1;
            break;
          case 79: /* down left*/
            y += 1; x -= 1;
            break;
          case 81: /* down right */
            y += 1; x += 1;
            break;
        }
      }
    if(key.c[1]!=59) xhairs(x, y);
  } while(key.c[1] != 59); /* F1 to stop */

  temp = ptr;
  /* restore the top of the current screen */
```

```
    for(i=0; i<14; i++)
      for(j=0; j<80; j+=2) {
        *temp = buf[i][j];
        *(temp+8152) = buf[i][j+1];
        temp++;
      }
    return sides;
}

/* Display a menu. */
menu(void)
{
  register int i, j;

  /* pointer to mode 4 graphics RAM */
  char far *ptr = (char far *) 0xB8000000;

  char far *temp;
  unsigned char buf[14][80]; /* hold the contents of screen */
  int choice;
  char items[][20] = {
    "BOX",
    "CIRCLE",
    "LINE",
    "FILL BOX",
    "FILL CIRCLE"
  };

  temp = ptr;
  /* save the top of the current screen */
  for(i=0; i<14; i++)
    for(j=0; j<80; j+=2) {
      buf[i][j] = *temp; /* even byte */
      buf[i][j+1] = *(temp+8152); /* odd byte */
      *temp = 0; *(temp+8152) = 0;  /* clear top of screen */
      temp++;
    }

  goto_xy(0, 0);
  /* wait until last button press has cleared */
  while(rightb_pressed() || leftb_pressed()) ;
  cursor_on();

  choice = mouse_menu(5, items, 0, 0);

  cursor_off();
```

```
    temp = ptr;
    /* restore the top of the current screen */
    for(i=0; i<14; i++)
      for(j=0; j<80; j+=2) {
        *temp = buf[i][j];
        *(temp+8152) = buf[i][j+1];
        temp++;
      }
    return choice;
}


/**********************************************/
/* Mouse interface functions.                */
/**********************************************/

/* Turn off the mouse cursor. */
void cursor_off(void)
{
  union REGS r;

  r.x.ax = 2; /* remove the cursor */
  int86(0x33, &r, &r);
}


/* Turn on the mouse cursor. */
void cursor_on(void)
{
  union REGS r;

  r.x.ax = 1; /* show the cursor */
  int86(0x33, &r, &r);
}

/* Return true if right button is pressed,
   false otherwise. */
rightb_pressed(void)
{
  union REGS r;

  r.x.ax = 3; /* get position and button status */
  int86(0x33, &r, &r);
  return r.x.bx & 2;
}

/* Return true if left button is pressed,
```

```
   false otherwise. */
leftb_pressed(void)
{
  union REGS r;

  r.x.ax = 3; /* get position and button status */
  int86(0x33, &r, &r);
  return r.x.bx & 1;
}

/* Set mouse cursor coordinates. */
void set_mouse_position(int x, int y)
{
  union REGS r;

  r.x.ax = 4; /* set position */
  r.x.cx = x;
  r.x.dx = y;
  int86(0x33, &r, &r);
}

/* Return mouse cursor coordinates. */
void mouse_position(int *x, int *y)
{
  union REGS r;

  r.x.ax = 3; /* get position and button status */
  int86(0x33, &r, &r);
  *x = r.x.cx;
  *y = r.x.dx;
}

/* Return the direction of travel. */
void mouse_motion(char *deltax, char *deltay)
{
  union REGS r;

  r.x.ax = 11; /* get direction of motion */
  int86(0x33, &r, &r);

  if(r.x.cx>0) *deltax = RIGHT;
  else if(r.x.cx<0) *deltax = LEFT;
  else *deltax = NOT_MOVED;

  if(r.x.dx>0) *deltay = DOWN;
  else if(r.x.dx<0) *deltay = UP;
```

```
    else *deltay = NOT_MOVED;
}

/* Display a one-line mouse menu and return selection. */
mouse_menu(int count, /* number of menu items */
           char item[][20], /* menu items */
           int x, int y) /* display position */
{
  int i, len[MENU_MAX][2], t;
  int mousex, mousey;

  goto_xy(x, y);
  t = 0;
  for(i=0; i<count; i++) {
   printf("%s  ", item[i]);
   len[i][0] = t;
   len[i][1] = t + strlen(item[i])*16;
   t = len[i][1] + 32;
  }

  do {
    if(rightb_pressed() || leftb_pressed()) break;
  } while(!kbhit());
  /* wait until button not pressed */
  while(rightb_pressed() || leftb_pressed()) ;

  mouse_position(&mousex, &mousey);

  /* see if mouse cursor is on a menu selection */
  if(mousey >= 0 && mousey < 8)
    for(i=0; i<count; i++) {
      if(mousex > len[i][0] && mousex < len[i][1])
        return i;
    }
  return -1; /* no selection made */
}

/* Return 1 when specified button released. */
void wait_on(int button)
{
  if(button==LEFTB)
    while(leftb_pressed()) ;
```

```
  else
    while(rightb_pressed()) ;
}

/* Reset the mouse. */
void mouse_reset(void)
{
  union REGS r;

  r.x.ax = 0; /* reset the mouse */
  int86(0x33, &r, &r);
  if((int) r.x.ax != -1) {
    printf("mouse hardware or software not installed");
    exit(1);
  }
  if(r.x.bx != 2) {
    printf("two-button mouse required");
    exit(1);
  }
}
```

You will be surprised at how much more exciting the paint program is to use because you can now draw "freehand" curves instead of just straight lines. For example, the picture shown in Figure 9-1 was created in just a few minutes. The picture in Figure 9-2 shows the mouse menu and the default graphics mouse cursor.

SOME ADDITIONAL ENHANCEMENTS

First, you might want to expand the **mouse_menu()** function so that more than one line of selections can be displayed. In fact, with careful thought, you can integrate the mouse into the pop-up and pull-down window routines developed in Chapter 1. If you enjoy using icons, you might want to change the menu function so that icons rather than words are displayed. Another enhancement is to create a routine that allows the mouse to "drag" a part of the screen from one place to another.

One final note: if you are interested in learning more about interfacing to the mouse, you will want to get the *Microsoft Mouse Programmer's Reference* (Redmond, WA.: Microsoft Press, 1989).

Figure 9-1

Sample output from the paint program:
Mountains with Tower at Sunset with Star

Figure 9-2

Example of a mouse menu

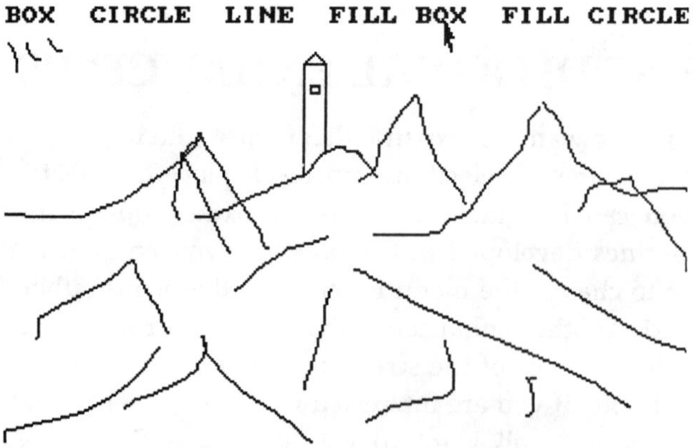

BOX   CIRCLE   LINE   FILL BOX   FILL CIRCLE

CHAPTER TEN

Creating Business Bar Graphs

This chapter develops routines that can be used to create one of the most common types of business graphs—the bar graph. The ability to display numeric data in visual form is very useful in many situations. As you will see, it is not as difficult to create bar graphs as you might think.

The chapter begins by developing a small toolbox of business-related graphics functions. The second half of the chapter explains how these toolbox routines can be used to create a simple, but useful, general-purpose bar graph program that allows up to three sets of information to be plotted on the screen at the same time. This chapter also develops a no-frills "slide-show" presentation program that displays graphs easily.

The examples in this chapter require a PC-type computer with a color graphics adapter. Video mode 4 is used because it works with all the color adapters. However, you can easily change the functions to work with other adapters.

PROFILE

REX JAESCHKE

A member of the ANSI C Standards Committee, contributing editor for "C Users Journal," convenor and chair of the Numerical C Extensions Group, publisher and editor of "The Journal of C Language Translation," C editor for "DEC Professional," lecturer, and author of *Mastering Standard C* and *Portability and the C Language*, Rex Jaeschke hardly needs an introduction!

Given Rex's extensive C background, I asked him what first brought him to the C language. "I had spent several years as an understudy to a systems programmer and I liked that level of programming. I liked being close to the machine and I always was fascinated with system software. First it was the operating system, then the linker, and eventually, the compiler. C was the language that opened up this world to me."

Because of Rex's diverse experience, I asked him to explain some of the common misconceptions that programmers have about C. "Perhaps the most common misconception is that the language is 'flawed' because it permits, even encourages the writing of bad code," said Rex. "Yes, it is possible to write poor code using C, but the problem lies with the programmer, not the language." Rex further elaborated, "I tell my introductory C students that C looks sufficiently like a high-level language that you can be fooled into thinking that it *is* a high-level language! However, to master and fully exploit C, you need to know many of the same things that a master assembly language programmer knows—something that not all programmers are capable of. Further, C assumes that you are a mature adult who's willing to clean up your own mess." "Remember," Rex said with a smile, "C says, 'Use me or abuse me as you see fit.'"

On the future of C, Rex commented, "The C curve has not yet peaked, despite what the OOP and C++ folk will tell you. Remember, the ANSI/ISO standard is finally done and is widely accepted. This gives programmers the ability to create portable code across a variety of implementations and environments." Rex added this final remark, "No doubt C++ will enjoy considerable success. But, both C and C++ will coexist for quite some time to come."

Rex Jaeschke lives in Reston, Virginia, with his wife and son.

NORMALIZING THE DATA

Before developing routines that plot data on the screen, you must understand how these values are translated into the appropriate screen coordinates. As you probably recall, the dimensions of the screen in video mode 4 are 320x200, with 320 being the horizontal dimension and 200 the vertical dimension. Assuming that the bar graph is displayed with the bars running vertically, the values of the information must be converted in such a way that they fit in the range 0 through 199. This conversion process is known as *normalization*.

To normalize a value, you must multiply it by some ratio that guarantees the result will be within the range of the screen. To accomplish this, the minimum and maximum values of the data to be plotted must be known. To compute the proper ratio, first subtract the minimum value from the maximum value. Then divide the maximum value of the range you wish to normalize to by this result. This ratio is then used to adjust each item of data. Assuming that the entire vertical range of the screen in video mode 4 is used, the ratio is computed using this formula:

normalization _ factor = 200 / (max-min)

Therefore, each item of data is normalized by this formula:

normalized _ data = raw _ data * normalization _ factor

DEVELOPING THE BAR GRAPH FUNCTION

Before developing the function that actually draws the bar graph on the screen, it is necessary to define exactly what it will do. First, it must accomplish its primary purpose of displaying the data in the form of a bar graph. The function will accept as input an array of floating-point values and transform them into their normalized integer equivalents. The function must be capable of being called repeatedly with different sets of data so that several sets can be displayed at the same time. To do this, the function must accept an argument that determines the spacing between the bars when two or more sets of data are plotted. The function must also plot each set of data in a different color. Finally, it must allow the thickness of the bars to be specified. The function **bargraph()**, shown here, accomplishes these goals:

```c
/* Display a bar chart. */
void bargraph(double *data, /* array of data */
    int num, /* number of elements in array */
    int offset, /* determine exact screen position */
    int min, int max, /* min and max values to be plotted */
    int width) /* thickness of the lines */
{
  int y, t, incr;
  double norm_data, norm_ratio, spread;
  static int color=0;
  int tempwidth;

  /* always use a different color */
  color++;
  if(color>3) color = 1;

  /* determine normalization factor */
  spread = (double) max-min;
  norm_ratio = 180/spread;

  incr = 280/num; /* determine spacing between lines */
  tempwidth = width;
  for(t=0; t<num; ++t) {
    norm_data = data[t];

    /* adjust for negative values */
    norm_data = norm_data-(double) min;

    norm_data *= norm_ratio; /* normalize */
    y = (int) norm_data; /* type conversion */
    do {
      line(((t*incr)+20+offset+width), 179,
        ((t*incr)+20+offset+width), 179-y, color);
      width--;
    } while (width);
    width = tempwidth;
  }
}
```

Let's look closely at this function. The function is passed the array of data, the number of elements in the array, the horizontal offset between the bars when multiple data sets are plotted, the minimum and maximum values of the data, and the width, in pixels, of the bars. The **static** variable **color** is used to ensure that each time **bargraph()** is called, a new color is used. In this way, multiple sets of data can be distinguished by the color with which they are plotted. Next, the normalization factor is computed. The value of 180 rather than 200 is used as the maximum screen height so that two lines of text information can be shown at the bottom of the graph. Although not necessary, it is usually more pleasing when a bar graph fills the entire display regardless of how many values are being plotted; a bar graph of a small number of values, for example, looks more appealing if the bars are spread out rather than bunched up at one end of the display. To accomplish this, the width of the screen (less some room for range labels) is divided by the number of values to be displayed. This value is then used to determine the horizontal position of the bars. Finally, the loop normalizes each value and plots a line of the specified thickness beginning at the specified offset.

When you are plotting multiple sets of data, the first set will be plotted using an **offset** value of 0. Subsequent sets must be plotted using some positive offset to prevent their bars from overlaying previously plotted bars.

You'll learn about the rest of these bar graph toolbox functions in the discussion that follows.

Drawing a Grid

One thing you will almost certainly want to show along with the bars is the range of the graph. You will also want to provide a baseline. The function **grid()**, shown here, does just that:

```
/* Draw the chart grid. */
void grid(int min, int max)
{
  goto_xy(0, 22); printf("%d", min);
  goto_xy(0, 0); printf("%d", max);
  line(10, 180, 300, 180, 1);
}
```

As you can see, like **bargraph()**, it leaves the bottom two lines of the display untouched. These bottom lines allow labeling and other information.

Labeling the Values

It is very common to label the values plotted on the screen. For example, if a bar chart shows five years of corporate profits, you will probably want to label each year. Although you can do this manually by using the **goto_xy()** and **printf()** functions, the **label()** function, shown next, will automatically place a label under each value. It accepts as input an array of strings (labels) and the number of entries. Each label is restricted to a length of 20 characters (including the null terminator), but this is not a severe restriction because in video mode 4, only 40 characters can be displayed on one line, making short labels desirable.

```
/* Display labels on the screen. */
void label(char str[][20], /* strings to display */
           int num) /* number of labels */
{
  int i, j, inc;

  inc = 38 / num;
  i = 2; /* initial horizontal starting point */
  for(j=0; j<num; j++) {
    goto_xy(i, 23);
    printf(str[j]);
    i += inc;
  }
}
```

The value of **inc** is determined by dividing the "magic number" 38 by the number of labels. In graphics mode 4, each character is 8 pixels wide. This means that about 38 characters can fit under the graph. Thus, the spacing between the labels is determined by the line **inc = 38 / num**, where **num** is the number of labels.

Drawing Reference Lines

In some situations, it is helpful to add horizontal lines at consistent intervals to aid in comparing widely separated bars. Generally, you will not want to use solid reference lines because they are too distracting. Instead, dotted lines are drawn. The function **hashlines()**, shown here, draws these dotted reference lines:

```
/* Draw dotted reference lines across the screen. */
void hashlines(void)
{
  int i, j;

  for(i=10; i<300; i+=5) {
    for(j=10; j<180; j+=10)
      mempoint(i, j, 3); /* one point every 5 pixels */
  }
}
```

Displaying a Legend

When multiple sets of data are plotted, it is a good idea to identify the color of the bar that goes with each set. One way to do this is to show a legend that contains the name of each set of data and the color used to display it. The function **legend()**, shown next, draws this legend. It takes as arguments a list of names and the number of names. It displays the name and a box filled with the color associated with that name across the bottom row of the screen. It uses the **fill _ box()** function developed earlier in this book to draw the colored box.

```
/* Show a legend. */
void legend(char names[][20],
            int num) /* number of names */
{
  int color=1, i, j;

  goto_xy(0, 24); /* legend goes on bottom line */
  j = 0;
  for(i=0; i<num; i++) {
    /* print the label */
    printf("%s    ", names[i]);

    /* Compute where colored box goes by
       converting cursor location into graphics
       coordinates. Each character is 8 pixels wide in
       mode 4 graphics.
    */
    j += strlen(names[i])*8+4;
    fill_box(j, 192, j+12, 198, color);
    j += 28;  /* advance to next field */
```

```
    color++;
    if(color>3) color = 1;
  }
}
```

A Simple Demonstration Program

The following program shows all the bar graph toolbox routines in action.
It produces the output shown in Figure 10-1. The program shows the
average price per share of three imaginary companies over five years.

```
/* A bar graph demonstration program. */

#include "dos.h"
#include "stdio.h"
#include "conio.h"
#include "ctype.h"
#include "stdlib.h"
#include "math.h"
#include "string.h"

#define XMAX 319
#define YMAX 199

void bargraph(double *data, int num, int offset,
              int min, int max, int width);
void grid(int min, int max);
void label(char str[][20], int num);
void hashlines(void), legend(char names[][20], int num);

void line(int startx, int starty, int endx, int endy,
          int color);
void fill_box(int startx, int starty, int endx, int endy,
          int color);
void mempoint(int x, int y, int color);
void palette(int pnum);
void mode(int mode_code);
void goto_xy(int x, int y);

main(void)
{
  double widget[]={
    10.1, 20, 30, 35.34, 50
  };
```

```
double global[]={
  19, 20, 8.8, 30, 40
};
double tower[]={
  25.25, 19, 17.4, 33, 29
};

char n[][20]={
  "Widget",
  "Global",
  "Tower"
};
char lab[][20]={
  "1987",
  "1988",
  "1989",
  "1990",
  "1991"
};

mode(4); /* 320x200 graphics mode */
palette(0);

grid(0, 50); /* display the grid */
hashlines(); /* display dotted reference lines */
label(lab, 5); /* label the graph */
legend(n, 3); /* show the legend */

/* plot the stock prices of the three companies */
bargraph(widget, 5, 0, 0, 50, 4);
bargraph(global, 5, 10, 0, 50, 4);
bargraph(tower, 5, 20, 0, 50, 4);

getch();
mode(3);

return 0;
}

/* Draw the chart grid. */
void grid(int min, int max)
{
  goto_xy(0, 22); printf("%d", min);
  goto_xy(0, 0); printf("%d", max);
  line(10, 180, 300, 180, 1);
```

```
}

/* Display labels on the screen. */
void label(char str[][20], /* strings to display */
           int num) /* number of labels */
{
  int i, j, inc;

  inc = 38 / num;
  i = 2; /* initial horizontal starting point */
  for(j=0; j<num; j++) {
    goto_xy(i, 23);
    printf(str[j]);
    i += inc;
  }
}

/* Draw dotted reference lines across the screen. */
void hashlines(void)
{
  int i, j;

  for(i=10; i<300; i+=5) {
    for(j=10; j<180; j+=10)
      mempoint(i, j, 3); /* one point every 5 pixels */
  }
}

/* Show a legend. */
void legend(char names[][20],
            int num) /* number of names */
{
  int color=1, i, j;

  goto_xy(0, 24); /* legend goes on bottom line */
  j = 0;
  for(i=0; i<num; i++) {
    /* print the label */
    printf("%s    ", names[i]);

    /* Compute where colored box goes by
       converting cursor location into graphics
       coordinates. Each character is 8 pixels wide in
       mode 4 graphics.
    */
```

```
    j += strlen(names[i])*8+4;
    fill_box(j, 192, j+12, 198, color);
    j += 28;  /* advance to next field */
    color++;
    if(color>3) color = 1;
  }
}

/* Display a bar chart. */
void bargraph(double *data, /* array of data */
    int num, /* number of elements in array */
    int offset, /* determine exact screen position */
    int min, int max, /* min and max values to be plotted */
    int width) /* thickness of the lines */
{
  int y, t, incr;
  double norm_data, norm_ratio, spread;
  static int color=0;
  int tempwidth;

  /* always use a different color */
  color++;
  if(color>3) color = 1;

  /* determine normalization factor */
  spread = (double) max-min;
  norm_ratio = 180/spread;

  incr = 280/num; /* determine spacing between lines */
  tempwidth = width;
  for(t=0; t<num; ++t) {
    norm_data = data[t];

    /* adjust for negative values */
    norm_data = norm_data-(double) min;

    norm_data *= norm_ratio; /* normalize */
    y = (int) norm_data; /* type conversion */
    do {
      line(((t*incr)+20+offset+width), 179,
        ((t*incr)+20+offset+width), 179-y, color);
      width--;
    } while (width);
    width = tempwidth;
  }
```

```
}

/* Draw a line in specified color
   using Bresenham's integer-based algorithm.
*/
void line(int startx, int starty, /* upper-left corner */
          int endx, int endy, /* lower-right corner */
          int color) /* color */
{
  register int t, distance;
  int x=0, y=0, delta_x, delta_y;
  int incx, incy;

  /* Compute the distances in both directions. */
  delta_x = endx-startx;
  delta_y = endy-starty;

  /* Compute the direction of the increment.
     An increment of 0 means either a vertical
     or horizontal line.
  */
  if(delta_x>0) incx = 1;
  else if(delta_x==0) incx = 0;
  else incx = -1;

  if(delta_y>0) incy = 1;
  else if(delta_y==0) incy = 0;
  else incy = -1;

  /* determine which distance is greater */
  delta_x = abs(delta_x);
  delta_y = abs(delta_y);
  if(delta_x>delta_y) distance = delta_x;
  else distance = delta_y;

  /* draw the line */
  for(t=0; t<=distance+1; t++) {
    mempoint(startx, starty, color);
    x += delta_x;
    y += delta_y;
    if(x>distance) {
      x -= distance;
      startx += incx;
    }
    if(y>distance) {
```

```
      y -= distance;
      starty += incy;
    }
  }
}

/* Fill box with specified color. */
void fill_box(int startx, int starty, /* upper-left corner */
          int endx, int endy, /* lower-right corner */
          int color) /* color */
{
  register int i, begin, end;

  begin = startx<endx ? startx : endx;
  end = startx>endx ? startx : endx;

  for(i=begin; i<=end;i++)
    line(i, starty, i, endy, color);
}

/* Write a point directly to mode 4 graphics RAM. */
void mempoint(int x, int y, /* coordinate of point */
          int color) /* color */
{
  union mask {
    char c[2];
    int i;
  } bit_mask;
  int index, bit_position;
  unsigned char t;
  char xor; /* xor color in or overwrite */

  /* pointer to mode 4 graphics RAM */
  char far *ptr = (char far *) 0xB8000000;

  bit_mask.i = 0xFF3F;   /* 11111111 00111111 in binary */

  /* check range */
  if(x<0 ¦¦ x>XMAX ¦¦ y<0 ¦¦ y>YMAX) return;

  xor = color & 128; /* see if xor mode is set */
  color = color & 127; /* mask off high bit */

  /* set bit_mask and color bits to the right location */
  bit_position = x%4;
```

```
    color <<= 2*(3-bit_position);
    bit_mask.i >>= 2*bit_position;

    /* find the correct byte in screen memory */
    index = y*40 + (x >> 2);
    if(y % 2) index += 8152; /* if odd use 2nd bank */

    /* write the color */
    if(!xor) { /* overwrite mode */
      t = *(ptr+index) & bit_mask.c[0];
      *(ptr+index) = t | color;
    }
    else { /* xor mode */
      t = *(ptr+index) | (char) 0;
      *(ptr+index) = t ^ color;
    }
}

/* Set the palette. */
void palette(int pnum)
{
  union REGS r;

  r.h.bh = 1;    /* code for palette select */
  r.h.bl = pnum;
  r.h.ah = 11;   /* set palette function */
  int86(0x10, &r, &r);
}

/* Set the video mode. */
void mode(int mode_code)
{
  union REGS r;

  r.h.al = mode_code;
  r.h.ah = 0;
  int86(0x10, &r, &r);
}

/* Send the cursor to the specified X,Y position. */
void goto_xy(int x, int y)
{
  union REGS r;
```

```
r.h.ah = 2; /* cursor addressing function */
r.h.dl = x; /* column coordinate */
r.h.dh = y; /* row coordinate */
r.h.bh = 0; /* video page */
int86(0x10, &r, &r);
}
```

A GRAPHING PROGRAM

You can use the bar graph toolbox functions to construct a program that
allows the creation of bar charts. The program lets you enter the number
of sets of data, the number of entries per set, the names and the labels
associated with the data, and the thickness and spacing of the bars. Once
the information has been specified, the program automatically draws the
bar graph. You can also instruct the program to save the graph to a disk
file for later presentation.

Figure 10-1

Output from the bar graph demonstration program

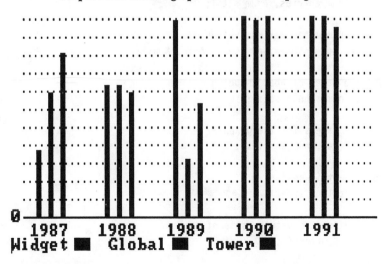

The main() Function

The operation of the graph program is outlined in the code to the **main()** function, shown here along with some macros and global variables:

```
#define MAX_SETS 3
#define MAX_ENTRIES 38
#define MAX_LABELS 20
#define MAX_NAMES 20

double v[MAX_SETS][MAX_ENTRIES]; /* holds the data */
char names[MAX_NAMES][20];
char lab[MAX_LABELS][20];

main(void)
{
  int num_entries;
  int num_sets;
  int min, max, i;
  int lines, offset;
  char save=0; /* save graph? */
  char ch;

  sin(0.1); /* to force Turbo C to link math library */

  /* read in the information */
  enter(v, &num_entries, &num_sets);

  /* find minimum and maximum values */
  min_max(v, num_entries, num_sets, &min, &max);

  /* get the names of what is being graphed */
  get_names(names, num_sets);

  /* get the labels for the graph */
  get_labels(lab, num_entries);

  /* get line thickness */
  lines = get_line_size();

  /* get the spacing between sets of data */
  offset = get_offset();

  /* save to disk file ? */
```

```
printf("save the graph to disk file? (Y/N) ");
ch = getche();
if(tolower(ch)=='y') save = 1;

mode(4); /* 320x200  graphics mode */
palette(0);

grid(min, max); /* display the grid */
hashlines(); /* display dotted reference lines */
label(lab, num_entries); /* label the graph */
legend(names, num_sets); /* show the legend */

/* plot the values */
for(i=0; i<num_sets; i++)
  bargraph(v[i], num_entries, i*offset, min, max, lines);

if(save) save_pic();
getch();
mode(3);

return 0;
}
```

As you can see, before **main()** begins, a number of variables that will have their values set by the user are declared. The array **v** is defined to be large enough to hold three sets of data with up to 50 values per set. (These dimensions are arbitrary, and you may change them if you like.) The function then reads in the data to display. Next, the minimum and maximum values to that data are found. After that, the grid, reference lines, names, and legend are displayed. Finally, the bars are plotted. Before exiting, the screen can be saved by using the **save_pic()** function developed for the paint program, if desired. Let's look at some of the functions used by the program that are not part of the bar graph toolbox already developed.

The enter() Function

The **enter()** function, shown next, is called with the address of the array that will receive the data and the addresses of the variables that will receive the number of entries and the number of sets. The function begins by prompting the user for the number of sets followed by the number of entries. It then reads in the information for each set.

```
/* Enter values to be plotted. */
enter(double v[][MAX_ENTRIES], /* data array */
      int *entries, /* number of entries in each set of data */
      int *sets) /* number of sets of data */
{
  int i, j, count, num;

  printf("How many sets of data? (1 to %d) ", MAX_SETS);
  scanf("%d", &count); fflush(stdin);
  if(count>MAX_SETS) count = MAX_SETS; /* prevent array overrun */
  *sets = count;

  printf("How many entries? (1 to %d) ", MAX_ENTRIES);
  scanf("%d", &num); fflush(stdin);
  if(num>MAX_ENTRIES) num = MAX_ENTRIES; /* prevent array overrun */
  *entries = num;

  j = 0;

  /* read in the values */
  while((j<count)) {
    printf("Data set %d\n", j+1);
    for(i=0; i<num; i++) {
      printf("%d: ", i+1);
      scanf("%lf", &v[j][i]);  fflush(stdin);
    }
    j++;
  }
  return count;
}
```

The min_max() Function

Since the **bargraph()** function needs to know the minimum and maximum values of the data to be displayed, a function that determines these values is required. Because multiple sets of data may be plotted on the same grid, it is necessary to check each set of data to ensure that the smallest minimum and the greatest maximum values are used. The **min_max()** function, shown here along with its two support functions, accomplishes this task:

```
/* Find the smallest minimum and greatest maximum values
   among all the sets of data.
*/
void min_max(double v[][MAX_ENTRIES], /* values */
     int entries, /* number of entries */
     int sets, /* number of sets */
     int *min, int *max) /* return minimum and maximum values */
{
  int i;
  int tmin, tmax;

  *min = *max = 0;

  for(i=0; i<sets; i++) {
      tmax = getmax(v[i], entries);
      tmin = getmin(v[i], entries);
      if(tmax > *max) *max = tmax;
      if(tmin < *min) *min = tmin;
  }
}


/* Returns the maximum value of the data. */
getmax(double *data, int num)
{
  int t, max;

  max = (int) data[0];
  for(t=1; t<num; ++t)
    if(data[t]>max) max = (int) data[t];
  return max;
}


/* Returns the minimum value of the data. */
getmin(double *data, int num)
{
  int t, min;

  min = (int) data[0];
  for(t=1; t<num; ++t)
    if(data[t]<min) min = (int) data[t];
  return min;
}
```

Since **min** and **max** are integers, you must make sure that your data falls within an integer's range.

The Entire Bar Graph Program

The entire bar graph program is shown here:

```c
/* A bar graph generator program. */

#include "dos.h"
#include "stdio.h"
#include "conio.h"
#include "ctype.h"
#include "stdlib.h"
#include "math.h"
#include "string.h"

#define MAX_SETS 3
#define MAX_ENTRIES 38
#define MAX_LABELS 20
#define MAX_NAMES 20

#define XMAX 319
#define YMAX 199

void bargraph(double *data, int num, int offset,
              int min, int max, int width);
void min_max(double v[][MAX_ENTRIES], int entries,
             int sets, int *min, int *max);
void get_names(char n[][20], int num);
void get_labels(char l[][20], int num);
void grid(int min, int max);
void label(char str[][20], int num);
void hashlines(void), legend(char names[][20], int num);

void line(int startx, int starty, int endx, int endy,
          int color);
void fill_box(int startx, int starty, int endx, int endy,
          int color);
void mempoint(int x, int y, int color);
void palette(int pnum);
void mode(int mode_code);
void goto_xy(int x, int y), save_pic(void);
int get_offset(void), get_line_size(void);
int getmax(double *data, int num);
int getmin(double *data, int num);
int enter(double v[][MAX_ENTRIES], int *entries, int *sets);
```

```
double v[MAX_SETS][MAX_ENTRIES]; /* holds the data */
char names[MAX_NAMES][20];
char lab[MAX_LABELS][20];

main(void)
{
  int num_entries;
  int num_sets;
  int min, max, i;
  int lines, offset;
  char save=0; /* save graph? */
  char ch;

  sin(0.1); /* to force Turbo C to link math library */

  /* read in the information */
  enter(v, &num_entries, &num_sets);

  /* find minimum and maximum values */
  min_max(v, num_entries, num_sets, &min, &max);

  /* get the names of what is being graphed */
  get_names(names, num_sets);

  /* get the labels for the graph */
  get_labels(lab, num_entries);

  /* get line thickness */
  lines = get_line_size();

  /* get the spacing between sets of data */
  offset = get_offset();

  /* save to disk file ? */
  printf("save the graph to disk file? (Y/N) ");
  ch = getche();
  if(tolower(ch)=='y') save = 1;

  mode(4); /* 320x200  graphics mode */
  palette(0);

  grid(min, max); /* display the grid */
  hashlines(); /* display dotted reference lines */
  label(lab, num_entries); /* label the graph */
  legend(names, num_sets); /* show the legend */
```

```
    /* plot the values */
    for(i=0; i<num_sets; i++)
      bargraph(v[i], num_entries, i*offset, min, max, lines);

    if(save) save_pic();
    getch();
    mode(3);

    return 0;
}

/* Enter values to be plotted. */
enter(double v[][MAX_ENTRIES], /* data array */
      int *entries, /* number of entries in each set of data */
      int *sets) /* number of sets of data */
{
    int i, j, count, num;

    printf("How many sets of data? (1 to %d) ", MAX_SETS);
    scanf("%d", &count); fflush(stdin);
    if(count>MAX_SETS) count = MAX_SETS; /* prevent array overrun */
    *sets = count;

    printf("How many entries? (1 to %d) ", MAX_ENTRIES);
    scanf("%d", &num); fflush(stdin);
    if(num>MAX_ENTRIES) num = MAX_ENTRIES; /* prevent array overrun */
    *entries = num;

    j = 0;

    /* read in the values */
    while((j<count)) {
      printf("Data set %d\n", j+1);
      for(i=0; i<num; i++) {
        printf("%d: ", i+1);
        scanf("%lf", &v[j][i]);  fflush(stdin);
      }
      j++;
    }
    return count;
}

/* Input the names of the sets. */
void get_names(char n[][20], /* array for the names */
               int num)  /* number of sets */
```

```
{
  int i;

  for(i=0; i<num; i++) {
    printf("Enter name: ");
    gets(n[i]);
  }
}

/* Input the label of each entry. */
void get_labels(char l[][20], /* array for the labels */
                int num)  /* number of entries */
{
  int i;

  for(i=0; i<num; i++) {
    printf("Enter label: ");
    gets(l[i]);
  }
}

/* Input distance between bars in pixels */
get_offset(void)
{
  int i;

  printf("Enter distance between bars in pixels: ");
  scanf("%d", &i); fflush(stdin);
  return i;
}

/* Input bar thickness in pixels */
get_line_size(void)
{
  int i;

  printf("Enter thickness of bars in pixels: ");
  scanf("%d", &i); fflush(stdin);
  return i;
}

/* Draw the chart grid. */
void grid(int min, int max)
{
  goto_xy(0, 22); printf("%d", min);
```

```
    goto_xy(0, 0); printf("%d", max);
    line(10, 180, 300, 180, 1);
}

/* Display labels on the screen. */
void label(char str[][20], /* strings to display */
           int num) /* number of labels */
{
  int i, j, inc;

  inc = 38 / num;
  i = 2; /* initial horizontal starting point */
  for(j=0; j<num; j++) {
    goto_xy(i, 23);
    printf(str[j]);
    i += inc;
  }
}

/* Draw dotted reference lines across the screen. */
void hashlines(void)
{
  int i, j;

  for(i=10; i<300; i+=5) {
    for(j=10; j<180; j+=10)
      mempoint(i, j, 3); /* one point every 5 pixels */
  }
}

/* Show a legend. */
void legend(char names[][20],
            int num) /* number of names */
{
  int color=1, i, j;

  goto_xy(0, 24); /* legend goes on bottom line */
  j = 0;
  for(i=0; i<num; i++) {
    /* print the label */
    printf("%s     ", names[i]);

    /* Compute where colored box goes by
       converting cursor location into graphics
       coordinates. Each character is 8 pixels wide in
```

```
      mode 4 graphics.
    */
    j += strlen(names[i])*8+4;
    fill_box(j, 192, j+12, 198, color);
    j += 28;  /* advance to next field */
    color++;
    if(color>3) color = 1;
  }
}
/* Display a bar chart. */
void bargraph(double *data, /* array of data */
     int num, /* number of elements in array */
     int offset, /* determine exact screen position */
     int min, int max, /* min and max values to be plotted */
     int width) /* thickness of the lines */
{
  int y, t, incr;
  double norm_data, norm_ratio, spread;
  static int color=0;
  int tempwidth;

  /* always use a different color */
  color++;
  if(color>3) color = 1;

  /* determine normalization factor */
  spread = (double) max-min;
  norm_ratio = 180/spread;

  incr = 280/num; /* determine spacing between lines */
  tempwidth = width;
  for(t=0; t<num; ++t) {
    norm_data = data[t];

    /* adjust for negative values */
    norm_data = norm_data-(double) min;

    norm_data *= norm_ratio; /* normalize */
    y = (int) norm_data; /* type conversion */
    do {
      line(((t*incr)+20+offset+width), 179,
        ((t*incr)+20+offset+width), 179-y, color);
      width--;
    } while (width);
    width = tempwidth;
```

```
    }
}

/* Find the smallest minimum and greatest maximum values
   among all the sets of data.
*/
void min_max(double v[][MAX_ENTRIES], /* values */
      int entries, /* number of entries */
      int sets, /* number of sets */
      int *min, int *max) /* return minimum and maximum values */
{
  int i;
  int tmin, tmax;

  *min = *max = 0;

  for(i=0; i<sets; i++) {
      tmax = getmax(v[i], entries);
      tmin = getmin(v[i], entries);
      if(tmax > *max) *max = tmax;
      if(tmin < *min) *min = tmin;
  }
}

/* Returns the maximum value of the data. */
getmax(double *data, int num)
{
  int t, max;

  max = (int) data[0];
  for(t=1; t<num; ++t)
    if(data[t]>max) max = (int) data[t];
  return max;
}

/* Returns the minimum value of the data. */
getmin(double *data, int num)
{
  int t, min;

  min = (int) data[0];
  for(t=1; t<num; ++t)
    if(data[t]<min) min = (int) data[t];
  return min;
}
```

```
/* Draw a line in specified color
   using Bresenham's integer-based algorithm.
*/
void line(int startx, int starty, /* upper-left corner */
          int endx, int endy, /* lower-right corner */
          int color) /* color */
{
  register int t, distance;
  int x=0, y=0, delta_x, delta_y;
  int incx, incy;

  /* Compute the distances in both directions. */
  delta_x = endx-startx;
  delta_y = endy-starty;

  /* Compute the direction of the increment.
     An increment of 0 means either a vertical
     or horizontal line.
  */
  if(delta_x>0) incx = 1;
  else if(delta_x==0) incx = 0;
  else incx = -1;

  if(delta_y>0) incy = 1;
  else if(delta_y==0) incy = 0;
  else incy = -1;

  /* determine which distance is greater */
  delta_x = abs(delta_x);
  delta_y = abs(delta_y);
  if(delta_x>delta_y) distance = delta_x;
  else distance = delta_y;

  /* draw the line */
  for(t=0; t<=distance+1; t++) {
    mempoint(startx, starty, color);
    x += delta_x;
    y += delta_y;
    if(x>distance) {
      x -= distance;
      startx += incx;
    }
    if(y>distance) {
      y -= distance;
      starty += incy;
```

```
      }
    }
}

/* Fill box with specified color. */
void fill_box(int startx, int starty, /* upper-left corner */
              int endx, int endy, /* lower-right corner */
              int color) /* color */
{
    register int i, begin, end;

    begin = startx<endx ? startx : endx;
    end = startx>endx ? startx : endx;

    for(i=begin; i<=end;i++)
        line(i, starty, i, endy, color);
}

/* Write a point directly to mode 4 graphics RAM. */
void mempoint(int x, int y, /* coordinate of point */
              int color) /* color */
{
    union mask {
        char c[2];
        int i;
    } bit_mask;
    int index, bit_position;
    unsigned char t;
    char xor; /* xor color in or overwrite */

    /* pointer to mode 4 graphics RAM */
    char far *ptr = (char far *) 0xB8000000;

    bit_mask.i = 0xFF3F;   /* 11111111 00111111 in binary */

    /* check range */
    if(x<0 || x>XMAX || y<0 || y>YMAX) return;

    xor = color & 128; /* see if xor mode is set */
    color = color & 127; /* mask off high bit */

    /* set bit_mask and color bits to the right location */
    bit_position = x%4;
    color <<= 2*(3-bit_position);
    bit_mask.i >>= 2*bit_position;
```

```
/* find the correct byte in screen memory */
index = y*40 + (x >> 2);
if(y % 2) index += 8152; /* if odd use 2nd bank */

/* write the color */
if(!xor) { /* overwrite mode */
  t = *(ptr+index) & bit_mask.c[0];
  *(ptr+index) = t | color;
}
else { /* xor mode */
  t = *(ptr+index) | (char) 0;
  *(ptr+index) = t ^ color;
}
}

/* Save the video graphics display. */
void save_pic(void)
{
  char fname[80];
  FILE *fp;
  register int i, j;
  int e=0;

  /* pointer to mode 4 graphics RAM */
  char far *ptr = (char far *) 0xB8000000;

  char far *temp;
  unsigned char buf[14][80]; /* hold the contents of screen */

  temp = ptr;
  /* save the top of the current screen */
  for(i=0; i<14; i++)
    for(j=0; j<80; j+=2) {
      buf[i][j] = *temp; /* even byte */
      buf[i][j+1] = *(temp+8152); /* odd byte */
      *temp = 0; *(temp+8152) = 0;  /* clear top of screen */
      temp++;
    }

  goto_xy(0, 0);
  printf("Filename: ");
  gets(fname);
  if(!(fp=fopen(fname, "wb"))) {
    goto_xy(0, 0);
    printf("cannot open file - press a key ");
```

```
    getch();
    e = 1;  /* flag error */
  }

  temp = ptr;
  /* restore the top of the current screen */
  for(i=0; i<14; i++)
    for(j=0; j<80; j+=2) {
      *temp = buf[i][j];
      *(temp+8152) = buf[i][j+1];
      temp++;
    }

  if(e) return; /* if file could not be opened, exit */

  /* save image to file */
  for(i=0; i<8152; i++) {
    putc(*ptr, fp); /* even byte */
    putc(*(ptr+8152), fp); /* odd byte */
    ptr++;
  }

  fclose(fp);
}

/* Set the palette. */
void palette(int pnum)
{
  union REGS r;

  r.h.bh = 1;   /* code for palette select */
  r.h.bl = pnum;
  r.h.ah = 11; /* set palette function */
  int86(0x10, &r, &r);
}

/* Set the video mode. */
void mode(int mode_code)
{
  union REGS r;

  r.h.al = mode_code;
  r.h.ah = 0;
  int86(0x10, &r, &r);
}
```

```
/* Send the cursor to the specified X,Y position. */
void goto_xy(int x, int y)
{
  union REGS r;

  r.h.ah = 2; /* cursor addressing function */
  r.h.dl = x; /* column coordinate */
  r.h.dh = y; /* row coordinate */
  r.h.bh = 0; /* video page */
  int86(0x10, &r, &r);
}
```

DISPLAYING GRAPHS

If you have requested that the bar graph program save the graph to a disk file, you can redisplay it by using the short program, called SHOW, developed in this section. The program displays the graph whose file name is specified as a command-line argument. For example, to display a graph called BACKLOG, you would use this command:

SHOW BACKLOG

The program uses the **load_pic()** function developed for the paint program to display a graph on the screen. (You can also use this program to display graphics images created and saved by the paint program.)

```
/* A simple graphics presentation program. */

#include "stdio.h"
#include "dos.h"
#include "stdlib.h"
#include "conio.h"

void load_pic(char *fname);
void palette(int pnum);
void mode(int mode_code);
void goto_xy(int x, int y);

main(int argc, char *argv[])
{
```

```
  if(argc!=2) {
    printf("usage: show <filename>");
    exit(1);
  }

  mode(4);
  palette(0);

  load_pic(argv[1]);

  getch();
  mode(3);

  return 0;
}

/* Load the video graphics display. */
void load_pic(char *fname)
{
  FILE *fp;
  register int i;

  /* pointer to mode 4 graphics RAM */
  char far *ptr = (char far *) 0xB8000000;

  if(!(fp=fopen(fname, "rb"))) {
    printf("Cannot open file\n");
    return ;
  }

  /* load image from file */
  for(i=0; i<8152; i++) {
    *ptr = getc(fp); /* even byte */
    *(ptr+8152) = getc(fp); /* odd byte */
    ptr++;
  }

  fclose(fp);
}

/* Set the palette. */
void palette(int pnum)
{
  union REGS r;
```

```
  r.h.bh = 1;   /* code for palette select */
  r.h.bl = pnum;
  r.h.ah = 11;  /* set palette function */
  int86(0x10, &r, &r);
}

/* Set the video mode. */
void mode(int mode_code)
{
  union REGS r;

  r.h.al = mode_code;
  r.h.ah = 0;
  int86(0x10, &r, &r);
}

/* Send the cursor to the specified X,Y position. */
void goto_xy(int x, int y)
{
  union REGS r;

  r.h.ah = 2; /* cursor addressing function */
  r.h.dl = x; /* column coordinate */
  r.h.dh = y; /* row coordinate */
  r.h.bh = 0; /* video page */
  int86(0x10, &r, &r);
}
```

SOME INTERESTING EXPERIMENTS

The value of the bar graph functions can be enhanced by parameterizing the dimensions and location of the graph so that graphs of different sizes and locations can be created. For example, it might be useful to create four small graphs, each using its own quadrant of the screen, as a way to display four sets of related information. You might also want to make the routines work with the higher resolution graphics modes. Finally, you may wish to add scatter and pie graph capabilities.

Expand *Your Skill Even More*

with help from our expert authors. Now that you've gained greater skills with **Art of C**, let us suggest the following related titles that will help you use your computer to full advantage.

Borland C++ Handbook
by Chris Pappas and William Murray

This handbook teaches C, C++, the Assembler, Debugger, Profiler, Windows programming, and the Whitewater Resource Toolkit. The authors cover the basics of writing simple assembly language programs and patches, then provide a solid foundation in Windows programming and the C++ compiler.
$29.95 ISBN: 0-07-881015-9, 896 pages, 7 3/8 x 9 1/4

Teach Yourself C
by Herbert Schildt

This bestselling concise volume on the programming language of 1990s uses numerous exercises and skill checks to make sure your programming abilities grow lesson by lesson. By the final chapter, you will possess a solid command of C programming principles.
$19.95 ISBN: 0-07-881596-7 681 pages

C: The Complete Reference, Second Edition
by Herbert Schildt

This renowned reference guide, revised to comply with the ANSI C standard, is the best and most complete source for C programmers at all levels. Comprehensive reference sections are conveniently organized by topic for quick fact-finding.
$28.95 ISBN: 0-07-881538-X 823 pages
Available in Spanish ISBN: 84-76155352

C++: The Complete Reference
by Herbert Schildt

Internationally known programming expert, Herb Schildt covers C++ in full detail starting with aspects common to the C and C++ languages. This example-filled book thoroughly discusses those features specific to C++ and includes several chapters on effective C++ software development.
$29.95 ISBN: 0-07-881654-8 594 pages

ANSI C Made Easy
by Herbert Schildt

This volume is ideal for anyone in the fast-growing C programming field, including students and beginning systems programmers. This Made Easy book includes step-by-step exercises that facilitate both quick and lasting comprehension.
$19.95 ISBN: 0-07-881500-2 450 pages
Available in Spanish ISBN: 84-76156030

Advanced C, Second Edition
by Herbert Schildt

Experienced C programmers can become professional C programmers with Schildt's nuts-and-bolts guide to advanced programming techniques. All the example code conforms to the ANSI standard and you'll find information you need on such topics as sorting and searching, queues, stacks, and linked lists.
$21.95 ISBN: 0-07-881348-4 353 pages

Born to Code in C
by Herbert Schildt

This book is for programmers who want to learn all the secrets of C from the pros. Each chapter contains a profile of a world-class C programmer who reveals the strategies and methodologies that have put him at the top and extensive code examples.
$28.95 ISBN: 0-07-881468-5 526 pages

▶ _____Osborne **McGraw-Hill** ■ Available at local book and computer stores.

Artificial Intelligence Using C
by Herbert Schildt

Add a powerful dimension to your C programs—artificial intelligence. Learn to use AI techniques that have traditionally been implemented with Prolog and LISP. Each chapter develops practical examples that can be used in the construction of AI applications.
$24.95 ISBN: 0-07-881255-0 432 pages

C: The Pocket Reference
by Herbert Schildt

The guaranteed remedy when a C command slips your mind is this handy guide that can help you speed up your C programming by providing vital C commands, functions and libraries—all conveniently arranged in alphabetical order.
$5.95 ISBN: 0-07-881321-2 128 pages
Available in Spanish ISBN: 84-76152175

Using Turbo C++
by Herbert Schildt

Borland's Turbo C++ with object-oriented programming is thoroughly covered in this introductory guide. Since Turbo C++ can be used with or without its C++ extensions, Schildt has carefully structured the book to cover both environments. Included are numerous interesting examples programs in C and C++.
$24.95 ISBN: 0-07-881610-6 755 pages

Turbo C/C++: The Complete Reference
by Herbert Schildt

Programmers at every skill level can benefit from this desktop encyclopedia which covers every Turbo C and Turbo C++ command, function, and programming technique. Schildt discusses the Turbo Debugger and Assembler in this comprehensive reference.
$29.95 ISBN: 0-07-881535-5 1016 pages

Osborne McGraw-Hill

Computer Books

(800) 227-0900

Bookmarker Design — Lance Ravella

You're important to us...

We'd like to know what you're interested in, what kinds of books you're looking for, and what you thought about this book in particular.

Please fill out the attached card and mail it in. We'll do our best to keep you informed about Osborne's newest books and special offers.

YES, Send Me a FREE Color Catalog of all Osborne computer books
To Receive Catalog, Fill in Last 4 Digits of ISBN Number from Back of Book (see below bar code) 0-07-881 _ _ _ — _

Name: _____ Title: _____

Company: _____

Address: _____

City: _____ State: _____ Zip: _____

I'M PARTICULARLY INTERESTED IN THE FOLLOWING (Check all that apply)

I use this software
- ☐ WordPerfect
- ☐ Microsoft Word
- ☐ WordStar
- ☐ Lotus 1-2-3
- ☐ Quattro
- ☐ Others _____

I use this operating system
- ☐ DOS
- ☐ Windows
- ☐ UNIX
- ☐ Macintosh
- ☐ Others _____

I rate this book:
- ☐ Excellent ☐ Good ☐ Poor

I program in
- ☐ C or C++
- ☐ Pascal
- ☐ BASIC
- ☐ Others _____

I chose this book because
- ☐ Recognized author's name
- ☐ Osborne/McGraw-Hill's reputation
- ☐ Read book review
- ☐ Read Osborne catalog
- ☐ Saw advertisement in store
- ☐ Found/recommended in library
- ☐ Required textbook
- ☐ Price
- ☐ Other _____

Comments _____

Topics I would like to see covered in future books by Osborne/McGraw-Hill include:
_____

IMPORTANT REMINDER
To get your FREE catalog, write in the last 4 digits of the ISBN number printed on the back cover (see below bar code) 0-07-881 _ _ _ — _

Osborne **McGraw-Hill**

Computer
Books

(800) 227-0900